Gardening Techniques

Gardening Techniques

AURORA PUBLISHING

This edition published in 1995 by
Aurora Publishing
Unit 9, Bradley Fold Trading Estate
Radcliffe Moor Road
Bolton BL2 6RT

Produced by Marshall Cavendish Books, London
(a division of Marshall Cavendish Partworks Ltd)

ISBN 1 85926 059 4

Printed in England

Some of this material has previously appeared in the Marshall Cavendish partwork *MY GARDEN*

Contents

Introduction

There are few pleasures to match the sight of a garden as it bursts into life in springtime – as the first buds open into full bloom, showing off their matching and contrasting colours; as the first signs of green appear on trees which have sat bare all winter and shrubs begin to show off their colours again; and as fruit and vegetables begin to ripen, ready for eating.

It is small wonder, then, that gardening is one of the most popular pastimes in the world. In climates both harsh and mild, wet and dry, wherever space has allowed, people have chosen to plant and maintain gardens.

Yet this most rewarding of pastimes, can also be the most frustrating if seeds refuse to sprout, trees refuse to bear fruit and plants wither and die. When things go wrong, gardening can seem a waste of both time and money. Often, problems which appear to be insurmountable in fact have simple solutions which, with a little background knowledge, will become apparent. The plant which fails to grow or

looks sick may be saved with the addition of some nutrient or companion plant, or by moving it to another part of the garden. And, while some plants may fail in your garden, it might provide ideal conditions for others to thrive in.

Selecting the right plants for your garden and caring for them properly are vital factors in creating a garden which will bring you maximum satisfaction.

That is where this book comes in. Gardening Techniques provides a comprehensive general introduction to the skills and information you will need to garden successfully. It explains in an easy-to-follow manner the basic techniques involved in sowing, planting, pruning, and propagation. It provides detailed information about the different soil types you might encounter, explaining how these types might be improved and which plants will be most likely to thrive in particular soil conditions. It offers detailed information about different plant types and tells where and how to use them and look after each type. It introduces the wide range of garden tools available and explains how to make the best use of them. A chapter on garden safety will help you to ensure that the pleasure of gardening is not marred by some avoidable mishap. A chapter on garden design will help you make the best

Introduction *(continued)*

use of the space available in your garden and add to the pleasure involved in gardening by helping you increase your garden's visual appeal.

In an age when people are becoming increasingly concerned about the state of the environment, gardening is a pastime which is guaranteed to make a positive contribution, albeit on the small scale of one's own front and back garden. It makes little sense to spoil the eco-friendly nature of this, most 'green' of pastimes by using excessive amounts of chemicals to protect your plants from pests and disease. Gardening Techniques is full of suggestions for organic pest and disease control which, as well as being better for the environment, will prove less expensive than artificial fertilizers and pesticides. Gardeners with a particular interest in this subject should turn to the chapter on Organic Pest and Disease Control. As gardening is the most seasonal of all pastimes, Gardening Techniques makes regular reference to the different times of the year. Gardeners should note that the timing of each season will vary according to where you live. In a warm climate, spring will arrive earlier and autumn will come later than in a cold climate. You should therefore adjust your own growing timetable accordingly.

Gardening Techniques serves as a useful introduction to or reminder of the basics of gardening and will be relevant to both beginners and experienced gardeners, whether you live in a warm or cool climate, whether your garden is large or small, formal or informal, and whether gardening is an all-consuming passion or a passing interest.

Sowing Seeds Indoors

Growing from seed is immensely rewarding. Not only is it the cheapest way to fill your garden with masses of blooms, but it is also easy to do.

Fill your garden with masses of summer flowers for a fraction of the cost of ready-grown bedding plants.

Growing plants from seed is not a difficult business and it is enormously satisfying to bring on a plant from seed right through to flowering.

Buying seed is, of course, cheaper than buying plants, even allowing for a certain outlay on pots and compost. Perennials, trees and shrubs are slow to grow from seed, and it is usually better to buy an established plant. Annual bedding plants and vegetables, on the other hand, are best raised from seed and this can be done with the minimum of space and equipment.

There is no need for a greenhouse or cold frames. A warm, light windowsill will do perfectly well. By following a few simple guidelines you can produce an excellent stock of bedding plants.

Tools of the trade

You will need compost, a few pots and trays and the seed. Apart from compost and seeds, every piece of equipment can be improvised.

Begin by clearing a table or draining board and set out the containers (seed trays or pots) needed for each batch of seed. Shallow (half) pots or plastic seed trays are best for sowing seed. The seedlings are 'pricked out' soon after their first leaves appear so a greater depth of compost would be wasted. The plastic punnets or trays in which you buy your fruit and vegetables from the supermarket are ideal. Yoghurt pots or old plastic cups will do the job too. With a screwdriver, punch holes in the bottom for drainage. Cut cups down to 6cm/2½in high if you want to be economical with your compost.

Most seed packets contain a generous amount and you will

Show lupins off to best effect in the middle of a border.

Easy-to-grow sweet peas make wonderful cut flowers.

Begonias, in beds or containers, will flower all summer long.

EASY STEPS TO SOWING SEEDS

1 *Fill the seed tray with compost almost to the top. Compress the compost with another tray.*

2 *Water thoroughly by setting ba of tray in a bowl of water. Leave for a few moments.*

6 *Lupin seeds are quite large. Sow two then discard the weaker seedling later.*

7 *Cover seeds with 1.5cm/½in of compost. Water lightly so the seeds are undisturbed.*

not need the entire contents. Sow some of the seed into a small tray or 'half tray' (15 x 20cm/6 x 8in) and save or give away the rest.

Some seeds, such as sweet peas, lupins and pot marigolds are best sown in individual pots, which allows them to grow on with their roots undisturbed right from the start. (Small yoghurt pots are quite big enough to start with.)

There are many brands of seed compost available, and one will work just as well as another. The advantage of these composts is that they are fine-textured and contain no strong nutrients which might upset tiny seedlings. So do not be tempted to make do with stronger potting composts. Invest in a little of the right compost and it will help you to avoid set-backs with your seedlings' growth.

See the light

The seed containers should be filled evenly with compost, including the four corners of trays. Fill them loosely to the top, then take a second container of the same shape and use its base to press down the compost, firming it to a level within 6mm/¼in of the top. If

3 *Alternatively, gently pour water over the seed tray (without disturbing the surface too much).*

4 *Begonia seeds are like specks of dust. A capsule that may come with the seeds helps sow them evenly.*

5 *Do not cover begonia seeds with compost. Cover with cling film to create humidity for germination.*

8 *A plastic bottle 'cloche' provides moist conditions for germination. For ventilation, open the bottle top.*

9 *Sow sweet pea seeds in moistened peat pots. These can be put straight into the ground at planting time.*

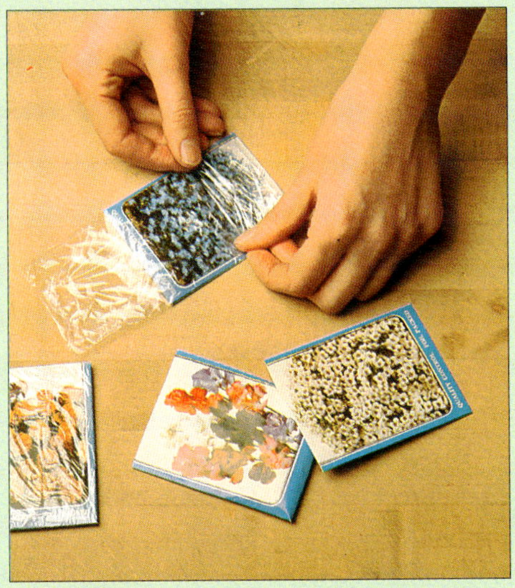

10 *Seal opened seed packets with cling film and store in a cool, dry place until next year.*

you leave the compost level much below that, the sides of the pot will reduce the light which reaches the seedlings. Maximum light and air are vital for healthy seedlings.

It is more practical to water the compost thoroughly at this stage. This avoids the need to water heavily after sowing, which can wash the seeds around on the surface of the compost and undo all your careful, even sowing.

The best method of watering is with a watering can with a good quality, fine metal rose on the end. Plastic roses are often very crude and spluttery, suitable only for garden use; it is worth buying a good rose that will fit your can. Alternatively, lower the pot's base gently into a bowl of water to soak the compost for a few seconds – *before* you sow your seeds. Allow the compost to drain a little before sowing.

Indoors or out?

Before rushing to sow, first check the seed packet for the precise instructions and requirements. For example, some annual flowers can be sown outdoors in situ. Others need to be sown indoors, but not covered with soil, since they require light for germination, for example, begonia.

To sow seed from a packet into the prepared container, shake the seed down to the bottom of the packet before tearing off the tip. This prevents spillage; generally seeds come in a sealed pack within the packet. Then, holding the packet on its side over the container, between thumb and middle finger, gently tap the packet with your index finger to produce a gradual trickle of seed. Move the packet around until the surface of the compost is thinly and evenly covered. Too thickly sown

WATERING

Small seedlings require very little water (except sweet peas), and there is no need to water often. As you grow them on and the plant develops, they will require more water. In the early stages, moistness is all that is necessary.

A cling film covering or home-made cloche helps provide a moist environment.

SUMMER SEEDS TO SOW NOW

Raise your own colourful bedding plants on your windowsill. Most of the plants will start to flower later than the plants from shops and garden centres, but they will reward you by flowering later into the season. These quick and easy seeds can be sown indoors and germinated on a windowsill.

Flowering plants:
African marigold
alyssum
aster
French marigold
busy Lizzie
mallow
lobelia
Livingstone daisy
nemesia
nicotiana
pansy
petunia
rudbeckia
salvia
tagetes
verbena
zinnia

For foliage:
Cineraria maritima
Kochia childsii and *K. tricophylla*
Ricinus communis

seed will produce crammed, crowded seedlings that are difficult to separate and pot on. They are also much more likely to go mouldy.

Do not feel you have to use the whole packet of seed. Save some for a later sowing, perhaps, or even for next year. Most seed will keep for 12 months in a cool place in an airtight container, even if it gives a slightly lower percentage of germination. Seal the packet in foil or cling film to help prevent deterioration.

Once the seed is sown it needs to be covered with the required depth of compost. (Check the seed packet details.) You can do this by using a loosely cupped hand as a sieve, shaking it over the pot to allow a thin trickle of compost to escape between your fingers. A very coarse kitchen sieve will do the job nicely too, but fine meshes hold back too much of the compost fibre.

Settling in

Give the containers a final watering to bed in the seed. Using a fine rose, pass the watering can once or twice quickly over the top; just enough to settle the surface. Try to make sure the can is already flowing before you spray it over the compost, to avoid the first, sudden spurts of water. This can splash in the earth and disturb the surface.

Find a warm and (in most cases) dark place to keep the containers until the seeds germinate. Once again, the seed packet will say whether a particular variety needs light and, sometimes, how long the seed will take to germinate. Some can sprout in just a few days, others take up to three weeks. (Some can take months, but these are usually hardy perennials rather than annuals).

Some seeds demand higher temperatures to germinate. In these cases, an airing cupboard provides an even, warm environment for germination, both day and night.

Covering up

To stop the compost drying out and save you the daily task of methodical watering, cover the containers. There are various methods. Glass used to be the traditional way, but, with small pots of seed, a little 'mob cap' made from polythene with an elastic band to hold it in

DON'T FORGET!

WHAT COMPOST?

The right compost is vital for successful seeds. Special seed composts, like John Innes, contain balanced nutrients and the correct texture.

For a modest outlay, this propagation kit (right), available from garden centres and shops, contains seed trays with lids and separate modules for pricking out. This kit allows you to grow 24-96 plants.

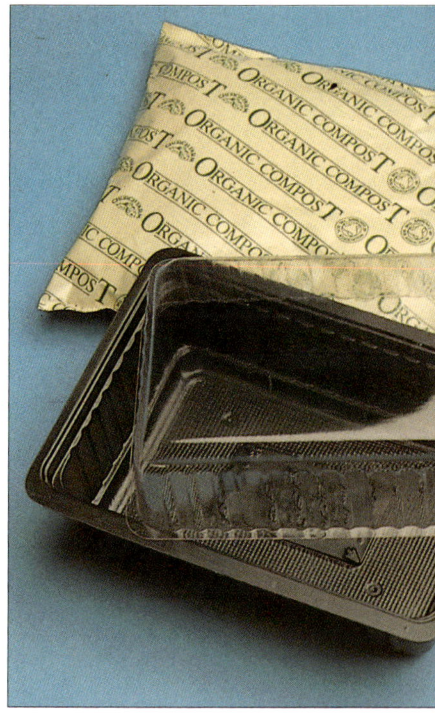

PROJECT PROPAGATING SEEDS ON A WINDOWSILL

The most ideal conditions for raising seeds are in a greenhouse or conservatory. This propagator box will give you excellent results from your windowsill. The foil acts as a reflector, so the seedlings receive all round light. This prevents 'legginess' – a common problem.

All you need is a cardboard box, kitchen foil, glue, sticky tape or stapler.

Choose a box which has a base area large enough for one or more seed trays but which can also fit near a light window. Cut the box as shown above.

Cover the inside with kitchen foil, shiny side outwards. Fix into position. Place seed trays in as shown. Remove from windowsill in frosty weather.

There are several variations of a more complete sowing kit on a smaller scale. This kit (left) contains seed tray, with drip tray and lid, seeds and compost. All you need to add is water and warmth.

Put together your own seed-raising kit for free. Recycle plastic vegetable and fruit packaging trays (below), yoghurt pots and margarine cartons. Don't forget to make some holes for drainage.

place will do just as well. Pierce a couple of holes to stop the air getting stale.

The condensation that builds up on the underside of the polythene drops onto the compost and keeps it moist. It will, however, need to be wiped off or turned over every other day or so. While you are doing this, keep a sharp eye open for the first emerging green shoots.

As an alternative to polythene covers, use very large clear plastic lemonade bottles with their bottoms cut off. These make splendid little 'greenhouses' and the screw-top serves as an excellent ventilator. For seed trays, use sheets of cling film or polythene pierced with a few fine holes for ventilation.

Timing counts

If you are growing annuals from seed without a cold frame, do not be tempted to sow too early. Without a cold frame in which to harden off young plants and accustom them to life outdoors, it is always best to sow at the end of the advised period on the packet. If you sow too soon your plants will be ready to go outside before the weather is warm enough and danger of frost is past.

Windowsills often have inadequate light which makes seedlings 'leggy'. To overcome this, make a propagator (far left) which maximizes the amount of light available. Plants which are grown late, but well, often overtake plants which were sown too early and have suffered setbacks.

The first shoots

Once the seedlings germinate and the shoots appear, uncover the containers and move them to a light windowsill which is also warm. A cold, draughty sill may kill off your seedlings. If this is the case, move them off the window-sill to a warmer position overnight when the temperature drops.

DON'T FORGET!

SHOW A LEG

Q Why do my seedlings often grow long stems in a lop-sided way?

A Seedlings grow towards the light. As soon as seedlings appear, turn the tray regularly so they receive even sunlight.

Modern, draught-proof and double-glazed windows are perfect. Here, the seedlings can continue to develop steadily until the first pair of 'seed leaves' are fully formed.

This is the time to separate the seedlings and prick them out into trays or pots. Whether you use one or the other at this stage is largely a matter of space. Trays allow you to put more plants into a smaller space, but when you come to plant them out there is more chance of disturbing the plants' roots.

One for the pot

Individual pots, however, allow the plants to develop a root system which can be lifted out without any disturbance or setback at planting time. For instance, sweet peas can be planted singly in peat pots. These can be planted straight into the ground, where they break up into the soil. Seedlings in individual pots can also be moved and spaced out individually as they grow on, to give them maximum light for bushier growth.

If you are limited to growing plants on your windowsills, then you might try modular trays. There are many brands available, but the basic idea is the same. A rectangular tray is divided into smaller units. Each plant has its own container, but the plants are held conveniently together. When you want to remove the young plants from the modules, simply press the bottom of the individual pocket to release the rootball.

Sowing Seeds Outdoors

Raising plants from seeds sown outdoors is easy if you know how. Make the most of a variety of seeds with these handy hints.

A vibrant display of Sweet Williams* (Dianthus barbatus) *can be grown from seed (left) at a fraction of the price of bedding plants. As this is a biennial, sow the seeds first in a nursery bed and allow the seedlings to develop into strong plants before moving them to their final flowering position. Sweet Williams thrive best in an open position and well-drained soil.

BIENNIALS

Name	Flowering	Planting spacings
Common daisy *(Bellis perennis)*	Mid spring to mid autumn	13-15cm/5-6in
Canterbury bell *(Campanula medium)*	Early to mid summer	25-30cm/10-12in
Siberian wallflower *(Cheiranthus × allionii)*	Late spring to mid summer	25-30cm/10-12in
Sweet William *(Dianthus barbatus)*	Early to mid summer	20-25cm/8-10in
Foxglove *(Digitalis purpurea)*	Early to late summer	30-45cm/12-18in
Honesty *(Lunaria annua)*	Mid spring to early summer	25-30cm/10-12in
Forget-me-not *(Myosotis)*	Late spring to early summer	15-20cm/6-8in

Whatever their size and shape, seeds need moisture, warmth and air to encourage germination. The majority germinate in darkness, while a few require light. They are therefore scattered on top of the soil or compost rather than being slightly buried.

Moisture is needed to soften the seed's coat and chemically activate the process of growth, while air is required to enable respiration in the roots and developing shoots.

Warmth controls when, and at what rate, the process of germination takes place. As long as the soil or compost is moist, but not waterlogged, and has an open texture to enable air to circulate, the only variable in the process of germination is the temperature.

Germination

The warmth needed to encourage seeds to germinate differs from one type of plant to another. Seeds sown in greenhouses can, of course, be given optimum temperatures to

HARDY ANNUALS

Name	Flowering	Sowing depth	Thin to
Love-lies-bleeding *(Amaranthus caudatus)*	Mid summer to mid autumn	3mm/½in	30-38cm/12-15in
Pot marigold *(Calendula officinalis)*	Early summer onwards	12mm/½in	25-30cm/10-12in
Cornflower *(Centaurea cyanus)*	Early summer to early autumn	12mm/½in	23-38cm/9-15in
Chrysanthemum carinatum (syn. *C. tricolor)*	Early summer to early autumn	6mm/¼in	15-23cm/6-9in
Clarkia elegans	Mid summer to early autumn	6mm/¼in	25-30cm/10-12in
Clarkia pulchella	Mid summer to early autumn	6mm/¼in	25-30cm/10-12in
Convolvulus tricolor (syn. *C. minor*)	Mid summer to early autumn	12mm/½in	23-30cm/9-12in
Larkspur Delphinium consolida (syn. *Consolida ajacis)*	Early to late summer	6mm/¼in	15cm-23cm/6-9in
Californian poppy *(Eschscholzia californica)*	Early summer onwards	6mm/¼in	23-30cm/9-12in
Gypsophila elegans	Early summer to early autumn	6mm/¼in	23-30cm/9-12in
Sunflower *(Helianthus annuus)*	Mid summer to early autumn	12mm/½in	30-45cm/12-18in
Candytuft *(Iberis umbellata)*	Early summer to early autumn	6mm/¼in	23cm/9in
Sweet pea *(Lathyrus odoratus)*	Early summer to early autumn	12mm/½in	23-30cm/9-12in
Poached egg plant *(Limnanthus douglasii)*	Early to late summer	3mm/⅛in	10cm/4in
Scarlet flax *(Linum grandiflorum)*	Early to late summer	6mm/¼in	30-38cm/12-15in
Virginian stock *(Malcolmia maritima)*	Summer (repeat sowings necessary)	6mm/¼in	15cm/6in
Night-scented stock *(Matthiola bicornis)*	Mid to late summer	6mm/¼in	23cm/9in
Love-in-a-mist *(Nigella damascena)*	Early to late summer	6mm/¼in	15-23cm/6-9in
Field poppy *(Papaver rhoeas)*	Early to late summer	6mm/¼in	25-30cm/10-12in
Mignonette *(Reseda odorata)*	Early summer to mid autumn	3mm/⅛in	23-30cm/9-12in
Black-eyed Susan *(Rudbeckia hirta)*	Late summer onwards	6mm/¼in	30-38cm/12-15in

Hardy annuals such as scarlet flax **(Linum grandiflorum** ***'Rubrum', left) are resilient plants which can simply be sown outdoors where you want them to flower. If they are to form part of a larger bed, make sure you take varying colour combinations into account before sowing.***

Encourage sweet pea seeds (right) to germinate rapidly by nicking them lightly with a knife before planting. This helps the hard seed coat to break down.

HARDY HERBACEOUS PERENNIALS

Name	Flowering	Sowing depth	Transplant to
Yarrow *(Achillea filipendula)*	Mid summer to early autumn	6mm/¼in	38-45cm/15-18in
Yarrow *(Achillea millefolium)*	Early summer to early autumn	6mm/¼in	30-38cm/12-15in
Anchusa azurea (syn. *A. italica)*	Early to late summer	12mm/½in	30-38cm/12-15in
Cupid's dart *(Catananche caerulea)*	Early to mid summer	6mm/¼in	30-38cm/12-15in
Shasta daisy *(Chrysanthemum maximum)*	Early to late summer	6mm/¼in	30-45cm/12-18in
Coreopsis grandiflora	Early to late summer	6mm/¼in	30cm/12in
Delphinium	Early to mid summer	6mm/¼in	45-60cm/1½-2ft
Globe thistle *(Echinops ritro)*	Mid to late summer	12mm/½in	45-60cm/18-24in
Blanket flower *Gaillardia aristata* (syn. *G. grandiflora)*	Early summer to mid autumn	6mm/¼in	38-45cm/15-18in
Avens *(Geum chiloense)*	Early summer to early autumn	3mm/⅛in	30-38cm/12-15in
Baby's breath *(Gypsophila paniculata)*	Early to late summer	6mm/¼in	45-75cm/1½-2½ft
Sweet rocket *(Hesperis matronalis)*	Early summer	6mm/¼in	38cm/15in
Oriental poppy *(Papaver orientale)*	Late spring to early summer	6mm/¼in	45-60cm/1½-2ft

encourage germination. Outdoors, this is dictated by the weather and especially by the area in which you live.

Spring is the traditional time of year for sowing seeds because the rising temperatures make germination possible. The range of ornamental plants for sowing outdoors is extremely wide and includes annuals, biennials, herbaceous perennials, trees and, of course, shrubs.

Annuals

Some annuals are half-hardy and must be raised under glass early in the year, ready for planting outdoors as soon as the risk of frost has passed. Hardy annuals have a tougher image and can be sown outdoors in the positions where they are to flower. Most are sown in spring.

Preparation for sowing hardy annuals should begin in the autumn of the previous year, when the soil is dug to a depth of about 25cm/10in (a spade's blade). Well-rotted manure and decayed garden compost can be dug into the soil at this stage, but remember annuals flower best in soil that is not too rich.

Winter weather breaks down large lumps of soil and by spring creates a fine tilth. In early spring, rake the ground level, further breaking down the soil. Firm light soils by systematically treading over them, but take care not to compact them too much.

Small and narrow flower beds at the side of paths can be sown without too much preparation. But large borders need to be carefully planned on paper first, taking into account the differing heights and colour combinations.

After raking and treading the surface, use a thin line of sand to mark out the areas for each type. Alternatively, mark the areas by using a stick to draw shallow lines.

A garden-line and the corner of a hoe or rake can be used to create drills in which seeds can be sown. Sow seeds thinly and evenly and use the back of a rake to cover them. Alternatively, shuffle along the

The hardy herbaceous perennial blanket flower* (Gaillardia aristata) *will provide a profusion of brilliant yellow blooms (above) for several years, if grown initially from seed in a nursery bed.

When preparing the soil in spring for sowing, first mark out the positions of the different plants you intend to sow with a thin line of sand (right). Then form drills with the side of a hoe. When the seeds are sown, use the back of a rake (inset) to cover them with soil to the required depth.

GROWING TIPS

SOWING WILD FLOWERS

Wild flower gardening is increasingly popular. Wild flower seeds, such as cowslips and wild cornflowers, can be bought from many garden centres, either as separate types or as mixtures.

Sowing wild flowers needs as much care as when handling garden flowers. Unless the soil is well prepared and moist, the seeds will not germinate.

Spring or late summer are the best times to sow the seeds. Alternatively, early autumn sowing is sometimes possible.

drill, with your feet on either side of it, gently pushing soil over the seeds.

If you need to lightly rake the surface at this stage, do this in the same direction as the drills. Raking across them may disturb and scatter seeds in the wrong places.

Place brushwood-type sticks over the area to prevent birds and cats scratching the seed. Alternatively, use black cotton stretched between canes inserted at the edges of the border. Extra protection can be given by threading pieces of tin-foil along the cotton.

During dry spells, keep the border moist. After germination, remove the sticks and, when large enough to handle, thin out the seedlings to the distances in the Hardy Annual table on page 1169.

Most of the plants in this table are true hardy annuals but some, such as Black-eyed Susan (*Rudbeckia hirta*), are short-lived perennials which are normally cultivated as hardy annuals.

Biennials

These are plants that are usually sown in shallow drills, about 30-38cm/12-15in apart, in a nursery bed in early summer for flowering during the following year.

During the first few months they germinate and develop into strong plants. Transfer them to their flowering positions in late summer or early autumn.

Many plants naturally have a biennial nature, but others although normally perennial are treated as biennials.

Herbaceous perennials

These are plants that live for several years, dying down to soil level in autumn and sending up fresh shoots the following spring.

They are raised by sowing seeds thinly in shallow drills in a nursery bed in late spring and early summer. The sowing depths are indicated in the Hardy Herbaceous Perennial table on page 1170.

After germination, thin the seedlings slightly so that they are not congested, and in late summer or autumn plant them into their flowering position. The spacings are also indicated in the table. These distances may need to be adjusted according to the height and vigour of a particular variety.

Trees and shrubs

Seeds of trees and shrubs are increasingly offered in seed catalogues and, although it takes many years for a reasonably-sized tree to be raised in this way, to do so always creates a lasting sense of personal achievement.

Seeds of some trees and shrubs are large, with thick coats that reduce the speed of germination. Therefore, it is often necessary to soften or remove part of the seed coat, or to submit them to alternating periods of cold and warmth before they are sown.

Some ways of encouraging the rapid germination of seeds are suggested below.

BRIGHT IDEAS

ENCOURAGING SEEDS

Soaking seeds in water helps to leach out chemicals that inhibit germination. Soak for up to three hours in hand-hot water. If the packet advises soaking for longer, change the water periodically. Some seed, such as clianthus, caragana and broom swell when soaked. If this happens, sow immediately – before they have time to dry out.

Seeds such as sweet peas and morning glory have hard seed coats that benefit from being chipped. Scratch the outer surface with a sharp knife, rub the seeds on fine sand-paper or, with small seeds, prick with a sharp needle.

Some perennials, such as a number of trees, shrubs and many alpines, need a cold period to break their dormancy. This used to be done by putting the seeds between layers of sand and leaving them outside for the winter. Today it is easier to use a refrigerator.

Sow the seeds on several layers of moist kitchen paper placed in a small plastic container with a close-fitting lid. Keep them at room temperature for about three days then place in the refrigerator for several weeks. Check periodically to make sure the kitchen paper has not dried out. Then remove the seeds and sow them in compost.

Seedlings

Seeds sown indoors in the last two or three weeks should have germinated by now. Here's what to do next.

As soon as your seedlings have produced their first pair of tiny green leaves it is time to give them a bit of space, or 'prick them out'.

Densely sown crops of seedlings are prone to damping off at this stage, so pricking them out while they are still small is very important. With tiny seedlings, it can be a rather fiddly job, but it is perfectly possible with a little practice.

As a general rule, prick out only the strongest seedlings and discard any that are weak or spindly. However, with mixtures prick out both strong and weak to ensure a good colour balance. Lobelia seedlings are tiny and are pricked out in small clusters, so some will inevitably be at a later stage of development than others.

Seedlings can be pricked out into pots, trays or modules (trays with their own internal divisions). Modules are economical on compost and space and are easy to handle. There

Growing plants from seed is not only immensely satisfying it is also very economical. Once your seeds have germinated you will be rewarded with trays full of densely packed seedlings (above). This is the stage at which you prick them out, to prevent overcrowding.

When the first two leaves appear the seedlings should be transplanted in order to give their root system adequate space to develop. The seedlings (left) have outgrown their tray and are being transplanted into another container where they will have adequate breathing space. The pansy seedlings (right) have been planted in individual containers until they are ready for planting out. Seedlings, like babies, cannot digest strong foods so plant in specially balanced seedling compost.

is also no disturbance to roots when the time comes to plant out, so the plants suffer no disruption to their growth.

Traditional seed trays (containing five rows of eight plants) are fine, but there will be a period, after the roots have been disturbed at planting out time, when growth is temporarily slowed down.

Which pot?

Pots can be used for seedlings, but they must be small (6-7.5cm/2½-3in across). A smaller pot is more economical on both space and compost and seedlings can later be moved to a larger one, if necessary.

To prick out seedlings, first fill your trays, pots or modules with compost, right up to the top. Press the compost down gently to leave space for watering. Make a hole with a pencil or a piece of fine cane. Then, using finger and thumb, take hold of the first seedling by one of its leaves. Use the pencil to gently tease up the root from the compost, then lower it into the prepared hole. Use the pencil again to bring the soil up to the root. When the tray is full, give it a thorough watering with tepid water through a fine rose. Seedlings hate an icy shower! Once the tray has drained, it is ready to go on the window sill.

The temperature needed now is not quite so high as it was for germination. Over the next few weeks it needs to be gradually lowered to steady the growth of your little plants. Remember, though, that the temperature should not vary too much. If you are growing your plants on the window sill, lift them away

Not all seedlings look the same. Some, like these cyclamen (left) are quite developed and already share a family resemblance. They produce 'true' leaves unlike most seedlings whose first pair of leaves bears no resemblance to their final form.

The cyclamen produces a root ball which can easily be replanted while the sweet peas (below) set out a long tap root which must be handled carefully. Make a deep hole and insert the seedling, taking care not to break the root.

DON'T FORGET!

VITAL NEEDS

To ensure that seedlings grow into compact, healthy plants remember to give them:

- maximum light
- maximum ventilation
- an even temperature
- soil that is moist but not saturated

PRICKING OUT SEEDLINGS

When your seed tray begins to look overcrowded, the time has come to give the seedlings a bit of room. The next stage in the process of raising seedlings is known as pricking out. It is a fiddly job because the seedlings are so small but it will pay dividends in the long run. The size of the seedlings depends on the plant. Some, like the begonias pictured below, have tiny seeds and very small seedlings. Cyclamen and sweet pea seedlings are larger and easier to handle. They can be transplanted into modular trays which have individual compartments for each seedling or into individual small pots.

1 ***Fill a modular tray with special compost suitable for seedlings and water well.***

2 ***Using a pencil, ease out the roots and lift by the leaves using thumb and forefinger.***

3 ***Make a hole in the compost with the pencil, insert the seedling and firm in.***

4 ***Using the blunt end of the pencil gently firm in the soil around the seedlings.***

5 ***Put a lid on the tray or cover pots with cling film to preserve moisture.***

OUTDOOR SOWING

Of course, the information on these pages applies only to seed sown indoors, and if the notes on your seed packet tell you to sow directly into the ground where the plants are to flower, you should follow this advice instead. Not all plants are automatically better suited to being nurtured indoors. Poppies, larkspur and pot marigolds will all produce far better plants when sown straight into the soil outdoors.

from the window into the room at night, so they do not get chilled. This is especially important at first, while the seedlings are getting established. Later, they will need to become accustomed to a colder night-time temperature before they go outside. A temperature of about 15-18°C/60-65°F is suitable for most new seedlings, reducing to 10–13°C/50-55°F later on.

While your seedlings are growing on, it is important to maintain as high a level of light as you possibly can. This will prevent the plants from becoming drawn and leggy. It is advisable to turn the trays or pots every few days so that both sides of the plants receive light and develop evenly.

At this stage bedding plants should be bushing out rather

WHAT DOES IT MEAN?

- **Pricking out** – spacing out seedlings in seed trays or pots.
- **Hardening off** – the process of acclimatizing tender and half-hardy seedlings raised indoors or under glass to the harsher conditions which exist out of doors.
- **Growing on** – the stage during which transplanted seedlings establish themselves and grow larger, before they are finally planted out of doors.
- **Damping off** – not a technique, but a fungus that can infect seedlings soon after they have germinated. For this reason, you should use only sterilized compost. Poor drainage and over-watering can also encourage the problem. Remove plastic coverings for a short period each day so that the atmosphere is not too humid. Always wash old pots and trays thoroughly before use, and water seedlings with fresh tap water.

Prevention is better than cure for controlling damping off. Keep tools clean and never use garden soil.

than making one tall shoot. If they are shooting upwards it means either that they are getting insufficient light or that they are too warm, or both. It may be necessary to pinch out the tops to encourage them to bush out.

Hardening off

As the days grow warmer it will be necessary to acclimatize your young plants to conditions out of doors. Hardening off is really just a matter of easing the transition from an 'intensive care' window sill to life in the real world of the flower bed.

Choose a mild, dull day to lift your pots and trays outside for a few hours. The temperature will not be too much of a shock, but they will not be used to the movement of air and it will take time for them to get used to transpiring, or breathing, at a faster rate. If your plants wilt the first time you put them outside, the chances are that they are having difficulty coping with the wind and sun. Try again on a balmier day. Eventually, after a few spells outdoors, they will be ready to take direct sun and wind. At this stage they will need more water than before.

A permanent cold frame is often a wooden construction with a glass top. This very professional looking example (right) is located in a sheltered spot by the side of a large greenhouse. The chains attached to the glass top allow the amount of ventilation to be controlled according to the specific requirements of individual plants. Because it is in sections there can be a degree of flexibility – so that some plants can have full ventilation while others are only exposed a little.

Cold frames

The more gently seedlings are hardened off the better, and the easiest place for this is in a cold frame. A cold frame is simple to construct and it will save you all the bother of lifting plants into the garden and back indoors each day. More importantly, a cold frame ensures that your plants are sheltered, receive maximum daylight and develop evenly.

Another advantage is that plants get plenty of ventilation. You can air your young plants constantly in clement

Once the seedlings have been transplanted they have to acclimatize to outside conditions. If you have a cold frame (below) it is easy to control the amount of air your plants receive and at the same time ensure they get maximum daylight. This ensures that your batch of seedlings develop evenly.

DON'T FORGET!

WATCH OUT FOR FROST!

One of the great enemies of bedding plants is late spring frost so it is important to insulate plants to protect them.

If your plants are in a frame, instead of bringing them indoors when a frost is forecast simply lay a sheet of newspaper over them before closing the frame. Cover the outside of the frame with opened-out cardboard boxes or a bit of old blanket, to provide a further layer of insulation.

Even when there is no threat of frost, get into the habit of closing your frame just as the evening begins to cool. You will then trap any heat that has built up during the day and preserve a higher night-time temperature.

TAKING CARE

Tiny seedlings are very fragile and some are so small they can be very difficult to handle. Seedlings should be pricked out when the first pair of leaves appear. Always try to lift the seedlings by these leaves. Never attempt to lift a seedling by the stem or roots as these are easily damaged and this may prevent the young plants growing into healthy adults.

weather and this is a great help in keeping fungal disease at bay.

Having transferred your plants to a cold frame, lift off the cover or prop it open whenever there is a suitably warm and sunny day. It should be open just as much as the plants can stand, to get that vital air through to them. This applies on a wet day just as much as on a dry one, but use a propped lid to let the rain run off and save the seedlings from becoming saturated.

A rain check

Once you have a cold frame you must keep an eye on the weather. When the sun shines, open the cover quickly so that plants are not roasted. At night, close the frame to protect plants from the chill or, even worse, frost. Once plants are acclimatized to the open air you can leave the cover off at night when the weather is mild.

Planting out

As soon as the risk of frost is past (May or June, depending on where you live), your plants should be planted out into their final positions to give them the maximum growing season. Left in their trays, they will stop growing as they will have used up all the nutrients in the compost.

PROJECT

BUILDING A SIMPLE COLD FRAME

A cold frame need not be large or permanent. It can be made from readily available materials and requires no special skill to assemble.

Site your frame in a warm, sheltered position that receives maximum light. For a frame measuring 1m/3ft 4in square, build up 48 bricks, layer by layer, on a flat surface, following the photographs. Make the joints of each layer overlap the joints of the previous one. There is no need to use mortar between the bricks so the frame can be dismantled easily and moved or stored for the winter.

Once you have built the walls of the frame, place a sheet of rigid clear pvc on top and secure around the edge using more bricks.

To ventilate the frame, remove the cover and place one of the securing bricks diagonally across each corner of the frame walls. Set the cover down again, resting it on the four bricks. Place the remaining four bricks across the corners of the cover, to hold it in place.

For a cheaper alternative to rigid pvc you could try using polythene, or a sheet of glass (in a wooden frame), though this can be risky with children around. Corrugated plastic is strong, but will leave a gap around the sides, even when closed.

1 *Using 48 ordinary household bricks, make a base for your cold frame.*

2 *Place a sheet of rigid clear pvc on top of the wall of bricks.*

3 *You will need another 8 bricks to secure the corners of the pvc.*

4 *To ventilate, simply raise the pvc up one level of the securing bricks.*

Summer Bedding

Bringing home a trayful of new plants for your garden can be so exciting. Here's how to plant them for maximum effect and long-lasting colour

Summer glory: a stunning and easy-to-achieve show of colour. Tall bedding dahlias in bright hues provide a backdrop for a mass of busy Lizzies in boldly clashing shades of pink and red.

Bedding plants are so called because that is the way in which they are used: they are 'bedded out' for display, another term for planting. The plants are mainly hardy annuals, capable of surviving outdoors all year round and half-hardy annuals.

Splashes of colour

The main use of bedding plants is to introduce colour to the garden throughout the summer, and as they are a temporary addition you can change the display every year.

Nearly all summer bedding plants have plenty of brightly coloured blooms, which is why they are so popular. They transform a flower bed into an attractive bank of colour, and just a few added to a border of shrubs works wonders.

So versatile, bedding plants need not be restricted to beds and borders, many grow happily in containers such as patio tubs, window boxes and hanging baskets.

Visual effects

Your local nursery or garden centre should have a wide variety of plants to whet your appetite, with contrasts in colour, texture, shape and size. You may like to arrange your

PLANNING A BORDER

An informal bedding scheme (above) is created by grouping several different varieties of bedding plants in random clusters; while a formal look (below) is achieved by setting colours together and using the silver-leafed cineraria as a feature plant.

CREATING A LOOK

It is a good idea to think about what sort of look you want to achieve with your new bedding plants *before* you start digging and planting. Put the plants out on the earth while they are still in their containers and move them around into different positions to give you an indication of the final effect. As a general rule, tall plants look best at the back, medium ones set mid-way, and small ones at the front where they will not be hidden. Use the list (right) to help you plan your scheme. All the plants listed are popular, easily available varieties.

PICK OF THE PLANTS

Tall
aster
bells of Ireland (moluccella)
Canterbury bell (campanula)
clarkia
dahlia – bedding type
schium
fuchsia
love-lies-bleeding (amaranthus)
lupin (lupinus)
salpiglossis
summer cypress (kochia)
sweet William (dianthus)
tobacco plant (nicotiana)
wallflower (cheiranthus)

Medium
African daisy (arctotis)
begonia – fibrous rooted
busy Lizzie (impatiens)
calendula (pot marigold)
cineraria (senecio)
coleus
cosmos (cosmea)
bellis perennis
dwarf sweet pea (lathyrus)
gazania
geranium (pelargonium)
love-in-a-mist (nigella)
nemesia
petunia
phlox
reseda (mignonette)
salvia
snapdragon (antirrhinum)
Star of the Veldt (dimorphotheca)
tagetes (African marigold)
zinnia

Short
alyssum
Californian poppy (eschscholzia)
candytuft (iberis)
dianthus – bedding
dwarf busy Lizzie (impatiens)
flower floss (ageratum)
lobelia
pansy
tagetes (French marigold)

plants quite formally, in tidy rows, or grouped informally around hardy perennials, shrubs and shrub roses.

Bedding plants really do look at their most glorious when displayed to show off their vibrant colours – it never seems to matter that 'clashing' colours sit side by side. Shocking pink, hot red and brilliant orange can look wonderful together in the flower bed.

If you want a less brazen effect, however, bedding plants look equally attractive when used as part of a more restrained colour scheme: pink and white is a popular combination, as is yellow and blue, or you could limit yourself to shades of one colour, against a backdrop of green shrubbery.

Buying for borders

In your enthusiasm to fill your garden with bright new plants, do not be tempted to buy at the first opportunity. Although bedding plants are sold by market traders, florists and some supermarkets, it is generally advisable to purchase them from a garden centre or nursery. Wherever you buy, it must have the proper environment and facilities for

GARDENERS' TERMS

Annuals – plants that will only last a season.

Biennials – plants which flower in their second season, then die.

Half-hardy annuals – annuals that cannot withstand frost.

Hardy annuals – annuals that can withstand a moderate frost.

Perennials – plants which live longer than two years.

Tender – liable to be damaged by frost. A tender plant should be brought indoors while there is a danger of frost.

The clash of orange, red, white and purple works well in this border (left). The different flowers – alyssum (white), lobelia (blue), salvia (red) and French marigolds (orange) – are planted in blocks, rather than being allowed to intermingle, making each colour more pure and intense. The vivid green leaves of the salvia and marigolds add an equally stunning fifth colour to the display.

keeping the plants in good condition.

Summer bedding plants are generally available to buy from mid-spring through to early summer. Bear in mind they must not be planted out until danger of frost is over, which is late spring in warmer areas and early summer in colder places. If you have no facilities for holding plants until planting time (for example, a frost-free greenhouse or garden frame) then do not buy them until you are ready to plant.

Small bedding plants, like pansies, are often sold in trays of 24 plants, though smaller quantities can be purchased in strips. Larger plants, such as pelargoniums, are usually sold singly in plastic or fibre pots.

Garden centres also sell ready-planted plastic containers, each with several plants coming into flower, which do not need planting out. They are simply placed in patio tubs or other ornamental containers to give an instant splash of colour.

Using differences in height and colour to the full – the tallish African marigolds stand over a strip of low-lying lobelia. The bold yellow pompons of the marigolds (below) contrast in colour and form with the edging carpet of sprawling mauve lobelia.

GARDEN NOTES

PLANTING DISTANCES

Before planting out water each plantlet, preferably the night before – but do not water the bed or planting will be a very sticky business.

The distance at which to plant will depend on the final size of the plants you have chosen. If planting in rows, stagger each row for the best effect. As a rough guide, use the list (left) to help you:

- small, slow growers: space about 15cm (6in) apart
- medium-sized plants: space about 23-30cm (9-12in) apart
- large plants: space about 30-38cm (12-15in) apart

Planning a scheme

A traditional summer bedding scheme, which is still popular today, consists of the main flower planted over a large area to form a colourful carpet: for instance, begonias, dorotheanthus or alyssum.

A few taller plants to give

PLANTING YOUR SUMMER BEDDING PLANTS

***1** Before you start any digging or planting, assemble everything that you need: plants, peat, bone meal, watering can, tools and gloves.*

***2** Clear the area set aside for new plants by digging out any spent ones and removing weeds and their roots from the soil.*

***3** Starting at the back of the bed, use a trowel to dig holes just bigger than the root balls of each plant. Space holes according to size of plant.*

***5** To remove each plant, turn the pot upside-down, supporting the plant between your fingers, and tap the base or gently squeeze the pot.*

***6** Position the plant in its hole and check that the roots are not bent or cramped before replacing soil. Firm soil around the plant with your hands.*

***7** If the plants were grown in polystyrene trays, separate them by gently pulling apart the roots. Plant these as before (step 6).*

GARDEN NOTES

FEEDING FLOWERS

Preparing beds and borders with the right balance of food will ensure a beautiful show of flowers all summer long. Bone meal is an organic fertilizer that releases its goodness slowly, so is specially good for shrubs and other slow-growing plants. Growmore is a general purpose fertilizer which acts more quickly than bone meal, but is suitable for annuals. Autumn is the ideal time for feeding soil with bone meal, but as bedding plants have fine root systems, springtime is perfectly adequate. Work the fertilizer into the top few inches of soil. Do not apply when the surface is dry.

height to the scheme, generally with attractive foliage, are planted at random in this carpet, contrasting with it in colour, texture and shape. These are known as dot plants, or feature plants, a typical example being silver-leaved cineraria. The bed can be given a low contrasting edging, if desired, such as sweet alyssum, ageratum or lobelia.

If you want to plant a long border which is viewed from the front only, you may prefer to arrange the various flowers in bold informal groups. Set the tallest ones at the back, medium-height plants in the centre and short plants at the front. There is no need to stick rigidly to this rule: to avoid a regimented effect, you can occasionally extend groups of tall and short plants towards the centre of the border.

Getting good results

Most summer bedding plants should be grown in a sunny position, although there are a few which will succeed in partial shade.

They grow in any type of garden soil provided it is well drained and not prone to lying wet over the winter. The soil should be reasonably fertile but not over-rich. Once a year, before buying and planting

4 ***Before planting your bedding plants, sprinkle a fine layer of bone meal into each hole and work it in ghtly with a garden rake.***

3 ***After all the plants are in place, hoe the soil around them to erase any footprints. Water the plants well ng a watering can with a fine rose.***

summer bedding, give the bed a light dressing of general purpose fertilizer, following the instructions on the pack, and lightly rake it into the surface.

Bedding plants are especially useful in new gardens which probably have a great deal of bare earth that needs to be covered quickly. They will give a good display of instant colour while you are doing some more long-term planning.

If your garden has just a few shrubs in it, use bedding plants to fill the spaces in between. Be sure to buy enough – over-planting looks better than under-planting, and helps to keep the weeds at bay, too.

WHAT WENT WRONG?

BORDER PROBLEMS

Q My summer bedding plants grew very well but produced few flowers. Do they need feeding?

A It sounds like you may have added too much fertilizer already. Follow the instructions on the packet carefully.

Q My bedding plants flowered well initially, but then produced very few blooms. Why?

A You probably didn't remove the dead flowers from the plants often enough. Remove them regularly to encourage flowering.

Q My summer bedding plants flowered beautifully but now the flowers are becoming mouldy. What did I do wrong?

A You might have over-watered. Water new plants daily until they start to grow, then only when dry.

A white begonia and a mauve and white fuchsia (above) make a very pretty match. Begonias are probably the 'ultimate' bedding plant. Easy to care for, they flower profusely all summer and come in virtually any colour.

There is no restriction on where to use your bedding plants. They work equally well in pots or tubs and in flower beds. If you use pots, do make sure they have adequate drainage, use a proper planting medium (not garden soil) and remember to water and feed the plants regularly.

FLOWERING PERIODS

Plan this year's display with reference to the chart below. Choose plants from the same colour band for planning simultaneous flowering or from different colour bands for consecutive flowering.

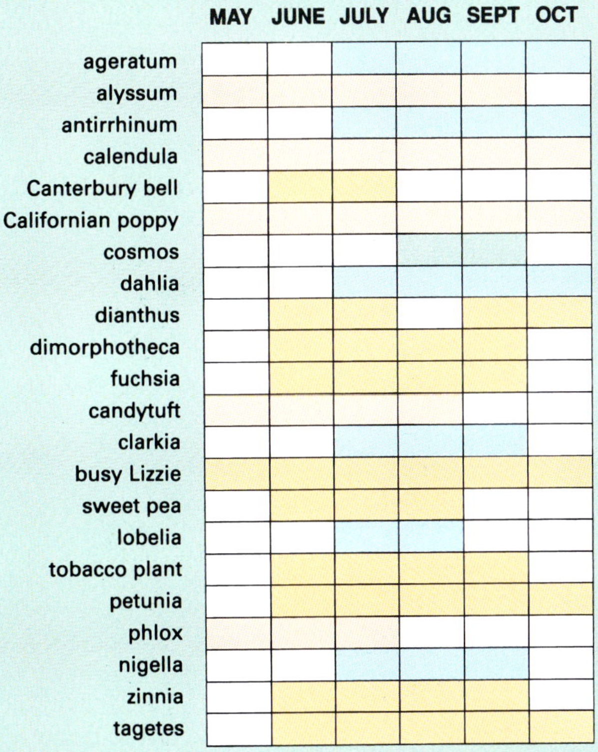

Note: All plants will be cut down by the first severe frost and weather will affect flowering.

Planning Your Garden

Plan a garden accurately on paper to achieve a layout which includes all the features you require. Some may be existing features, others new.

When changing an established garden, you must first decide what to keep. Shrubs and trees that screen off neighbours are worth retaining, but you may want to lay a new lawn, patio and path (above).

Whether you have a brand new plot with nothing in it, or an established garden, the first step is to measure up the site and draw an accurate scale plan of it.

If the garden is already established you will have to decide which features you want to retain. Incorporate these on the plan. Do not go into fine details, such as all the plants in beds or borders – just outline the planted areas.

All important permanent features should be included, such as paths, lawn, patio, garden shed, trees and large specimen shrubs.

Anything not required and that is to be cleared away should not be included on the scale plan.

An established garden may

already have a number of features that you want. With a brand new plot you can plan from scratch and this is perhaps more exciting.

Circular lawns (above) create an illusion of width in a narrow garden. The central birdbath catches the eye and is a focal point.

Principles of design

Some features are common to virtually all gardens, so let us consider these in some detail, starting with a few simple design principles.

To create an effect of distance have at least one focal point at the end of a view. This could be a tree, a specimen shrub, a seat, a statue or a sundial to draw the eye.

If the garden is long then divide it into several self-contained areas, but still aim for some long views.

Small rectangular gardens can be made to look larger by having curved lawns and borders. Circular lawns spanning a plot help to create the impression of width in long narrow gardens.

Try to have at least one hidden area with a path disappearing into it. This could be created with a trellis or fencing screen, a screen-block wall or a hedge.

Such an area helps to create an element of surprise in a garden, and should be attempted even in the smallest plot. Even something as simple as a small seat placed behind a group of tallish shrubs will give you a secluded, 'secret' area for sitting quietly.

Traditionally, vegetable and fruit plots are sited at the end of a garden, but if you have a large plot it may be more sen-

MEASURING THE SITE

The plot and house have to be measured up and transferred to paper.

You should start by measuring the outside perimeter of the house and transferring this to the graph paper.

But first you will need some simple equipment, including a strong tape measure (a steel tape is probably best); several long lengths of cord or nylon; some pointed wooden stakes about 30cm/12in in length; some 1.2m/4ft long bamboo canes; and a large right-angle triangle made of three lengths of wood (the formula for making this is three, four, five).

Establish a base line from which to measure. Generally, the most convenient is the wall of the house that faces the largest part of the garden.

Working from this wall, run lines (which can be marked with canes) at right angles to it until they meet the boundary of the plot.

If the sight line is interrupted, say by shrubs or other plants, then insert canes along the line. Each cane must be exactly in front of the preceding one when viewed with the eye close to it.

These lines are measured and then transferred to the graph paper. The boundary points can be marked on the paper with dots.

Then from points along these first lines you can run 'branch lines', at right angles, to other parts of the boundary. Measure these distances and transfer them to the plan.

When a garden is all round a house, or on several sides of it, the other house walls must be used as further base lines to make more right-angle measurements.

When all necessary dots have been made on your graph paper you can join them up to outline the perimeter of the plot.

Then, from the base lines, measure in a similar way to any other permanent features that will be retained. Include these on your plan.

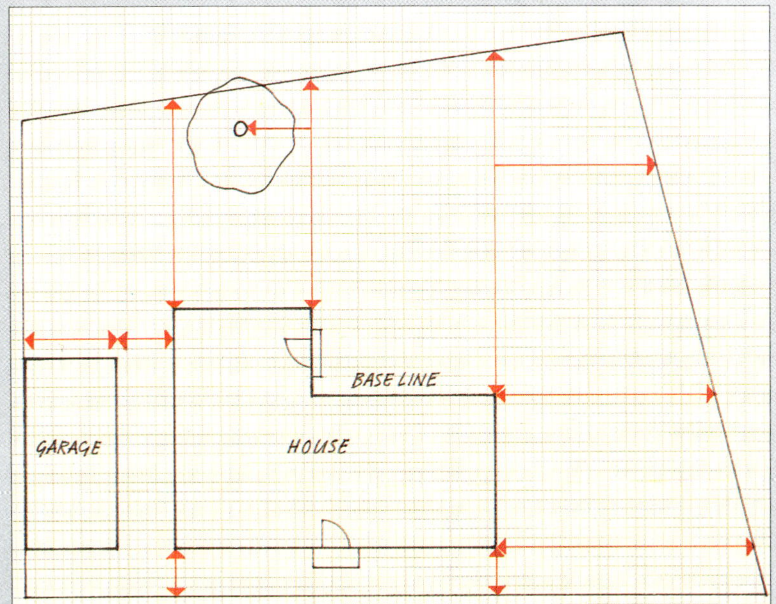

Take right-angle measurements to establish your boundaries. The scale here is 1 inch to 10 feet but the illustration has been reduced down.

DRAWING A GARDEN PLAN

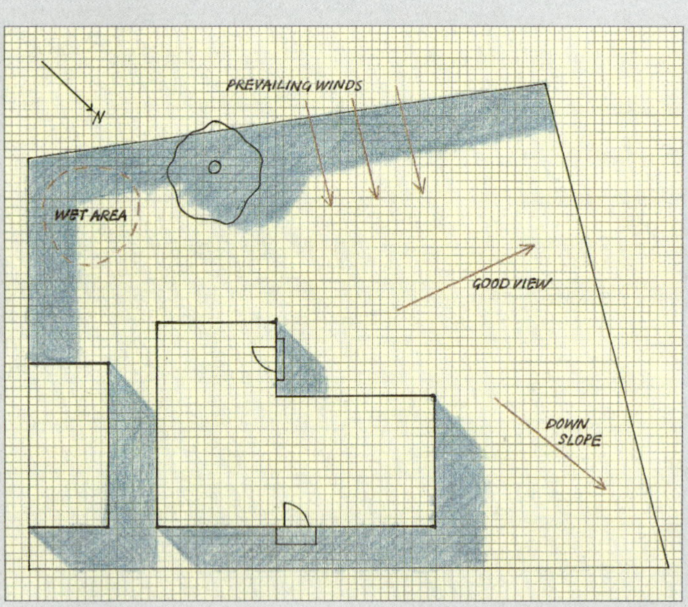

You will need to draw a scale plan of your plot, showing the house and garden. This is best done on graph paper, using a soft pencil so that you can easily erase any mistakes you make.

The larger the paper the better, as the easier it will be to draw a really accurate plan of the whole site.

You should choose a scale that will enable the entire plot to be drawn on one sheet of graph paper. Convenient scales are 1.2m or 2.4m to 2.5cm (about 4ft or 8ft to 1in), but on graph paper with one-inch squares that are divided into tenths it makes sense to use a scale of 10ft to 1in. (approximately 3m to 2.5cm).

Firstly, draw the perimeter plan on the paper, together with the house and any permanent features that are to be retained, including trees and outbuildings.

Then clip a sheet of tracing paper over the graph paper to draw in other features. These can include slopes and mounds, good views, eyesores, the direction of the prevailing wind, suntraps, boggy areas and so on.

Another sheet can be placed over this on which to draw in variations and other details. This enables you to build up and alter at will the plan until you are completely satisfied with it. Then it can be transferred to the graph paper to form a master plan.

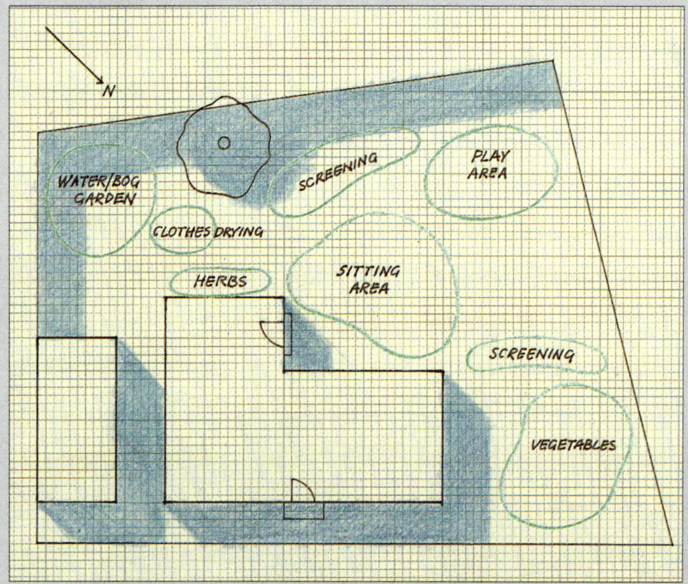

A well-kept vegetable patch (above) can be happily integrated with flower beds in a small garden.

By creating a variety of separate areas, the owner has made the most of this garden (left). Shrubs and trees provide privacy and screen unsightly sheds. The curved borders and lawn make the rectangular area seem bigger. A seat has been included and the pond provides a feature of interest at the far end. The washing line runs alongside the path.

Buddleia (right) is a fast-growing shrub that soon provides a splash of colour.

sible to have them somewhere nearer to the house.

Vegetable gardens can be made to look very ornamental, especially if laid out in geometric beds with grass or gravel paths between – they certainly do not have to be an eyesore and hidden away.

Areas for sitting

Some sort of sitting and outdoor living area is important and most people opt for a patio. This should be sited in the sunniest part of the garden, ideally adjacent to the house.

Many people like a lawn as well, but in a small garden constant use can turn this into a threadbare mud patch.

An open area other than a patio (which, in any case, may be partially enclosed to shelter it from the wind) is strongly recommended. It gives a sense of space in a garden and avoids that 'shut-in' feeling. A small garden, especially, needs this. The alternative to a lawn is a gravel area, constructed from pea shingle over a firm bed of well-rammed soil.

Sun and shade

A garden should have both sunny and shady areas, to suit people and plants. On a brand new site, plan at the outset for some shady areas. Include a group of small trees or large shrubs, both of which should

TIMETABLE OF JOBS

This is a suggested order of priority:

- Plan the garden on paper.
- Mark out any new features on site with bamboo canes or wooden stakes. Informal shapes can be marked with flexible lengths of hosepipe, rope or string.
- Carry out any construction work (avoid winter), such as the laying of patios, paths and gravel areas, and the building of walls and pools.
- Erect fences and pergola.
- Create a new lawn: from turf between mid-autumn and mid-spring, provided the ground is not frozen or very wet, or from seed in spring or early autumn.
- Dig and prepare beds and borders for planting.
- Plant permanent plants. If these are in containers it can be done all year round, provided the ground is not frozen or very wet. Hardy bulbs should be planted out during the autumn.

Broom (left) is a shrub that can be planted for a quick effect. This is **Genista hispanica,** *which is commonly known as Spanish gorse.*

A small, square garden (below) can be made functional yet attractive, with a central paved area and a variety of plants in containers, borders and protruding beds. A table and bench provide somewhere for tea, and the eye is caught by the lamppost and its surrounding variegated shrub.

cast dappled shade.

A garden exposed to full sun for much of the day can be an uncomfortable and glaring place, and you will not be able to grow the huge range of shade-loving plants.

For a quick effect, plan for some groups of large, fast-growing shrubs, such as buddleias or different varieties of brooms and pyracanthas.

Other features

These are some of the basic elements of good garden design but you may well require other features. However, do not be too adventurous. Bear in mind that some garden features can be very labour intensive and involve you in considerable time and money spent on maintenance.

A rock garden is a case in point. You will need to spend a lot of time on it weeding, if you want it always to look good.

A practical alternative, and one perhaps more appropriate in the garden of a modern house, is to have a small gravel area in which to grow alpines or rock plants. The gravel looks good and prevents weeds from growing.

Choose a sunny, well-drained part of the garden for this. It can have a few specimen rocks set in it and will make a very attractive and labour-saving feature.

A pond is a very popular feature but avoid it at all costs if you have small children. Instead, start off with a sunken sandpit for the toddlers, then when they grow up a bit convert it to a pond by removing the sand and lining it with a plastic or rubber pond liner.

Remember, though, a pond needs a fair amount of attention to keep it looking good. And it must be sited in a sunny part of the garden away from the shade of overhanging trees and large shrubs.

Practical points

A clothes drying area is important for many people. In a small garden, especially, a collapsible rotary drier set on a patio or lawn is often the most convenient solution.

If you want a greenhouse and have a fairly large garden, then it makes sense to site it near the house if you are going to run electricity and water to it. Running these services a considerable distance down a garden can be very expensive.

Besides, a greenhouse gen-

A contrast between hard landscape and rich borders (right) can be very effective. Here, pale gravel, square paving stones, circular stepping stones and the white statue are set off by the dark background of cypresses and bright floral arrangements. The light, Mediterranean feel is enhanced by the brown amphora and a spiky succulent in a matching brown jar.

erally needs frequent attention, which it may not get if sited too far from the house.

Pergolas are extremely popular and are well worth having. They are attractive in their own right, especially when spanning a path, and make ideal supports for climbing plants. Pergolas can also be built against unsightly outbuildings, such as concrete garages, to help hide them.

Making changes

In a well-established garden you may have some or all of these features. It is up to you which of them you retain.

Never be afraid to get rid of any features that you do not like or require. Some people are reluctant to dig up paths, lawns, shrubs or trees, but remember that all of these, and other features, can be replaced if need be.

For a garden to be successful, it has got to be what you want, not what the previous owners required.

However, good advice on taking over an established garden is to leave it alone for a complete year. This will give you ample time to decide which features you want to retain and what you would like to replace.

Also, it will allow you to assess the plants. You may, for instance, have some attractive shrubs, whose beauty was not obvious when you moved in.

The garden may be rich in bulbs and herbaceous perennials; remember these have a period of dormancy and so may well be hidden under the soil when you take over the house.

Most very old, worn-out shrubs are not worth keeping, but some can be rejuvenated by cutting them back hard in late winter or early spring. Roses respond well to this, as do shrubs like rhododendrons, laurels and yews.

Do, however, try to retain as many large shrubs and other plants as you can, for these help to create a real sense of maturity in a garden.

Buying

Don't be tempted to rush ahead and buy whatever plants catch your eye. Make sure you know the pitfalls before you splash out – it will pay dividends in the long run.

These container-grown conifers (above) are given the best growing conditions in a nursery where specialists in the plant industry pride themselves on growing most of their stock on site.

Garden centres (left) are the convenient – and tempting – way to buy just about everything you need for your garden. Like a supermarket, it is all too easy to fill your trolley with bags of goodies from the well stocked and clearly laid out shelves. This is a good reason for arming yourself with a list, although the garden centre is also a good place for picking up ideas.

From leafing through a catalogue in the comfort of your armchair to browsing in open-air markets, because there is such a wide choice of plants available it is easy to buy unsuitable ones.

What's on offer

The number of diverse plant retail outlets has increased enormously, each with their advantages and disadvantages.

Garden centres are where most people do their garden shopping. A good centre is well laid-out so you can easily find what you are looking for. These places do get crowded and tend to run out of stock towards the end of popular gardening periods. They usually have a good supply of container-grown plants, so you should find what you want at most times of the year.

Nurseries are more specialized than garden centres and are probably best for shrubs and conifers, heathers or specimen trees. They usually grow their own plants.

Mail-order catalogues are by far the most convenient way to buy from the comfort of your home. Catalogues are helpful and informative, allow you to choose at leisure, and provide an extensive range of plants, often with their own exclusive varieties. Bulbs, too, can be bought with confidence from growers who specialize in mail order. If you order growing plants such as shrubs by post, direct from a nursery, you must be prepared to plant them as soon as they arrive.

On your doorstep

The main advantage of ordering shrubs or conifers from a specialist grower by this method ensures they are delivered straight to your door at the best time for planting. You can also rely on good specimens.

Local markets generally have at least one stall which sells bedding plants and bulbs, and sometimes small shrubs and heathers as well. Market stalls are certainly convenient and generally inexpensive, but the range is often restricted to popular varieties of bedding and vegetable plants. Do not expect a huge success rate, as often these plants are greenhouse-reared and then displayed in often cold and windy conditions.

Stately selection

The gardens of British **stately homes** present a wonderful opportunity to admire plants in established beds and borders; many have their own plant stalls. Since many of these gardens are famous for growing plants, a visit to one of them can be an excellent chance to widen your own plant selection. The plants will usually be in good condition and, if the garden you are visiting is close to home, you know it stands a good chance of growing well in your own garden. Remember, however, that some of the plants may be specialized and may require particular conditions to be really successful.

Department stores, supermarkets and DIY suppliers sell a variety of plants, seeds and bulbs. They are convenient and generally inexpensive, but the plants may grow prematurely and die quickly.

Stocking up on shrubs

Shrubs, including roses, conifers and small trees, form the design backbone of most gardens. They are the permanent features which spread as they mature and around which other plants are arranged.

Since they are so important you will want to buy the best ones that you can afford. The biggest plant is not necessarily the best. On the other hand, small specimens may be too weak to establish successfully. At best, small plants will take years to make an effective contribution to your garden.

There used to be different

> **DON'T FORGET!**
>
> **BE PREPARED**
>
> Before you go to buy your plants:
> - Make all the necessary preparations for the plants, such as preparing soil and adding bone meal.
> - Check the plants will grow easily in your particular garden soil.
> - Work out a planting plan, taking into account the ultimate size of the plants.
> - Write out a list of the plants you need to buy.

This magnificent herbaceous border (above) belongs to one of the many private houses which open their gardens to the public. Plants are often for sale in the grounds.

Market stalls (below) are usually stocked with popular bedding plants grown in the local area so your purchases should settle into your garden easily.

Most nurseries and garden centres stock container-grown shrubs which can be planted at any time of the year. Look for healthy specimens like these (left). There is plenty of foliage and no leaf discolouration. Several strong stems are growing from the base. When you are ready to plant a container-grown shrub, ease it out of the pot and tease out any long roots which have wound themselves around, being careful not to disturb the root system.

planting seasons, depending on whether your shrub was deciduous or evergreen, but the widespread use of container growing has changed that nowadays. Basically, plants are available in one of the following four ways.

Self-contained

Most container shrubs can be planted at any time of year and are clean and easy to handle. If you plant during the summer months be sure to keep them well watered. If it is not possible to plant immediately – if the soil is frozen, for example – keep the pot damp, but do not waterlog it.

When choosing your shrub, check that the soil is firmly settled in the pot, not loose. There may even be a few weeds or some moss growing, which indicates that the shrub has been in the container for some time. A few fine roots growing out from the base of the pot are also a good indication. Too many, however, or weeds on the surface, suggests lack of care.

Exposed roots

Root-balled shrubs have been dug up from a field with a ball of soil around the roots, held in place with hessian or plastic. They can be left for several weeks before planting, as long as the soil is kept moist. It is best, however, to plant them in the appropriate seasons: evergreens in autumn or mid-spring; deciduous shrubs between autumn and spring when the weather is kind; conifers in early to mid-spring. Do not cut away the wrapping until the planting hole is ready. The ball-root method is best for larger shrubs with well-established root systems, but it can be rather messy. Make sure the wrapping is not torn and that the soil is moist.

When you are choosing ball-rooted or container-grown plants look for specimens which have good, even growth and healthy-looking stems and leaves without weeds.

Bare-rooted plants must be dormant when you buy them, so avoid any that are coming into leaf. Even though the roots are bare, they should

> **GARDEN NOTES**
>
> **CHOOSING SHRUBS**
>
> There are several points to bear in mind when choosing shrubs:
> - Look for a good shape with no straggly shoots.
> - Check leaves and stems for disease or pests.
> - Check the root system as much as possible, according to the type of shrub you are buying.

Annual bedding plants like these (left) are bought in trays or plastic strips. They should be sturdy looking and not too straggly or tall. It is better to buy specimens which have plenty of buds rather than flowers. Do not buy them too early as frost may kill them.

not have been allowed to dry out, so avoid any that look very parched. You must be ready to plant them at once, between late autumn and early spring, so do not buy if the soil in your garden is frozen hard. They are, however, much cheaper than the previous two types, and you do have the opportunity to inspect the root system.

This sorry-looking spider plant (above) is pot-bound. Left too long in a too-small container, the roots have twisted round the inside of the pot and the plant's growth has been severely stunted. Check for signs of this by looking under the pot for straying roots.

Similarly, the poor specimen on the left has been in its container for too long. The roots have forced their way through the plastic base and are very dried out.

Container-grown shrubs must be kept moist, especially in the summer when they dry out quickly.

Pre-packed roses, like bare-rooted plants, must be dormant. They are usually inexpensive, but you may have to wait longer before you start to enjoy good results.

Perennial interest

Herbaceous perennials and biennials have a vital part to play in your garden display and must be selected with equal care. Both are widely available, container grown. Look for healthy, well-proportioned specimens with no weak, stems or signs of damage from pests or disease.

Smaller plants grown from cuttings or seeds may be a year or two old and will take longer to contribute to your garden, but they are often cheaper.

Quick colour

Annuals bring an instant colour lift to your garden but even though they are short-lived you will get a better display if you choose well. They come in trays, polystyrene strips or individual pots

Check that the plants are fairly even in size – not straggly or 'leggy'. Choose plants that are in bud, not in flower. If the leaves are unhealthy-looking, leave well alone. Make sure the roots have not grown through the bottom of their containers, as this indicates that they have been in them too long. The compost should be evenly moist.

Finally, do not buy bedding plants until you are ready to plant them. Half-hardy annuals are often on display too early and if you have not got room to keep them under glass for a few weeks while they acclimatize, they may be ruined by a late frost.

Bulbs, corms, tubers

If you order these by post from a specialist grower, they should arrive in good condition, and at about the right time to plant. Do not keep them indoors too long, as the conditions don't suit them. If you choose loose bulbs in a shop or garden centre, try to buy them as soon after they come in as possible.

A good bulb should be firm and plump, with no black or grey mould. Avoid any showing signs of growth, or those with shrivelled skins.

GARDEN NOTES

VALUE FOR MONEY

- Shop around to find the best value for money. Your nearest garden centre may not be best for bargains.
- Perennials are better value than annual bedding plants as they last for several years.
- Nurseries usually supply good quality, more reliable plants because they are specialists in the field.

Shrubs

Shrubs are the backbone of garden design but they can also be some of the most beautiful feature plants – so choose them with care.

Shrubs are hard-working garden plants that can be ornamental features as well as practical attributes in your garden. They are part of the permanent framework of the garden and, once they are well established, there is little extra maintenance that you need to perform to keep them healthy and flourishing.

Average soil conditions will suit most shrubs which will grow well in sun or shade. Except in severe drought conditions, or when newly planted, they do not need regular watering. Some may need a little pruning to make them flower well but apart from that they offer much decorative value for little effort on your part.

What is a shrub?

Shrubs have tough, woody stems that do not die back in winter. The many stems or branches grow from near ground level and provide an overall bushy shape to the plant. There is no central or dominant, leading stem.

When you set out to buy shrubs from a garden centre in winter or spring when some of them may be bare and leafless, look for their unmistakable well-branched outline.

Decorative displays

Some shrubs are evergreen, with leaves all year round. While others are deciduous and lose their foliage in winter. Some, like forsythia, burst into flower early in spring. Others will dazzle you in autumn with russet coloured foliage. Many produce coloured fruits that are decorative and attract birds too.

Shrubs are the backbone of a good garden plan. They clothe and shape it, softening edges and adding colour and fragrance. A garden quickly looks established once the shrub framework is planted.

Best of all, they provide their attractive flowers, foliage, or their autumn fruits with the minimum of routine care. Some simply need removal of dead and damaged wood and a light pruning to keep them within bounds before the beginning of the growing season in spring, while

Shrubs form the framework of good garden design. Use them to create a layout to which you can add your personal stamp – choose colours, textures and even statues to complement the shapes and shades of the shrubs.

If you have a sheltered, sunny spot fill it with a Choisya ternata – Mexican orange blossom (left) – and lose yourself in the wonderful aroma of the white flowers which first deck the dark, glossy leaves in late spring and again in autumn. It is a slow growing shrub which is easily kept in check, making it suitable for all gardens.

Although often similar in height, dwarf conifers are trees not shrubs. They have one central trunk while shrubs have many branching stems. Shrubs and conifers make an extremely attractive display (below) and it can be remarkably colourful. Ranging from smoky blue-green to bright yellow-green and maroon they are lovely on their own, but mix them with a few well chosen flowers and the whole ensemble really comes to life.

GARDEN NOTES

WHAT IS A SHRUB?

Shrubs have tough, woody stems that do not die back in winter. They differ from trees in that they are generally not as tall and they do not have a central trunk. All their branches grow from near ground level, and create a bushy shape.

others need special pruning to make sure that they produce a mass of beautiful flowers.

Because shrubs are such popular and useful garden plants there are many that are easily available at garden centres and nurseries. Their popularity means that they are usually inexpensive and you can be sure that you are buying healthy, reliable and garden-worthy plants.

You may, however, wish to include in your garden shrubs that are not so widely available. They may be expensive and you would find them at specialist nurseries, but make sure they do not require too much extra attention or special situations that you cannot easily provide.

Shrub or tree

While the growth habit of trees is usually dominated by a central leading stem (the trunk or bole) with a head of branches sprouting from the top, shrubs do not develop this central stem. Instead their many stems branch at different angles to the ground and make a rounded shape.

There is, however, an area of overlap between shrubs and trees. Holly, hazel, hawthorn and some willows may develop into trees or into shrubs depending on how you prune and maintain them. Beech, for example, is often grown as a hedge. Similarly, Leyland cypress is clipped into shrub-like shapes to make hedging.

The other difference between shrubs and trees is in

Lighter than air, the arching branches of the Tamarix pentandra 'Pink Cascade' (above) seem coated with a fine pink dust which looks as if it might be blown away in the slightest breeze.

height. Trees may offer as much ornamental value as shrubs, but most take up a great deal of space when they reach maturity. They may take many years to reach full height (this can range from a couple of metres up to 40m/100ft or more), so seem to have shrub-like proportions at first. Once they are mature they are likely to be too big for your garden; they may block out light and will certainly be difficult to underplant successfully, as they drain the soil of moisture.

Shrubs can grow tall and wide, but they do respond well to pruning and maintenance, so you can control their ultimate size. They will not attain tree-like heights, they range in height from under 30cm/1ft up to 6m/20ft.

Shrubs in the garden

Shrubs can be purely ornamental features for you to admire and use in the garden. Flowers are their most obvious advantage. Shrubs flower over a long period from spring through to late autumn, and some even flower in winter, making them essential to keep year-round colour in a garden.

Coloured bark or stems, evergreen foliage or variegated leaves, autumn leaf colour, coloured fruits or berries and a pretty fragrance are among the decorative charms that shrubs bring to the garden. Additionally, many shrubs will do well when planted in containers on balconies and patios. Pieris, camellias, formosa and lavender are included among these.

Beyond the purely ornamental, shrubs can be used to define the space in your garden. They introduce changes of height in a border or terrace area, and can also be used to enclose parts of the garden. In a large garden you can use shrubs to guide your eye to particular views or vistas.

GARDEN NOTES

TIME TO MOVE

If a shrub has outgrown its space it can be transplanted provided you follow a few rules.

- Move deciduous trees between autumn and spring. Larger shrubs are best moved after they start to shed leaves.
- For evergreens early autumn or late spring is best. Water in thoroughly.

Shrub screens

They also work well, if planted in groups or straight rows, as hedges or windbreaks. In a small garden, they are ideal plants to make screens around unsightly sheds or utility areas. Some shrubs grow very low and scramble across the ground. These can be used to a gardener's advantage too, as they will stabilize and decorate banks that may be difficult to maintain under grass.

Many shrubs hold their foliage throughout the year, offering you permanent colour and shape. Evergreen shrubs

Some shrubs have a prostrate habit and are excellent as ground cover. Stranvaesia davidiana 'Prostrata' (below) has white flowers in summer and berries in winter.

Lithospermum diffusum, also known as Lithodora diffusa (right), is another shrub with a spreading, prostrate habit. It looks like an alpine, proving that shrubs are an extremely diverse group of plants. Some look like trees and others, like this one, are small enough to grow in rockeries. It has a height of 15-30cm/6-12in and spread of 60cm/2ft. Masses of vibrant, violet-blue, star-shaped flowers are produced in summer. This species likes a soil that is slightly acid.

are most suitable for hedges or screens, as they offer permanent cover or privacy. They do drop some leaves, usually in spring, but not on as large a scale as deciduous shrubs.

The leaves of evergreens are usually glossy and there are many evergreen shrubs with golden and white variegations that will offer you added colour. Although decorative in their own right, evergreen shrubs also provide a useful backdrop for many other garden plants.

Deciduous shrubs

These plants look bare and twiggy in winter, when they lose their leaves, but their soft and fresh spring shoots and leaves, followed by flowers and possible autumn leaf colour, more than make up for this seasonal lack of beauty.

Some shrubs, including many of the dogwoods, have exceptionally beautiful stems that create an eye-catching winter feature.

Hardy or tender?

Hardy shrubs will not need any protection during winter or outside the growing season. Some, like *Convolvulus cneorum,* a shrubby bindweed that is not invasive, and abelia *(A. grandiflora)* are hardy in most situations, but in very cold districts they may need a sheltered position.

Tender shrubs are those that need protection in winter, either by mulching their roots with straw or by placing a seasonal barrier of protective netting or insulation around them. Some may have to be kept inside or in a conservatory over winter.

On the borderline are shrubs such as the pretty yellow-flowered wall plant, *Fremontodendron* 'Californian Glory'. It will need a sheltered or sunny position to survive in very cold areas.

Sub-shrubs

This term is applied to plants that have a woody base and soft stems. They are perennials whose soft stems die back in winter. Like shrubs they have bushy shapes, but are generally low-growing.

Included in this group are the low-growing rock rose *Helianthemum alpestre,* and the lovely little rockery plant *Lithospermum diffusum.*

Conifers are usually classified as trees, but many of the compact, slow-growing specimens are used as shrubs in garden situations. True dwarf conifers are valuable additions to the shrub repertoire.

They do remain small and are genuinely slow-growing, but they may revert back to their true type and grow too tall for your purpose. If your rockery dwarf conifer starts developing vigorous shoots, cut them back before too much growth is made.

Size and scale

Most garden centres and nursery catalogues estimate the size a shrub will reach either when mature or up to ten years after planting. In a

Many tiny shrubs, like the Helianthemum oelandicum or rock rose, look more like little alpines. The rock rose (above) loves a well-drained, sunny spot and is ideal for brightening up a rocky patch or a dry bank. Its open-faced, five petalled, bright yellow flowers appear from early to mid-summer.

BRIGHT IDEAS

EARLY FLOWERS

Some early flowering shrubs that offer delightful flowers and do well in most conditions include the following:

- Quince (*Chaenomeles × superba*) provides cup-shaped flowers on bare stems in early spring, with edible fruits in late summer. Grow it against a sunny wall. After flowering, prune it lightly but do not cut away all the fruiting stems. (1.5 × 1.5m/5 × 5ft)
- Winter hazel (*Corylopsis pauciflora*) offers attractive, delicately scented yellow flowers that seem to drip down from its bare stems. The flowers need protection from early sun. (0.9-1.5 × 0.9m/3-5 × 3ft)
- Mahonia japonica is a huge evergreen shrub with decorative spiky leaves and long trails of yellow scented flowers in late winter, early spring (up to 2 × 3m/6½×10ft)
- Laurustinus *(Viburnum tinus)* is an evergreen with bouquets of small white flowers in spring. (2.7 × 1.8m/9 × 6ft)

As well as being extremely decorative, many shrubs have very practical applications. The Fagus sylvatica 'Purpurea' (right), better known as the purple beech, makes a perfect hedge. Beech is one of the border-line shrubs that doubles up as a tree. When trained into a hedge it is a shrub but when allowed to grow tall and straight it is a tree. When kept clipped these hedges do not drop their dead, brown leaves in winter but remain densely covered in foliage.

The beauty of shrubs is that they are generally hardy. The frosted plants (left) look magical and the colours are tinged with blue. Libertia chinensis, Nandinia domestica and euonymous have been used here.

Skimmia japonica (below) is a very versatile shrub. From early until late spring it produces abundant clusters of star-shaped white flowers. The rich green foliage is highly aromatic throughout the year and bright red fruits are produced in autumn.

small garden you need to know the ultimate size the shrub will reach: you do not want to have to uproot an expensive and cherished plant because there is no room for it.

You can control the size and shape of most shrubs by careful pruning or keeping them in bounds when they do get overly large. Do this on a regular basis, rather than making a severe cut-back when the shrub is well-established.

Most shrubs will grow in average garden soils but to grow vigorously and flourish they should be planted in a site which is well prepared and has good drainage. The planting hole should be well dug to a depth of up to 30cm/1ft to allow for the plant's root system. Early spring or late autumn are generally the best times to plant shrubs. Apply a little fertilizer to the planting hole along with plenty of good garden compost and a handful of bonemeal. Water the plant in well and keep it well watered, especially in drought conditions and in the first year of its planting.

GARDEN NOTES

PRUNING SHRUBS

- Many shrubs need pruning to increase their flowering capacity. Deciduous spring and early summer flowering shrubs should be pruned immediately after flowering. Cut back old wood with faded flowers to encourage new growth. Flowering currant (*Ribes sanguineum*), forsythia (*Forsythia spectabilis*) and mock orange (*Philadelphus*) are included in this group.

  After pruning, new growth will quickly appear and it is on this new wood that the buds for next year's flowers will be made. If the plants bear fruit later in the season prune lightly after flowering and enjoy the fruits.

- Prune most late summer flowering shrubs in spring. They produce their flowers on shoots grown immediately after pruning. Cut them back hard so that they make plenty of new wood in spring to carry their flowers. Included in this group are the butterfly bush (*Buddleia davidii*), pheasant berry (*Leycesteria formosa*) and the tamarisk tree (*Tamarix pentandra*). Winter-flowering shrubs simply need pruning to tidy up any dead or diseased branches after flowering in early spring.

Another plant with attractive berries is Mahonia japonica, (right), but these appear in summer. Sprays of pretty yellow flowers decorate the spreading branches from mid-winter until early spring, introducing a touch of summery colour to your garden in the wintry months. These shrubs are excellent as specimen plants as they are sure to provide year-round enjoyment. This particular species grows to about 2m/6½ft and has a wide spread of approximately 3m/10ft so make sure it has enough room.

SHRUB CHOICE

Shrubs, whether evergreen or deciduous, are a good choice for a new garden, to fill empty space and make an immediate impact. They create an excellent background for bedding plants and, if well chosen, provide year-round interest. Here is an attractive selection.

PLANT NAME	ATTRACTION	SIZE
abelia *Abelia grandiflora*	fragrant flowers in summer	height and spread up to 1.5m/5ft
common camellia *Camellia japonica*	spring flowers and evergreen leaves	bushy, up to 3m/10ft high
Californian lilac *Ceanothus 'A. T. Johnson'*	beautiful blue, showy spring flowers	1.5-3m/5-10ft high
Mexican orange *Choisya ternata*	slow-growing, shade-tolerant bush with orange-scented flowers in spring and autumn	up to 3m/10ft but can be pruned hard after spring flowering
mezereon *Daphne mezereum*	early spring flowers, purple-red and scented, on leafless branches; berries in autumn	up to 1.5m/5ft
silk tassel bush *Garrya elliptica*	fast-growing, with grey-green catkins in winter and spring	up to 3m/10ft but can be pruned
griselinia *Griselinia littoralis*	fresh green leaves; makes very good hedging in coastal areas	up to 2.4m/8ft wide and tall but can be kept in bounds if trimmed regularly
Oregon grape *Mahonia aquifolium*	evergreen with fragrant yellow spring flowers and grape-like fruits; shiny dark green leaves turn reddish-purple in autumn	90cm-1.8m/3-6ft tall
Jerusalem sage *Phlomis fruticosa*	grey foliage; whorls of yellow summer flowers	low-growing, up to 1.2m/4ft
pieris *Pieris formosa* 'Wakehurst'	new leaves have a red blush of colour; white flowers appear in late spring	height 1.2-1.5m/4-5ft or more
firethorn *Pyracantha rodgersiana*	good wall or screening shrub, with clusters of white flowers; orange berries in autumn	erect; 2.4 × 2.4m/8 × 8ft, but depends on how it is pruned
rosemary *Rosmarinus officinalis*	a culinary herb with aromatic leaves and pretty blue flowers in early spring	bushy, up to 90cm/3ft
viburnum species	many have good flowers, some scented, in early spring and through the year	up to 3m/10ft but can be pruned

The catkins, weighted down by a fresh new snowfall, droop heavily from the Garrya elliptica (above) in winter and spring. It prefers a sheltered spot as long severe frost may damage the plant. Generally they are frost hardy.

Some shrubs enjoy particular soil conditions. Azaleas, rhododendrons and camellias, in particular, prefer a lime-free or acid soil. To provide the right conditions you may need to make an acid bed or plant them in containers with ericaceous compost.

It is less work and less expensive if you grow shrubs that thrive in your particular region. Otherwise you might have to give them extra attention to make sure they do well in a climate or soil that does not quite suit them.

Viburnus tinus, a winter flowering viburnum (below) is an evergreen. Pretty pink buds open into white flowers. Some varieties have pink-flushed flowers. This is ideal as a specimen shrub.

Fruits

Fruit trees look good in blossom and produce a very satisfying crop. Today's dwarf varieties make them very suitable for a small garden.

Apple trees can be very compact. They fruit well, the fruit is easy to pick and they are a convenient height for pruning. The variety in the foreground is 'Greensleeves', which has crisp, juicy apples from mid to late autumn. It is a good pollinator of other apple trees.

DON'T FORGET!

TIP BEARERS

Some apple trees, such as 'Worcester Pearmain' and 'George Cave', are tip bearers, which means they need a completely different system of pruning. If you prune them as you would spur-forming apples, you will simply cut off all the flower buds and get no fruit.

There is nothing to compare with the taste of your own home-grown fresh fruit. Supermarket fruit may spend up to three years in carbon-dioxide-filled cold stores before it reaches the shops, so for flavour you should grow your own.

The work involved in growing fruit trees is not enormous. The important thing is to do it regularly and at the right time. Nowadays fruit trees can be made to crop heavily when only a few feet high, so there is no longer any need to stretch awkwardly up from the top of a tall ladder.

Choose your tree carefully. However pretty the blossom, a tree which does not bear fruit properly is a waste of space and time. Make sure you get a tree which suits your local climate and the available space. Take as much advice as you can get, and buy from a reliable nurseryman who is willing to help you choose or visit a good garden centre.

Tree shapes

Fruit trees, especially those which require more heat to do well, can be very successfully grown against walls. The traditional shapes for a wall are the fan and the espalier. There is also the cordon, which allows you to grow several different varieties in a small space. Wall trees are usually bought ready-trained but you can buy 'maidens' and train them into shape on a wall. A later issue looks in detail at wall-trained fruit trees.

Free-standing shapes of tree include the bush and dwarf pyramid, which are small and are easy to work on. Half-standards are proper trees on a 1.3m/4ft trunk, while standard trees have a 1.8-2.1m/6-7ft trunk suitable for an orchard. All these can be bought from nurserymen, and fans and bush shapes are on sale at garden centres.

An alternative is a 'family tree', which has several varieties of fruit (all apples or all

pears) on one tree. It usually comes as a half-standard.

'Ballerina' trees are a natural form of free-standing cordon, which do not have to be trained. They crop well on a single upright stem.

Size and situation

The habit and size of a fruit tree is entirely dependent upon its roots. Trees are grafted onto different kinds of rootstock according to whether a bush, a fan or a large tree is required. Some fruits are more successful when trained into certain shapes, and you will not find all varieties available in every shape. The following is a rough guide.

Apples do not really need wall heat and are better grown in the open as trees. Dwarfing rootstocks produce very small trees which have a relatively short life, and some always need staking. Trees on more vigorous stocks are longer lived and withstand poorer soils. The more dwarf the plant, the sooner it will begin to crop properly. Dwarf trees begin to crop when they are two to six years old.

Pears are naturally very big trees, and to keep them smaller they are grafted onto quince stocks. Quince C is used for wall fruit and smaller trees. Quince A is used for trees on poor soil where more vigour is needed.

Plums, greengages and damsons were traditionally very large trees, which made them unpopular. However, they are now available on dwarfing rootstocks, making them suitable for smaller gardens. They can be grown on walls or in the open. In colder areas they are best grown against walls.

Cherries also used to be large trees, suitable only for large gardens or tall walls. The new Colt stock has made cherry growing (and picking!) a much easier business. The newer Inmil stock is even more dwarfing. Dessert cherries require more warmth than cooking (sour) cherries, and grow well against a wall.

Other fruits. Apricots and peaches can be grown on sunny walls in the south of Britain, but the quality of the fruit is never great outdoors. They are better grown under glass. The same is true of figs, except in the warmest counties and inner London. Figs, however, do make a very ornamental addition to any wall border as a foliage plant.

Medlars and mulberries are large trees, while quinces rarely grow higher than 6m/20ft; all have a low return of fruit. It is best to regard them

All cherries (above) are beautiful when in blossom. This is 'Stella', the only self-fertile sweet (dessert) cherry.

'Conference' (below) is the hardiest all-round pear. The pears cook well and, if kept, they make good eaters.

GOOD VARIETIES

Look out for the following excellent varieties. All the cherries and plums are self-fertile, but most apples and pears will need a pollen partner to set fruit.

Apple
Cox's Orange Pippin, James Grieve, Laxton's Superb, Lord Lambourne, Newton Wonder. Egremont Russet and Charles Ross are self-fertile.

Pear
Doyenne du Comice, Doyenne d'Été, William's Bon Chrétien, Conference, Beurré Hardy.

Plum
Victoria, Czar, Merryweather Damson, Early Transparent Gage.

Cherry
Morello, Stella, Kentish Red, May Duke.

as ornamental plants with an incidental fruit value.

The fruits of the flowering quince, *Chaenomeles,* can be used as a substitute for those of the larger true quince, *Cydonia.* But flowering quince, or japonica as it is known, is still grown principally as an ornamental plant.

Pollination

It is important to realize that not all fruit trees are self-fertile. You may need a second variety of the same fruit in the garden, with which the first tree can cross-pollinate, in order for fruit to be set.

Not all varieties are compatible with each other, for technical reasons, and you need to check in a book or with the supplier to see that you buy suitable trees.

The need to grow two trees in order to set fruit was one reason why people moved away from fruit growing; it took up too much space. But now, with modern dwarfing stocks, you can grow, say, four varieties of apple as cordons on a wall 2.4m/8ft long.

If you want just one tree, it is safest to choose a self-fertile variety which can fertilize its own flowers and set fruit by itself. This is reliable, but it limits your choice of varieties as there are far fewer self-fertile varieties.

Family trees have two to four compatible varieties grafted on to the same main stem, so cross-pollination is no problem. You can even get dessert and cooking apples growing on the same tree.

Apples: most need a second variety to cross-pollinate, and it must be one which flowers at the same time within the long apple-flowering season. There is often a suitable pollinator in a nearby garden, so you may get a good crop with just one tree. 'Grenadier' (early cooker) and 'Spartan' (late eater) are two self-fertile varieties.

Pears : all are better with a

PLANTING A FRUIT TREE

Plant bare-root trees in frost-free weather from late autumn to early spring. Dig a hole big enough to take the roots. Add humus.

Drive in a stake and plant the tree alongside it. Fix the trunk to the stake with a tie after returning the soil and firming it down.

Apple varieties grown on dwarfing rootstocks (above) remain compact. This is 'Lord Lambourne', which produces juicy, sweet dessert apples from mid to late autumn. It flowers early and will flourish on heavier soils than 'Cox's Orange Pippin'.

THE EFFECT OF DWARFING ROOTSTOCKS

Dwarfing rootstocks largely determine the eventual size of a tree. Soil is another major factor; on poor soil you need a more vigorous (less dwarfing) stock.

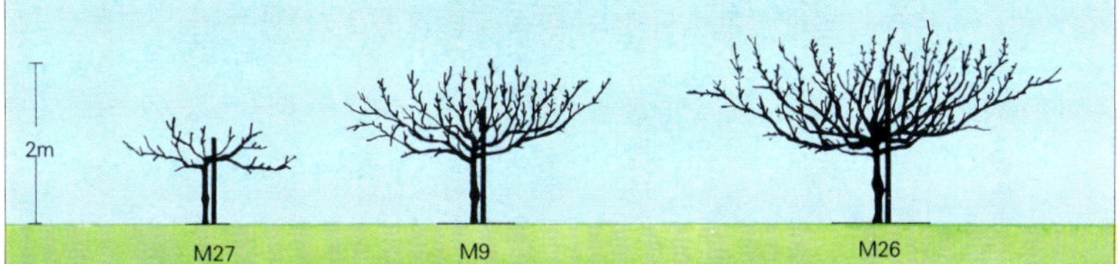

Apples (after ten years):
M27 1.8m high × 1.8m spread/6ft × 6ft. Can be grown in pots.
M9 3m × 3m/10ft × 10ft.
M26 3.6m × 3.6m/12ft × 12ft.

Plums (after ten years):
Pixy 2.4m × 2.4m/8ft × 8ft.
St Julien A 5m × 5m/16ft × 16ft.
Myrobalan B Large orchard tree.

'Ballerina' apple trees (left) have a single upright stem. This variety is 'Bolero', growing on the vigorous, semi-dwarfing rootstock MM106.

Trees are generally pruned after fruiting and before flowering. Secateurs cope with thin branches.

second tree to cross-pollinate. Pears are less commonly grown by neighbours.

Plums: most are self-fertile, but a few of the best are not, so make sure you know what you are buying.

Cherries: most need a compatible tree to set fruit, but 'Morello' (cooker) and 'Stella' (dessert) are self-fertile.

Avoiding frost

In cold areas there is always the risk that late frosts will destroy the blossom on fruit trees, and with it the year's crop of fruit. This is one reason for growing fruit on a wall, which gives some protection.

However, some varieties not only flower later but also actually resist the frost better, so make sure you buy suitable varieties if you live in a cold area or a frost pocket.

Usually plums flower first in the season, followed by cherries, pears and then apples.

Planting

A fruit tree should offer you high returns for many years, so it deserves good planting. Always take out a generous, deep hole for the roots, and add plenty of good compost or well-rotted manure, and a slow-release fertilizer. Do not use fresh manure or the tree may shoot too hard.

Trees on very dwarfing rootstocks, such as M27, should be staked for all their lives, so use a stout stake, treated with a preservative. Drive it into the hole before you plant the tree, to avoid damaging any roots.

The point where the graft has been made should always be a few inches above soil level after planting the tree.

Pruning

Once fruit trees are established, pruning settles down to an annual programme. All you need are secateurs, a small saw and a little understanding of the principles.

Fans and espaliers, however, need considerable training in the initial years, until the framework of branches has been built up. If you do not enjoy this sort of precise work, it may be better to go for the easier cordon, bush and half-standard shapes, where pruning is simpler.

Generally speaking, apples and pears are pruned in winter, with a little summer pruning as well if you have time. Plums and cherries are pruned rather less, and the work must be done in late summer or early autumn while the trees are still in leaf.

Fruit trees, like all plants, have their own range of pests and diseases, such as scab and codling moths. Whatever the problem, it is always easier to deal with it on smaller trees or wall-trained specimens. It is no harder to look after fruit trees than, say, roses, or any other strictly managed plant. Even so, it is always best to select disease-resistant varieties wherever possible.

WHAT WENT WRONG?

POOR CROPPER

Q In my new garden there are two good, productive apple trees and one weak, poor one. Should I replace the poor one?

A No, not until you have identified the varieties. The poor tree may be the pollinator for the other good trees. Removing it might stop the good trees cropping well.

Herbaceous Perennials

Lovely herbaceous perennials are the backbone of many gardens, providing long-term colour and blending well with annuals and existing shrubs.

Herbaceous perennials are hard-working, decorative plants that can generally be left undisturbed for many years. Once you have planted a selection of them you can sit back and enjoy the display with just the minimum of maintenance in the future.

The term 'perennial' is the name for a large group of very diverse plants that live for many seasons. You do not have to replace them or sow fresh seeds each year. Most of them take a rest from above-ground activity in winter, but when they spring into action in the growing season they provide a fine display of colour.

Herbaceous perennials are essential foundation plants in a garden as they provide much ornamental value for relatively little outlay. Most are tolerant of average conditions, but if you have a particularly dry or damp garden it is wise to choose those that will suit it.

Herbaceous perennials come in a range of shapes and sizes and differing flower colours, but their general behaviour is similar. They live for many seasons, producing flowers with consistent vigour, and in autumn most of them lose their stems and leaves. Underground, their root systems continue to live and many increase in size, spreading into clumps from the roots.

GARDEN NOTES

PLANTING OUT FROM POTS

Container-grown plants can be put out at any time of the year but between spring and autumn is usually the best time. Dig a hole sufficiently deep and wide to allow a full spread of the root system. For a large plant, mix some moist peat and some bonemeal with the soil in the planting hole. Ease out the roots from the pot, keeping the soil ball as complete as possible, and set in position. Depress the soil around the plant slightly to help it collect moisture, and water.

Garden value

Perennials are great value because they have long flowering periods. They come in a wide range of heights and are therefore versatile plants in any garden layout. They are relatively inexpensive to buy and they grow in size, providing you with extra plants over the years. Some herbaceous perennials form clumps and mats of vegetation that make good ground cover in a border, suppressing weed growth.

Some border perennials have green leaves during winter and these are the ones that will fill the gaps in the garden left by perennials that die back. Hellebores, including Christmas rose, have flowers and leaves through the year. Epimediums, too, hold their lovely autumn leaves until spring when delicate flowers dance above the new foliage.

Reliability

For gardeners the main attraction of herbaceous perennials is their general reliability and adaptability to a wide range of garden conditions.

In spring, when the soil is beginning to warm up and the growing season begins, herbacious perennials are on sale at garden centres, but they hardly look their best at this stage. All you can see in the pot is a few shoots and a clump of leaves. It is hard to believe

A border of herbaceous perennials, showing the variety of height and form that can be achieved. In the foreground are low-growing, mauve asters. In the centre is bright red montbretia. At the back are hollyhocks in two colours and the tall spikes of bear's breeches (Acanthus).

that this Cinderella will turn into a choice garden plant. In autumn, also a good planting time, there is little to see on most herbaceous perennials.

Are they hardy?

Most herbaceous perennials are hardy and will survive the winter without any frost protection. A few, such as red hot pokers, may need the crown

protecting in cold areas, with a layer of straw or bracken, or even a layer of weathered ash. Just a few, like dahlias, are tender and will be killed by frost; these must be lifted and given winter protection (as stored tubers in the case of dahlias), then replanted the following year.

From autumn to early spring is a good time to take root cuttings. Pot them up and keep them frost-free. Plant them out next autumn.

Some people feel that perennials leave too many gaps in winter when the majority die back. You can minimize this by clever planting with a few that do not die back, or with spring bulbs and winter flowering perennials. Today, most perennials are planted into mixed borders rather than in borders solely devoted to perennials, so gaps are not likely to be too noticeable. One of the pleasures of these plants is the discovery of new shoots and leaves starting into growth after a dormant period.

CHOICE PERENNIALS

- *Hellebores* grow to about 60cm/2ft and flower in winter or spring. Leave them undisturbed if possible. Hardy and evergreen.
- *Pulmonaria* (lungwort) has speckled foliage, is evergreen and hardy, flowers in early spring to early summer, does well in shade and is good ground cover. A useful front of border plant.
- *Sedum spectabile* has fleshy leaves and flowers late in autumn. It does well in hot and dry conditions and makes good ground cover in the middle of a border.
- *Aquilegia* (columbine) is not always very vigorous but is easy to replace with seedlings. The flowers are very graceful.
- *Rudbeckia* makes a splash of strong colour in late autumn and does well in sunny or shady sites.
- *Dianthus,* (which includes pinks and border carnations) provides a good show at the front of a border.
- *Lupins, hollyhocks* and *delphiniums* are favourite choices for the back of a border, or to give an island bed height. They need staking and may need replacing if they lose their flowering vigour.
- *Crocosmia* (montbretia) provides orange or red flowers in late summer. It will need dividing as it spreads quickly.
- *Japanese anemones* are excellent border perennials, providing dainty pink or white flowers on long stems that are self-supporting.

Two choice perennials that will add colour to any flower bed. The bright pink of Sedum spectabile 'Autumn Joy' (above) and the bi-coloured flowers of the aptly-named Dianthus 'Snowfire' (below) which can be grown as an annual.

Height and shape

When you decide to plant perennials there are a number of

factors you need to consider. First you should choose plants to suit your particular colour plans. Knowing their eventual height and shape is also important. If a plant is going to spread into a large space, it is no use planting anything too close to it. On the other hand, you do not want unsightly gaps in the soil, so spread is a necessary dimension to know.

Perennials vary greatly in height. Some, including delphiniums, traditional border giants, grow to 1.5m/5ft or more. They should be planted at the back of a border. There are many perennials that grow to medium heights (between 90cm/3ft and 1.2m/4ft), including Japanese anemones and day lilies *(Hemerocallis)*. Then come the vast majority that are up to 60cm/2ft high. For the front of a border or for growing on rockeries there are many perennials that do not grow taller than 15cm/6in, but they spread out wide to form ground-covering mats of flowers and leaves.

Good company

Perennials used to be planted in traditional one-sided borders that backed onto walls or hedges. Although glorious in the summer growing season, they were a depressing sight in winter. Today, perennials are usually combined with shrubs, bulbs and bedding plants in mixed borders that can give all-year pleasure.

Island beds, that can be seen from all angles, are popular for perennial plantings. Such beds offer all round light and good airflow. They are often very informal in style. Remember, though, when planting such a bed, that it will be seen from all directions. You can avoid using stakes by selecting varieties that are strong enough to support themselves, or will prop each other up.

Where to plant

The best site for most perennials is an open sunny position where their leaves can have as much light as possible. This makes it easier for them to make the food necessary for growth and flower production.

They need a well-drained soil but will want watering in extremely hot conditions. There should be a good flow of air around the perennial border to avoid a build up of pests and diseases. However, exposed and windy sites are not suitable for these ornamental plants. The best soil to grow a wide range of perennials in is a medium loam that has been enriched with well-rotted compost or fertilizer. Whether you plant two or ten perennials in a border, they will all be competing for the sun, moisture, air and soil – so you should ensure that there is enough to go round when you plant them out. Space them out well.

The show of colour produced by an imaginative planting of herbaceous perennials in a mixed border (above) can be quite stunning. This picture was taken in late summer when the chosen flowers were at their best. They contrast pleasingly in height, form and colour with the clumps of ornamental grasses.

Almost anything that will keep the frost away can be used to protect delicate perennials. Here (below) dry leaves and stems are being placed on a wire frame over the crowns.

General care

Although herbaceous perennials are not particularly demanding plants, they do need

PROJECT **DIVIDING PERENNIALS**

Every three or four years you should rejuvenate perennials by lifting them in autumn and dividing them. When the plant is out of the ground, place it on a sheet of plastic and use two forks to lever it apart. Replant the sections of the root on the outer edge of the plant. Add a little slow release fertilizer and water them in. In spring you will have the bonus of extra plants.

The older roots at the centre of the plant will be less vigorous (producing fewer leaves and blooms if left to grow) and should be discarded.

some care and attention. You will need to feed your perennials with a general compound fertilizer in early spring when growth begins, and then again in mid-summer.

A mulch of organic material soon after the first feed helps to conserve moisture and discourages weeds. Apply the mulch thickly to a depth of 7.5cm/3in. Perennials in mulched beds usually need watering only in exceptionally dry conditions, when they will need the same attention from sprinklers and hoses as your other garden plants.

In late summer and early autumn it is usually necessary to cut back dead flowers and dying stems and leaves from some of your more unsightly perennials. You can tidy up beds and borders at the same time, hoeing out any weeds.

A bonus with some early flowering perennials, such as lupins and delphiniums, is that they will flower again in later summer if they are deadheaded as soon as their first flowers fade.

Problem perennials

A few perennial plants do present problems, but you can find ways to avoid these. Some, for example, do much better than others and become garden thugs, swamping and overwhelming slower and gentler-growing plants. Avoid perennials such as *Archillea ptarmica* 'The Pearl' as it is a very invasive plant. To keep it under control you will have to divide it every year.

Some older varieties are prone to diseases such as rust and mildew. Michaelmas daisies, in particular, are affected by mildew, but this can be largely avoided by buying new varieties that are disease resistant. Some perennials lose their vigour after a few years and so are not such good value. Lupins, for example, should be replaced every few years. Hollyhocks get rust spots on their leaves: this can be controlled by spraying but it may be simpler to replace with new plants.

Tall perennials need staking to prevent them flopping over in winds or after rain. Some of medium height also need staking and this can be time-consuming and a bit unsightly in the middle of an ornamental border. Avoid perennials that are too tall or choose varieties that are known to be self-supporting, such as the Belladonna hybrid group of delphiniums rather than those with very tall spikes. Try *D. belladonna* 'Blue Bees'.

GROWING TIPS

GROWING FROM SEED

Some perennials can be grown from seed but it is a lengthy and often challenging process. If you think it is worth growing from seed, you are wise to buy from a reliable seed merchant or your plants may be of uneven or poor quality. Sow indoors or under glass from mid-winter.

Tall-growing hollyhocks (far right) are fairly sturdy but should be staked unless in a sheltered site.

Tall perennials will need staking against rain and wind damage. Whatever form of support is used it should be put in place early to avoid damaging the plants. There are several options. Ready-made frames can be bought from garden centres. A framework of twiggy pea sticks, carefully inserted in a clump to a height of 90cm/3ft, will soon be covered by foliage. Single tall spikes can be staked with a bamboo cane, but the best option for groups of flowers is to form a 'cage'. Insert three canes and circle them with wire or garden twine (right).

The epimediums form excellent ground cover. Epimedium × perralchicum (right) has evergreen heart-shaped leaves and produces yellow flowers in spring.

Acid Lovers

In most gardens, the soil type dictates which plants will thrive and which will fail. Here's how to make the most of a garden with acid soil.

Gardening without understanding your soil is like cooking without any temperature controls. You will only learn by trial and error after many dishes have been burnt. Similarly with soil – if you do not know your soil type many plants will die and a great deal of effort and money wasted before you discover the best plants for your garden. Once you know the facts, the door to successful gardening will be opened for you and you can buy plants which will flourish year after year.

If you discover that your soil is acid you will be amazed by the possibilities. Far from being limited by your soil it should encourage you to use suitable plants more creatively. Rhododendrons, azaleas and heathers are ericaceous, which means they thrive on acid soils and perish on soils which are limy and alkaline.

You can often tell at a glance whether the soil in your area is acid. If there are lots of thriving rhododendrons around (above) there is a good chance that it will be but do a soil test to make sure. Guesswork may prove expensive and frustrating. This sad-looking peony (right) has become chlorotic (its leaves have turned yellow) because it has been grown on chalky soil.

If acid-loving plants are grown on an alkaline soil they soon become yellow (chlorotic) and sickly. Depending upon the plants and the degree of lime in the soil, they can either die quite quickly or linger on for years looking miserable and worthless. This is because some of the nutrients in the soil, particularly iron, are bound up by the lime and are made unavailable to acid-loving plants. Without these nutrients, the plants slowly starve to death.

Know your soil

The first thing to do is to test the pH value of the soil. Very often you can tell quickly just by looking in the neighbouring gardens whether the soil in your district is acid. If there are lots of rhododendrons and heathers there is a good chance it will be, but it is still worth testing.

You may find that, while most of your garden is acidic, there is limy soil around the house walls, or that an old vegetable patch has been heavily limed. Do test your soil first, so as to give your new and expensive plants the best possible chance of survival.

Test kits are inexpensive and are available from all garden centres, nurseries, and some department stores. The pH scale measures acidity and alkalinity. A reading of 7 is neutral. Below that it is acidic, and the likelihood is that an acidic garden soil will be in the range of pH5-6.5, which is fine for acid-loving plants.

Only very rarely do you find soil with a reading lower than pH5. A pH reading of about 7 means the soil is unsuitable for lime-hating (calcifuge) plants. If your soil is close to pH7, however, it may be worth trying to acidify pockets of soil in the garden which will enable you to grow acid-lovers. If the reading is above pH8, however, it is not worth the effort and expense. It is far better to garden within the natural limitations of your soil.

THE ACID TEST

To be sure of the acidity or alkalinity of your soil, test the pH value. A value of about 5-6.5 is ideal for acid loving plants. The soil must be below 7 as the soil above 6.5 is too limy.

Improving your soil

In trying to improve a soil to make it suitable for acid-loving plants, it is worth remembering that there are other qualities of acid soils which also need to be sought after and encouraged.

The first of these qualities is an open texture. Most acid soils tend to be peaty or sandy, and they usually have a crumbly texture which contains plenty of air. Think of the crumbly leaf mould on the floor of an oak wood. Indeed, acid leaf mould, which you can

If your soil is limy you can still grow acid-loving plants in containers. Use a proprietary compost which has the correct acid balance and all the nutrients the plants will need. The rich colour of the hydrangea (below) assures you that it is not suffering from any mineral deficiency.

GARDEN NOTES

ERICACEOUS COMPOSTS

Ericaceous is the gardening term for plants in the erica, or heather, family and most other acid-loving plants. If you intend to grow acid-loving plants such as azaleas or small rhododendrons in containers, perhaps because your garden soil is alkaline and the lime would damage them, then use a proprietary ericaceous compost. It is far superior to a peat and grit mixture because it also has all the nutrients necessary for sustained growth which are lacking in peat alone.

Acid-loving plants hate a rich compost, but need minerals to survive.

make yourself by composting leaves, is the ideal additive for improving your soil. It is far better than peat because it contains more nutrients.

Alternatively, well-rotted garden compost will do, as long as it is not too rich. Green peat can be bought conveniently and easily, but it is definitely second best and, as it is a limited resource, it should be used only where necessary.

Sand, grit or pine needles can be used to open up the texture of heavier soils. Do make sure that you use sand that is not alkaline, though. Builder's sand, for example, can often be very limy.

Keep it moist

The second quality needed by acid-loving plants is adequate drainage and a good moisture content. If your soil is acidic and sandy, you will need to add as much organic matter to the soil as possible in order to build up the humus content and help to retain moisture.

Use anything you can get hold of, from leaf mould and

CLASSIC PLANTS FOR ACID SOILS

At first glance the new red leaves of this pieris look almost like flowers.

Kalmia angustifolia 'Rubra' is a bushy shrub with clusters of deep pink flowers.

The bright blue star-shaped flowers of lithospermum are produced in profusion.

- Rhododendron species and hybrids vary from 15cm/6in to 3.6m/12ft high. Most flower in the spring.
- Azaleas, part of the rhododendron family, come in two main kinds: Kurume azaleas are evergreen, flower in early spring and grow to a height of 30-60cm/1-2ft; deciduous azaleas flower in late spring and grow to a height of 75cm-2.1m/2½ft-7ft.
- Camellias flower mainly in early spring and grow to a height of 1.5m-2.1m/5-7ft. They require a sheltered position to flower well.
- Pieris are attractive evergreen shrubs with a lily-of-the-valley type flower and beautifully coloured new foliage.
- Magnolias prefer a deep, humus-rich soil.
- Hydrangeas are best in a moist, rich soil, sheltered from cold winds. They do well near the sea. Hydrangeas will grow on lime, but too much makes them chlorotic and alters the colour of the flowers from blue to pink.
- Eucryphia is a small group of narrow, mostly evergreen trees suitable for the smaller garden. The attractive white flowers, like single roses, appear in late summer and early autumn.
- The snowdrop tree (*Styrax japonica*) is a shrub or small tree with masses of white 'snowdrops' hanging from the branches in early summer.
- Enkianthus is an attractive group of slow-growing shrubs carrying coppery bells in late spring and followed by excellent autumn colour. These grow to 1.8-2.4m/6-8ft.
- Calico bush (*Kalmia Latifolia)*, is a medium sized evergreen shrub with clusters of deep pink-red flowers in early summer.
- Fothergilla, a group of small spring-flowering shrubs, have white bottle-brush flowers followed by attractive autumn colours.
- Pernettya, small but spreading evergreen shrubs, are grown for their colourful berries. Male and female plants are needed to produce berries.
- Gaultheria is a group of (mainly) small creeping evergreens with bright autumn berries.
- Leucothoe, small shrubs for shade, have arching evergreen stems and attractive foliage. The form 'Rainbow' has leaves of cream, yellow and pink.
- Willows include species with very attractive foliage, stems and catkins.
- *Cornus canadensis* is a good small carpeting shrub for moist shade. The stems bear starry white flowers. It is slow to establish.
- Heathers are colourful, low evergreens requiring an open peaty soil and full light. They flower in early spring and autumn.
- Lithospermum is a beautiful sprawling shrub which looks particularly well amongst heathers. The flowers are produced from late spring and are a most vivid blue. Look for the varieties 'Grace Ward' and 'Heavenly Blue'.
- The blue poppy, Meconopsis, is a perennial plant with stunning flowers which it produces in late spring and early summer. In warm areas pick a cool spot for planting.

CARE OF ACID-LOVING PLANTS

Your tap water, which probably contains far too much lime, may not be suitable for watering acid-lovers. Lime-free rainwater is a far better bet. Collect it in a water butt, if you have room for one.

If plants become chlorotic (yellow), use Sequestrene in diluted or powder form, following the manufacturer's directions carefully.

A water butt collects rainwater which will be suitable for most acid-loving plants.

Apply diluted Sequestrene to the roots of large plants, using a watering can.

If a smaller plant is suffering sprinkle dry Sequestrene on the roots and water in.

Acid soils tend to be peaty or sandy and they usually have an open texture which acid-loving plants are particularly fond of. To enhance the texture of your soil make a mulch of well rotted acid leaves, pine needles or ordinary garden compost and apply it annually around the base of your plants (above). This will also improve the drainage and moisture content of the soil.

A raised bed is an ideal home for acid-loving plants in a limy garden. Make a wall with bricks, stones or even peat blocks and fill it with acid components such as grit, acid loam soil and garden compost. It need not be as big as the grand example (left), but the effect you will achieve can be just as spectacular.

compost to peat. It will all help. Dig plenty in before you plant, and be prepared to mulch the soil annually.

Self-contained

One way of growing acid lovers on an alkaline soil is to use raised beds or containers. Containers filled with ericaceous compost remain permanently acidic – and camellias in tubs can look wonderful in a courtyard. They will need gentle feeding over the years, however, and they will need soft water at all times. If your tap water is limy (look for scale in the kettle) then you will need to collect rainwater for your acid containers.

A simpler solution is to create raised beds of acid soil on top of your existing garden soil. These will naturally stay much damper than containers because of contact with the ground.

Raised beds

Raised beds can be made using low walls of brick or stone (not limestone of course) or even with peat blocks. To be successful a depth of not less than 25cm/10in is required. Fill your beds with a mixture of whatever acid components you can find or afford. Grit, leafmould, garden compost, acid loam soil or peat will all be suitable for this.

Over the years worms will tend to bring up lime into the acid soil, but periodic top-dressings of leaf mould or peat will help to keep up acidity.

GARDEN NOTES

HERBACEOUS ACID LOVERS

Many popular border plants will happily grow on an acid soil, giving plenty of scope for colour-scheming. Choose from the following: Lilies, shooting star, dog's-tooth violet, fritillary or chequered lily, toad lily, astilbe, blue poppy, gentian, false spikenard, blood root and ferns.

Chemical solutions

The use of Sequestrene may also be beneficial. This is a chemical powder which is diluted with water and is then watered onto the soil around plants which show signs of lime intolerance. It simply makes the lacking minerals directly available to the plants. In this form these elements cannot be 'pinched' by the lime in the soil. The benefits can be dramatic, but it is an expensive way of helping lime-hating plants, and should be used only in addition to basic soil improvement.

Over-acidity can be conveniently corrected by the application of lime. Spread it on the soil surface in winter and simply allow the rain and frost to dig it in for you.

Soil Types

For successful, satisfying gardening, you need to know what kind of soil you have and how to make the most of it.

It does not matter whether you are a complete beginner or consider yourself a bit of an expert; unless you know your soil you will never obtain the best results from your garden. Every plant has different preferences – for instance, some thrive on an acid soil while others do not.

Soil is made up of four basic components which are present in varying amounts.

Organic matter is essential to any fertile soil. It is composed of decaying plants and animals and puts back into the soil what the plants have taken out (worms help by pulling leaf litter underground as they tunnel). It is also referred to as humus.

Air is necessary to ensure that the organic matter is broken down and to prevent waterlogging, while **water** carries the nutrients to the plant and clings to the soil particles. Some soils are less able to hold water than others: sand for example drains very quickly giving the plant less time to take it up.

The glorious hydrangea (above) is a mixture of colours because the soil is limy and alkaline and is turning the blue hydrangea pink. The hydrangea would be purely blue on an acid soil.

Minerals are the rock particles in the soil and they are chiefly responsible for the texture. When these vital components are well balanced good humus results and the soil is healthy and fertile.

Soil texture

The soil is made up of pieces of material of different sizes. A soil which is made from large,

FROM TOP TO BOTTOM

There is usually a distinct difference between the top layer of your soil, the topsoil, and what lies below it, the subsoil. Depending on how well established your garden is and what are the geological qualities of the area, the topsoil may vary from a couple of inches to several feet deep. There may even be a range of different soil types and this can work to your advantage as well as against you. Gravel under clay provides good drainage and chalk under acid neutralises acidity. Take care not to bury the topsoil under the subsoil when digging.

TOPSOIL

Topsoil (the dark, shaded part of the diagram, left) can vary in depth from a couple of inches to several feet. More open in structure and darker in colour, it is organic material and rich in nutrients. Plants, especially small ones, feed mostly from this layer. Worms are vital because they mix up the material.

SUBSOIL

Lying below the topsoil, subsoil is a less rich layer, providing water and a firm anchorage for larger plants, trees and shrubs.

coarse particles is known as 'light' while a 'heavy' soil is made up of tiny grains. Ideally the composition should be somewhere between the two: a mid-textured soil is known as a loam.

The way soil particles are held together is known as the structure. A clay soil has minute particles which cling together in clumps. Other soils form flat layers or plates, but the best structure is one which is crumbly. This is known as a 'good tilth'. A crumbly loam has the perfect structure and texture but you must also find out how acid or alkaline your soil is in order to decide which plants you will be able to grow. This can be done very cheaply and easily with a soil testing kit. It will only take a few minutes and may save you years of unsuccessful attempts.

Whatever your soil, you will not be able to change either the structure or the acid/alkaline balance completely. But do not despair. Even if you have a heavy clay or a highly alkaline soil you can still improve it enormously. Finding out all you can is the first step.

Basic soil-types

Peat It is rare to find a garden soil that is very peaty, but it does occasionally happen. The area has at some time in the past been wet and boggy, like the fen lands of East Anglia.

Dark in colour, with a light and spongy texture, peaty soils have a high fibrous content – if you squeeze a handful it will fall apart easily.

Peat soils are capable of absorbing and retaining large amounts of water, which they can hold right up to the surface. Drainage can sometimes be a problem but generally it is a soil which is easy to work and very fertile.

This open texture and high moisture content is ideal for growing hydrangeas, rhododendrons, pieris and the many kinds of heathers. Primulas and lilies do well, and so does blue poppy (meconopsis).

All these plants appreciate

This magnificent scented lilac border flourishes where most plants would flounder. Lilac grows well on thin, starved chalky soils.

This aptly named 'Fireglow' azalea is a member of the rhododendron group of plants and, like its relatives, it grows well on acid, peaty soils.

Roses, like this delightful hybrid tea 'Le Havre', grow particularly well on clay soils; although some roses will grow quite happily on sandy soils too.

	How to recognise	Advantages
CLAY	A heavy, sticky soil. A squeezed handful will stick together and retain its compressed shape.	Usually rich in nutrients. A clay subsoil is ideal for making ponds.
SAND	Light, crumbly and free-draining. A squeezed handful will fall apart easily.	Fast to warm up in spring. Lawns will drain freely, and borders can be worked on all winter if the weather permits. Does not stick to tools.
CHALK	Limy soils vary a great deal, from thin, stony loam over chalk bed to a deep clay soil. But they all have a high pH value (= alkaline).	A moderately limy soil will grow a wide range of plants.
PEAT	A dark, fibrous and spongy soil. A squeezed handful will not hold together. Water may sometimes be squeezed out.	Ideal for acid-loving plants and those which need a high moisture level at all times.
LOAM	Brown or red, medium-weight soil, with plenty of organic matter. A squeezed handful will hold together but can be made to crumble easily.	A loam soil of neutral pH (7) is the ideal soil for growing a wide range of plants, especially vegetables.

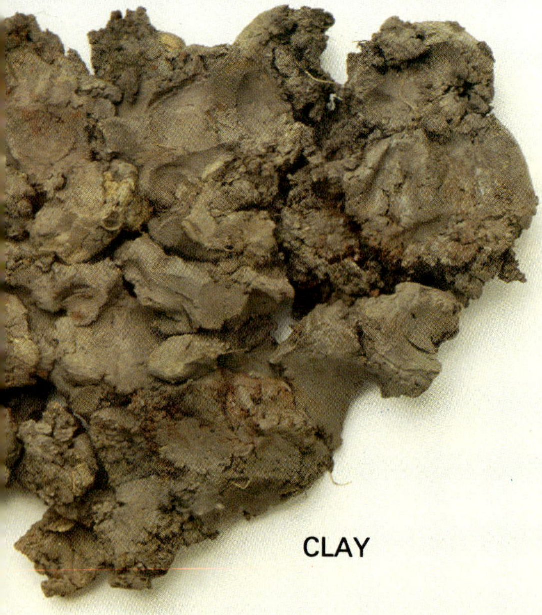

CLAY

SAND

PEAT

CHALK

LOAM

isadvantages	Will grow/won't grow
low to warm up in spring. Lack f free drainage is hostile to nany kinds of plants. Difficult to veed, and compacts easily in orders and under lawns.	Good for roses, irises and many water-side plants. Unsuitable for rhododendrons, heathers, tenders shrubs, bulbs and alpines.
an be very lacking in nutrients, equiring the addition of much rganic matter and fertilizer. ries out quickly, even when nulched.	Grows most things, but poor for moisture-loving plants such as many primulas, hostas and bergenias.
ften dry, thin and starved, over ock. Will not support acid-loving lants at all. Some plants ecome 'chlorotic' (yellow eaves).	Good for lilac, cistus and hebes. Bad for most heathers, rhododendrons and hydrangeas.
onstant high moisture level is ad for tender/drought-loving lants which need sharp rainage. Lawns can be poor.	Good for rhododendrons, azaleas, heathers, lilies and primulas. Bad for cistus and dianthus. Extra lime needed for good vegetables.
oam can be acid or alkaline, and nerefore plant choice is limited ccordingly.	Alkaline loams will NOT support acid-loving plants.

moisture, but some of them, especially those in the heather family, must have another of the qualities of peaty soil: acidity. If a soil is acid, it means it is lacking in lime, a substance which some plants will not tolerate. Soil acidity is measured on the pH scale. Rhododendrons and heathers prefer a pH of about 5-6.5.

GARDEN NOTES

ACIDITY AND ALKALINITY

The term pH (potential of Hydrogen) is a scale for measurement of the chemical alkaline/acidity level of soil. The full scale runs from 1 to 14, but most garden soils are within the range of 4 to 8. When a soil contains enough lime or chalk to give a pH value of over 7, it is said to be alkaline. A pH balance of 6.5 or less is acid. A pH reading of 7 is neutral.

Lime Soils containing lime can be very varied. At worst they can be dry, thin and stony, over solid chalk or limestone. But at best they are excellent, rich, loamy soils, which happen to be alkaline.

The only way to be sure whether a soil is alkaline is to test its pH value, and see if it is above pH7.

There are very few limitations of a rich but alkaline soil. It will not grow plants such as rhododendrons, pieris and summer-flowering heathers, because they must have acid soil. But it will grow good roses, vegetables, lawns and an enormous range of flowers and shrubs.

Extreme alkalinity may, however, cause yellowing of the leaves (chlorosis) in some plants such as camellias. Blue-flowered hydrangeas also turn pink on limy soils.

Thin, dry alkaline soils over chalk are more of a problem, and can be very limiting. They tend to be lacking in nutrients and are often stony and difficult to work and are sticky and soft in wet weather. Not all plants flounder on limy soils, some prefer it: cistus, rosemary and carnations (the dianthus family), will be perfectly happy there.

Sand Crumbly and free-draining, sandy soils are without doubt the easiest to work with. Tools keep themselves clean with almost no effort, and the soil warms up quickly in spring which means it is suitable for early crops.

Although this type of soil is good for growing alpines, and shrubs and perennials of doubtful hardiness, the real problem with sand is likely to

In hot and dry weather, clay will shrink and crack, because of its poor drainage. Plants with shallow root systems such as these dwarf herbaceous plants (top) cannot cope with the extreme conditions that clay produces. Roses or hardy shrubs make a better choice for clay beds.

Rhododendrons are unable to extract vital nutrients from chalky soils, such as this shrub (above), which is showing its suffering with yellowing, or chlorotic, leaves.

PROJECT

TESTING YOUR SOIL

Soil testing kits can be bought from garden centres and other gardening outlets. They take only minutes to do and can save you years of trial and error in trying to grow the wrong plants on the wrong soil. These kits test the pH value of your soil; pH is simply a scale, ranging from 4–8, which measures the acidity or alkalinity of your soil. The range of 3–6.5 indicates acidity, 7.5–8 alkalinity, 7.0 is neutral.

Remember to test several parts of your garden to get an overall view and if you are treating the soil, test after treatment and compare the results.

A rich, neutral loam is the ideal soil and if you are lucky enough to have it in your garden you will be able to grow practically anything. It has an excellent moisture content and a good crumbly texture. Plenty of organic material ensures that your plants get maximum nutrition, so there is less need to feed. Here it has been used to create a beautiful flower-filled garden.

be dryness. The topsoil, and even the subsoil, can be so free-draining because of its open texture that, in times of drought, thirsty plants will soon wilt for want of a good drink of water and even trees, with their extensive roots may show signs of suffering.

The topsoil, of course, can be made to hold more water by adding some humus to it. Nutritional enrichments – fertilizer – is often necessary, too, in large quantities.

Most plants will grow well on sandy soil but be careful with shallow-rooted varieties. So long as it is on the acidic side (with a pH value below 7), even summer heathers and rhododendrons thrive. They enjoy the open texture of sandy soils; for your part, give them sufficient water and they will do very well.

Clay Probably the hardest type of soil to deal with. In winter, clay is cold, wet and sticky, so that you cannot work on the garden for fear of compacting the soil into a solid mass. Plants can literally drown when clay soils become waterlogged. In summer, clay can dry out and crack. Because of poor drainage, the moisture will simply evaporate. It is never easy to weed. Seedling weeds seem to be stuck to the soil in winter and baked on during a dry summer.

Good for roses

Clay soil is not all bad news, however. It can be very fertile, it is well supplied with plant foods, and they are not drained away by a heavy rainfall. Roses grow best of all, along with a good range of shrubs and perennials. And the texture can be improved with effort over the years. It will never make a light, open soil, so it is better to stick to plants which will tolerate clay successfully, rather than try those which will just survive and never look at their best.

Clay soils can be either on the acidic or alkaline side, but generally the lime-loving plants like lilac and cistus do best on it. Often a heavy loam topsoil will be found overlying a clay subsoil, and this is a satisfactory combination.

Loam The ideal soil for gardening, loam will grow much the widest range of plants. It posesses all of the good points of sandy and clay soils but few of their disadvantages. It can be acidic or alkaline, which will limit the choice of plants a little, but, broadly speaking, you can grow anything on loam. Certainly a medium acidic loam will grow rhododendrons perfectly well.

Best of all

The advantage of loam is that it has a high content of organic matter, which is full of nutrients and holds water well. A handful of an average loam, when squeezed, will have enough fibre and moisture to stick together afterwards, but will not be so sticky that you cannot easily make it crumble again.

This is just what growing plants need for healthy foliage and root systems. For vegetables you could not do better.

Cold Frames

A cold frame is useful in a garden that is intensively cultivated, but is invaluable for nurturing plants where space is limited.

A cold frame is halfway between a greenhouse and cloches, with some of the uses of each. You can use a cold frame to propagate many kinds of plants or to produce greenhouse crops, like tomatoes and other salad vegetables, out of season.

Alternatively, you can force spring bulbs for the house or overwinter young plants. A frame can also be used to house specialist collections of plants that need protection from the wet in winter, such as some alpines and bulbs. You can even heat a cold frame to keep frost-tender plants alive through the winter.

The basic choice is between wooden- and aluminium-framed cold frames, and between glazed or solid sides.

Choosing a frame

Aluminium-framed, PVC-glazed frames are the cheapest to buy and the most readily available in garden centres.

They are rather lightweight, so are not suitable for a windy site unless well anchored. These frames are most suitable for growing edible crops early and late in the season, as they provide good light. They may be cold in winter, though.

Wooden-framed cold frames are difficult to find nowadays but are usually made of red cedar or a similar wood that has been treated to prevent rotting. The same wood is used for the solid sides of the frame, as glass or plastic sides would not carry the weight.

These are the best frames to choose if you plan to overwinter young plants, alpines or bulbs, as the solid sides retain heat better and plants are less likely to freeze. They are probably the best frames for general purposes.

Making your own

You can make your own cold frame quite easily from old window frames, or from Dutch

The newer types of aluminium-framed mini greenhouses, cloches and cold frames are glazed with good-quality plastic, rather than the traditional glass, making them cheaper, lighter and safer to use.

lights which are sometimes available from nurseries. Dutch lights are like large picture frames containing a single sheet of glass.

To make the cold frame, the glass lights are laid flat over dwarf walls made of timber planks, old railway sleepers, brick or breeze blocks.

Dutch lights should always be firmly secured to avoid damage on windy nights. To do this, drive a nail into each corner of the light's wooden framework, and corresponding nails into the base it lies on. Use short lengths of flexible wire to link the pairs of nails.

VEGETABLE CALENDAR

Early spring Sow radish, spring onion, early carrots, lettuce, broad bean 'The Sutton', early peas.
Mid spring Sow French beans, lettuce, beetroot, herbs, asparagus peas. Slightly later, plant French or runner beans, sweet-corn, outdoor tomatoes, cucumbers, canteloupe melons, courgettes.
Late spring Remove lights.
Early autumn Pull out summer crops as they finish. Replace lights and sow endive, winter lettuce, winter-hardy spring onion, lamb's lettuce, and the Chinese vegetables, green-in-the-snow and pak choi. Plant cabbage 'Hispi', cauliflower 'Alpha' or 'All The Year Round'.

Siting

A sheltered site is essential for cold frames. In a windy position they may be damaged by flying debris. In strong winds, the frame itself may even be lifted and blown about.

As regards orientation, few people with small gardens have much choice. For general-purpose use, anywhere the frame receives direct sun for at least half the day is adequate.

If buying a frame for a particular purpose or where there is a choice of sites, some aspects are better than others.

South-facing sites are best for edible crops, which need plenty of warmth and light. For propagation, an east- or west-facing site, or one shaded during the middle of the day prevents young plants from becoming scorched.

Avoid east-facing sites for overwintering plants, as the early morning sun in winter can damage plants that have been frosted overnight.

How to use frames

Few people use cold frames exclusively for one purpose, however. Most of us use them for a bit of everything throughout the year.

A typical general-purpose cropping plan might start in spring with an early crop of salad vegetables or the propagation of hardy annual flowers for the garden. In summer, this might be followed by a crop of melons, tomatoes or cucumber (when the lights are removed), and then by late vegetables, shrub cuttings or young plants kept under cover for the winter.

Edible crops

By providing protection from the weather, cold frames are a useful way of extending the growing season. They make it possible to sow early crops about six weeks earlier than you could in the open. They can be used again in late summer for fast-growing crops that mature in the autumn, or

This aluminium-topped frame (above left), in which shading panels are interchangeable with ones of glass or plastic, is one of the many kinds now available. For greater ventilation flexibility, the 'glass' side panels also slide open.

A long-lasting frame can be made by using bricks (above) for the sides. The back wall needs to be a brick or two higher than the front so that the frame slopes towards the south. Old windows can make good covers or, as here, a purpose-built top with sliding or removable glass or plastic panels.

Making your own cold frame (right) is not a difficult task. Metal-framed boxes supported on a couple of layers of bricks are simply topped with Dutch lights which can be removed when necessary or propped open to allow ventilation. Potatoes, carrots, beans and peas have been successfully nurtured in these makeshift frames.

those that remain in the ground over the winter for use in early spring.

In summer, cold frames are often used to grow frost-tender crops, such as tomatoes. These can be planted from mid spring onwards in mild locations. When the plants reach the glass, a month later, the lights are removed, leaving the crops to grow up like those in the garden.

Plants like cucumbers and melons, which in greenhouses are trained up canes or strings, may be allowed to ramble over a raised framework of wire netting in a cold frame. They should not be left to run over the ground as the developing fruit may rot.

By early autumn, summer crops will be virtually finished. You will need to clear out the frame, put the next crop in and replace the lights.

Keen gardeners can install insulated electric warming cables (above) in their cold frame. This type of dry heating, which can keep moisture-loving fungus diseases at bay, should be thermostatically controlled for economy.

The protection of a cloche or cold frame is particularly valuable for the early sowing of salad vegetables such as lettuce (above left) or radishes.

A cold frame is the best place for starting off indoor hyacinths (left) since it protects the bulbs from the rain and prevents them from becoming waterlogged, which might otherwise happen when they are started off in the garden.

Hardy annual flowers, such as nasturtiums and sweet peas, can be sown in early spring in trays placed in a cold frame, for transplanting into the garden about four to six weeks later on.

Softwood cuttings of many easy rooting shrubs can be taken in midsummer, in the same way as you would geranium cuttings. Take cuttings of cornus, hebe, lavender, cistus, ribes, roses and perennial herbs. Strike them in deep pots filled with a mixture of John Innes seed compost and a little sharp sand.

Hardwood cuttings of the same type of plants can be taken from early to late autumn. Take cuttings 15cm/6in long and carefully remove the soft tips of the shoots.

Many spring bulbs are grown in pots or bowls for winter decoration indoors. After potting the bulbs in autumn, put them in a cold, dark place (like the garage) to root. Move them to the cold frame when the first green shoots appear, and only take them indoors when the first flower buds appear and start to show colour.

After flowering, bulbs can be returned to the cold frame for protection and storage while the foliage dies down.

Overwintering

After being propagated, many young herbaceous flowers and shrubs are still too small to plant straight out into the garden. They are best potted into 9cm/3½in pots and kept under cover in the cold frame for their first winter. They can be

Summer bedding plants (above) can be protected from spring frosts in a cold frame. It is equally important to have some form of shading to prevent dehydration of young plants in bright spells of spring sunshine.

To prevent diseases, ventilate the cold frame whenever weather allows by propping up the lights with blocks of wood or sturdy flower pots (above right). However, ensure that the plants do not dry out by keeping them moist but not waterlogged.

planted out the following spring or in early summer.

Frost-tender plants and half-hardy perennials, such as fuchsias and pelargoniums, may be kept over the winter in a cold frame if it is heated enough to prevent them freezing. A small electric heater or a paraffin heater can be used.

Special collections

Collectors of choice alpines and bulbs often use cold frames to house their collection all year round.

To make it easy to look after, the floor of the frame is excavated to 15cm/6in and the soil replaced with sharp sand. This produces a sand bed in which pots can be plunged to their rims. By keeping the sand moist, plants need much less watering. During summer the lights are removed, though they may be replaced to provide sufficient light and warmth in very wet weather.

Collections of shade-loving plants, such as ferns and choice woodland species, are housed in much the same way. They require a north-facing cold frame which remains cool and shady all year.

Management

From autumn to late spring, keep frames covered. To prevent diseases, however, ventilate whenever the weather allows, propping up the lights on blocks of wood. Do not let plants remain dry for long – they should be just moist – and avoid overwatering.

In summer, remove the lights and check plants regularly to see if they need watering. During hot spells it is useful to have shading to protect alpines or plants that are being propagated. Shading lights are like Dutch lights in which the glass has been replaced with shading fabric.

PROPAGATION CALENDAR

Early spring Sow hardy annual flowers.
Mid spring Sow summer cabbage, sprouts, summer cauliflower, sprouting broccoli, lettuce, French and runner beans, courgettes and sweet-corn for transplanting.
Late spring Sow autumn cauliflower for transplanting.
Early summer Sow biennial flowers eg wallflowers, forget-me-nots and Canterbury bells, herbaceous perennial flowers, winter-flowering annual pot plants eg cineraria, calceolaria, exacum, Christmas cherry, *Primula malacoides* and *P. obconica*.
Mid summer Take softwood cuttings of perennial herbs, shrubs and roses.
Late summer Sow spring cabbage for transplanting.
Early to mid autumn Take hardwood cuttings of perennial herbs, shrubs and roses.
Late autumn to late winter Sow seed of alpines, hardy trees and shrubs.

Lean-to and Mini Greenhouses

Mini-greenhouses give an exciting new dimension to gardening. Learn what types to look for, how to look after them, and what plants to grow.

Few gardens are too tiny for a small lean-to greenhouse – sometimes called a planthouse. One can usually be fitted in against a wall or a fence, or even against the house.

For those with slightly more space, who prefer a traditional, free-standing greenhouse, there are miniature versions of the standard greenhouse – mini-greenhouses. They can be erected in a sheltered but sunny part of any garden.

Although small, lean-to and mini-greenhouses will help you grow plants that make your garden more colourful. They are also excellent for growing tomatoes, cucumbers and other salad crops.

Shapes and sizes

Planthouses (the smallest lean-to greenhouses) are about 60cm/2ft in depth, 1.5m/5ft to the eaves and 1.8m/6ft to the ridge, and in length they range from 1.2m/4ft to 1.8m/6ft. They have a sliding door at the front. Some have hinged ventilators in the roof area, while others rely on the door being left open to create ventilation.

Mini-greenhouses with a traditional ridged roof are about 1.8m/6ft wide, 1.5m/5ft to the eaves and 2.1m/7ft to the ridge. Lengths vary from 1.2m/4ft to 1.8m/6ft.

Standard-sized lean-to greenhouses are 1.8m/6ft to 2.1m/7ft in depth, sometimes more. A compromise between this and the smallest planthouse – and one that suits many gardeners – is a 'compact' type about 1.2m/4ft wide. This has just enough space for a path and staging.

Unlike planthouses, in which plants have to be tended from outside, with the door open, the compact allows the gardener to work inside the greenhouse. This type is ideal for fitting to the rear of a garage, or against or even on a single-storey, flat-roof extension where you have access.

Siting the greenhouse

Lean-to greenhouses need an aspect between south-east and south-west; they must not be shaded by buildings for most of the day, nor overhung with trees that create shade and drip water long after the rain has stopped.

Free-standing types also need a site away from shade and overhanging trees, as well as shelter from northerly and easterly winds. Orientate the greenhouse so that the ridge is east-to-west; this ensures that tall plants on one side do not

A compact lean-to greenhouse (above), at the end of an extension. This walk-in type has a sliding door at one end, a hard path, staging for pots and a bed below this for planting or putting down growing-bags.

A shelf (below) can be fixed at whatever height is convenient.

> **GROWING TIPS**
>
> **REDUCING HEATING COSTS**
>
> To save heating costs early in the year, sow half-hardy summer-flowering bedding plants on windowsills indoors. After germination – and when the seedlings have been pricked out – place the containers in your lean-to or mini-greenhouse.
>
> Most seedlings take 7-14 days to germinate. Starting plants on windowsills indoors therefore saves two to three weeks of heating the greenhouse.

A mini-greenhouse (right), erected on a lawn. It has a sliding door at one end and a ventilation window on either side of the roof. For greater rigidity the aluminium frame is braced with struts on the sides and ends. Staging runs along one side and there is room for more on the other side, as well as shelving above it. The central area can be paved if there is not a hard base. This greenhouse is certainly small but a lot can be packed into the available space.

create shadows on the plants growing on the other side.

With free-standing greenhouses, it is equally important to position the door so that it is on the westerly side (or on the southerly end if it has to be orientated north-to-south) so that cold air is less likely to blow in through the door.

A flat, firm piece of ground is essential. One that slopes in several directions will strain the building, resulting in doors and ventilators that do not fit and producing unwelcome draughts in winter.

A planthouse (below) in the tiny back garden of a modern house. This small lean-to greenhouse against a wall takes up very little space, extending only 60cm/2ft into the garden itself.

Mini-greenhouses usually have a path down the centre, and plants are put directly in the soil or in growing bags on either side. Lean-to greenhouses, however, are usually erected on concrete or paving.

Aluminium greenhouses are often supplied with an aluminium base surround that screws or slots together, as well as to the greenhouse. This is securely anchored to the ground by corner brackets set in concrete. Strong anchorage is vital, especially for free-standing greenhouses situated in exposed areas.

Heating

If the greenhouse is to be used to grow plants throughout winter – or for raising summer-flowering bedding plants in spring – warmth is essential. This is usually provided either by a small paraffin heater or by an electric fan or tubular heater.

The movement of air from a fan heater can help control fungal diseases. Both electric heaters create dry heat and can be controlled by thermostats. A paraffin heater produces humidity, which can encourage fungal diseases but is less likely to shrivel thin-leaved plants. If plants suffer from a dry atmosphere, place a tray of water on the floor.

Gas and solid-fuel heating systems are also available, but these are unsuitable for lean-to and mini-greenhouses.

Ventilation

Ventilation is just as important as heating – many plants are killed by excessively high temperatures in summer. If the greenhouse manufacturer offers an option of additional ventilators at the base and in the roof, take advantage of it.

The lower ones are often made up of adjustable louvres, while those in roofs are hinged windows. In free-standing greenhouses, try to have a roof ventilator on both sides, so that when ventilation is needed the one on the leeside can be opened. Whenever possible, avoid cold air blowing into the greenhouse.

Gadgets that automatically open and close windows and

STAGING AND SHELVING

Staging – a bench on which plants are placed – can be fitted into all greenhouses, even tiny lean-to types. It enables more plants to be placed in a greenhouse, as well as raising them to waist height where they can be more easily seen and tended. Two-tier staging makes even better use of the space, but remember that the lower shelf will be shaded and therefore may only be suitable for the storage of pots and boxes.

Once installed, most staging is permanent, but some hinges upwards to make it more adaptable. The surface of staging is either solid and perhaps made of plastic-coated steel trays, or slatted and made of fine-mesh plastic-covered or galvanized wire. In wooden greenhouses, it may also be formed from slatted wood.

The solid-surfaced type is better in summer, when it can be covered with sand to encourage the retention of moisture and humidity around the pots. In winter, however, when a better circulation of air is needed around pots to defeat attacks of damp-loving diseases, the slatted type is better.

Shelving is narrower than staging and is used to support pots and plants 23-30cm/9-12in below the eaves. In aluminium greenhouses, shelving is usually secured to the glazing bars by special brackets designed by the manufacturer.

In wooden structures, brackets and wires can be secured to the wood.

It is important to shade plants in the summer. Here (above) an inexpensive, home-made green hessian blind has been hung from the roof vent.

louvres are available. They are often activated by heat-sensitive wax in a cylinder that exerts pressure on a piston. The device can be adjusted to make the ventilator open when the desired inside temperature is reached, usually about 13°C/55°F. The weight of ventilators varies, so be sure to buy an opener that suits your greenhouse.

Electric extractor fans (similar to those used to remove steam from kitchens) are another way to reduce the temperature. In free-standing greenhouses, install one in the glass opposite the door.

Summer shade

Small greenhouses are more likely than large ones to suffer from rapid and excessive fluctuations in temperature during summer. Apart from opening the ventilators and leaving the door open, shading is essential to prevent plants becoming scorched.

The simplest and cheapest form of shading is to paint a proprietary shading liquid directly on the outside of the glass. It is resistant to rain and can be scrubbed off in autumn. Unfortunately, this type of shading also makes the greenhouse dull when the sky is overcast.

Roller blinds attached to the outside of the greenhouse and formed of green, fine-meshed, weather-resistant plastic are better, as they can be rolled up and down to suit variations in weather. Alternatively, the plastic can be held in place with clips or drawing pins.

Conserving heat is essential, especially if the greenhouse is used in winter and early spring to raise summer-flowering bedding plants.

Winter heat

Heat can be kept in by fixing 'bubble' sheeting to the inside of the glass, especially on northerly and easterly sides. It traps air between the plastic and the glass.

The bubble sheeting is held in place by a range of fixings, including double-sided adhesive pads, drawing pins and

Modern aluminium staging (below). Pots can be placed on the slatted metal top or, if the slats are removed, in a bed of damp peat or sand which will help keep them moist.

special clips that are made for aluminium greenhouses.

Both white and green 'bubble' insulation is available. The green often makes the greenhouse too dark in winter, although if left in place in summer it creates shade.

What temperature?

The range of plants that can be grown in a tiny greenhouse depends, like all other greenhouses, on its temperature.

Unheated greenhouses – often known as cold-houses – allow you to grow certain plants that you could not grow outdoors. Cool-houses, where the temperature never drops below 7°C/45°F, will extend still further the range of plants that you can grow.

Stove houses are even hotter – often 24°C/75°F and above – and are essential for the care of tropical plants. A stove house, however, is very expensive to run in winter, has unnecessarily high temperatures for raising plants in spring and is not needed for food plants in summer.

An agreeable temperature compromise – and one that saves money – is just to heat the greenhouse in late winter and spring, when sowing seeds and raising young plants. In summer, the natural heat of the sun alone will speed the growth of plants such as tomatoes and cucumbers.

Once your greenhouse is installed, you will want to pack it with plants. Both the time of year and the greenhouse's temperature influence the plants you select.

Starting off

The following plants and the routine are an example of what you can do in a small greenhouse heated in late winter and spring, but unheated from late spring onwards.

Raise half-hardy summer-flowering bedding plants to brighten flower beds and containers on patios. This is important to many gardeners.

During late winter and early spring, sow seeds of summer brighteners such as ageratum, antirrhinum, *Begonia semperflorens*, lobelia, nicotiana, petunia, marigolds and zinnias in 15-20°C/59-68°F.

After germination, prick off the seedlings when large enough to be handled into trays, seedboxes or pots. Slowly lower the temperature, ventilate more freely and by late spring accustom the plants to outside conditions. However, these plants are susceptible to frost, which in many areas may still occur until the first week of summer.

If a cold frame is available, place these plants in it from mid-spring onwards – covering with hessian on cold nights – so that the greenhouse can be used to establish other plants. Tomatoes in summer save on the food budget.

A cheap but effective form of insulation in winter is to attach lengths of bubble wrap (above) to the inside of the glass.

An enormous number of seedlings (below) can be brought on in a greenhouse, for planting out later in the garden. This will provide you with an excellent, early display of flowers.

Growing tomatoes

Tomato seeds sown in 16°C/61°F in early spring develop plants producing fruit about four months later – sometimes earlier. However, as you will probably not need more than six plants, it is easier to buy established plants as soon as the greenhouse is free of bedding plants. These are best planted in growing-bags. A 1m/3½ft long bag accommodates about three plants.

Make sure the greenhouse is heated until frosts have passed. Supports are available for plants in growing-bags. Feed and water tomatoes regularly for a good crop.

Containers

Containers now come in all shapes, sizes and materials. Filled with a variety of attractive plants, they can add interest to every corner of the garden.

The great beauty of containers is their versatility. They allow you to garden anywhere – even places where there is no soil. They are also the perfect way to personalize your garden without breaking the bank. You can stand containers on paths, by front and back doors, on balconies or flat roofs. Window boxes are wonderful for brightening up the outside of a small house or flat. Hanging baskets suspended from strong brackets are ideal for enlivening a plain stretch of wall. For supporting several hanging baskets, you can also buy maypole-like structures with arms branching out of the top.

Ringing the changes

Because containers are portable, you can switch them around whenever you fancy a change of scene rather like rearranging the furniture in your house, though the larger, heavy containers will need to be moved using a trolley or when they are empty. You can use a succession of containers – or a succession of different plants in the same container – to provide something new to look at all year round. Spare plants in containers can be used to fill a gap where a plant has died or perhaps is not looking its best.

From the design point of view, an attractive container helps make the most of a special plant, and provides a good

Terracotta is a very popular material for containers – and it need not be limited to conventional flower pots. Here, an old chimney pot (above) is the basis for a delightful display of red ivy-leaved geraniums (pelargoniums) and blue lobelia. This is an ideal choice of plants for a sunny spot but always be sure to keep pots well watered in hot weather, up to twice a day in long hot spells.

focal point in a corner, or at the end of a path. Containers also add character to a garden in their own right. You can choose ones that complement the style of your house – ultra-modern, traditional or cottagey. Or they can team with a particular style of planting: Mediterranean-look terracotta is ideal on a patio or for planting sub-tropical plants and herbs; stone is excellent for showing off alpines and rock plants; rustic wood is useful for shrubs like camellias. Containers come in a huge range of materials, shapes and sizes. You will probably keep the same ones for many years, so it pays to think carefully about which ones to buy.

Low-cost containers

Plastic containers are the cheapest, but they tend to be short-lived. The cheaper plastics become brittle in sunlight, and crack after a few years out in the garden. They may even fall to bits completely when you try to move them, so take care if you move this kind when there are plants growing in them. Some plastic containers are designed only for use indoors or in a conservatory, so check the label or ask when you buy if you are not sure. If you are on a tight budget, plastic flower pots are the cheapest of all containers. Large sizes can double as tubs, and you could always tuck in a few trailing plants around the edge to hide the plastic.

When it comes to choosing containers for your garden, you can really let your imagination run riot! In this case, an old mangle (right) has been painted bright red and filled with colourful bedding plants.

An old wheelbarrow that has outlived its usefulness need not be thrown away. With a simple coat of paint, it can be given a new lease of life as an unusual plant holder. This white-painted wheelbarrow (below) is host to a cheerful display of geraniums and petunias.

Traditional terracotta

Terracotta containers are popular. Clay flower pots are available in various sizes, often with optional saucers. They cost more than plastic pots do, but they are still a lot cheaper than many other types of container. You can also find decorative terracotta urns with raised patterns, and strawberry pots with planting pockets in the sides. When buying terracotta containers,

Plant containers should harmonize with the style of your garden. Here, the classic formality of a Versailles tub (above) perfectly complements the modern simplicity of this seating area. The white-painted slats match those on the seat surround.

BRIGHT IDEAS

PLANT RELAY

Plunge pots of short-lived flowers like spring bulbs and some annuals up to their rims into a larger container filled with gravel. Then you can lift out and replace plants when they finish flowering without disturbing the display.

look for a label stating whether they are frost-proof or not. Pots that are not frost-proof, especially those with a neck, may crack if they are left out in the garden full of compost during winter – the water in the compost expands when it freezes and splits the pot. All is not totally lost if this happens, however, since the cracks can be repaired using special adhesives (from DIY or craft stores). Broken terracotta pots also look good laid on their sides by a gravel path and used for growing sedums or sempervivums.

This simple, stylish container (left) would look good in any modern setting. The understated look is emphasized by a cream and white colour scheme made up of nicotiana surrounded by a mass of white begonias.

Rustic look

Wooden tubs, half barrels and troughs are delightfully rustic. All wooden containers are liable to rot after a time, so treat them with wood preservative (choose one that is not poisonous to plants) and line the inside of the container with heavy-duty polythene before filling with compost.

Stone containers are expensive. Old stone sinks, carved from a whole chunk of rock, are now almost collectors' items, as are stone animal feeding troughs. Even so, many alpine enthusiasts like to get the real thing to show off their treasures to perfection. Synthetic stone, or reconstituted stone, is ground-up stone that has been moulded into the required shape.

Recycled and homemade containers are another option. Old chimney pots can still sometimes be bought from those builders' merchants who sell reclaimed old materials (look in your local directory, or ask a DIY shop or builder). Stood on end and filled with compost, they make lovely containers. For a similar, cheaper, effect you can use modern clay land drains.

Clever fake

A discarded modern sink can be transformed into a fake stone one by plastering it outside with 'hypertufa' – a mixture of peat, gritty sand and cement that weathers to a rough stony finish. First clean the sink well inside and out. When it is dry, coat the outside with a layer of outdoor adhesive to provide a 'key' – as hypertufa will not stick to a smooth surface. Then mix equal parts of each ingredient in a bucket with enough water to make it just sloppy, and

Plastic pots in shapes and designs similar to old metal ones can be 'antiqued' to give a similar look to the real thing (left). Just paint a dark grey paint over a dry lighter grey, and rub away part of the top coat while still wet to give 'highlights'.

paste it over the outside of the sink. If you want a really rough texture, use moss peat (also known as sphagnum peat or bog peat) instead of the cheaper sedge type. Allow several weeks for the 'stone' to set really hard. Once it is firm to touch, you can artificially 'age' it by painting it with natural yoghurt, or spraying it every few weeks with diluted liquid plant feed. Attractive outcrops of lichens and mosses will soon start to grow.

Recycling

The same fake stone 'recipe' can also be used to coat other containers such as clay flower pots. You can even use it to make containers. One way is to fashion the basic shape from scrunched-up chicken wire (fine mesh metal garden netting), and coat it with a stiff hypertufa mixture. Alternatively, use two cardboard boxes to make a mould for a sink-shaped container. Choose two boxes that fit one inside the other, leaving a 2.5cm/1in gap all round. Spread a 2.5cm/1in-thick layer of hypertufa over the inside base of the larger box, then stand the smaller box inside. Trowel the remaining mixture into the gap between the two, and firm it gently down so there are no air pockets. Leave the hypertufa for several weeks before attempting to remove the cardboard boxes as it will take a long time to dry.

To prepare a container for planting, first clean it inside

GARDEN NOTES

REPOTTING

Every now and again permanent plants growing in containers need to be either replanted or potted up to remain healthy. Small perennials growing in soil-based composts should be replanted after 3-5 years. Fruit trees and bushes, shrubs, bamboos, trees and conifers need moving to a slighty bigger container every year or two. After replanting, water them often to stop their leaves browning. Containers of annuals should be emptied when the flowering season is over.

For real budget gardening, empty paint pots can be turned into very effective containers (below). Remember to clean out the insides thoroughly first, and to drill drainage holes in the bottom.

Don't Forget!

PLANT MAINTENANCE

In summer, follow these watchpoints:

- check compost daily and water when dry
- feed plants regularly with liquid or soluble plant food, following maker's directions
- ask a neighbour to water containers when you are away

In winter, take these precautions:

- empty, clean and store all plant containers not in use
- in freezing weather either wrap planted containers with sacking or newspaper to insulate roots, or sink up to rims in the garden
- ensure plants are not standing in puddles or under drips
- move containers of non-hardy plants into a conservatory or greenhouse

(to remove any disease organisms left by previous plants) and outside (for appearance). Check there is at least one, and preferably several, drainage holes in the base. These are essential to allow excess water to run away.

Winter care

Good drainage is vital for containers that will remain outside with plants in them over winter – waterlogged roots quickly rot and cause plants to die. If holes are needed in wood or metal, you can make them with an electric drill and the relevant bit. Holes can be made in plastic by heating up the tip of a skewer with a lighter or over a gas ring and pressing it through the base of the pot.

The next job is 'crocking'. Containers that have big drainage holes in the bottom should have large pieces of broken clay flower pot (crocks) placed over the holes to stop the compost clogging them up. Place crocks curved side down, so water can run out but the compost cannot. Plastic pots with small drainage holes do not need crocking. Some plants, like alpines, need especially well-drained growing conditions – pour a 5cm/2in layer of gravel over the crocks before filling the container with compost.

The right compost

The compost you use depends on the kind of plants you will be growing. For annuals, peat-based composts are ideal. If you are planting bulbs, or shrubs that will remain in the containers for several years on end, a soil-based John Innes compost is best. John Innes No. 3 (often called JI3) contains more plant food than JI1 or 2 and is best for established plants. Young plants should be planted in JI1. In either case, mix 10 per cent gritty sand or fine gravel with the compost to help drainage and provide weight (this helps keep the pots upright in windy weather). If you are growing lime-hating or acid-loving plants such as camellias, use a special ericaceous compost, again mixed with 10 per cent grit. And for growing alpines, which need well-drained but moisture-retentive compost, make up your own mixture of one third each of JI3, gritty sand and coir fibre (also called coco peat).

If you are planting a single specimen in a container, simply treat it as if you were repotting a houseplant. Partly fill the container with loose compost. Knock the plant carefully out of its pot, tease out a few of the larger roots from the base of the rootball, stand it in the pot leaving 15mm/½in between the top of the rootball and the top of the pot, and refill around the roots with compost. Gently firm down the compost and water well.

Group arrangement

If planting a group of different plants together in a large container, first arrange them *outside* the container. Do not plant them until you have the best possible combination of shapes, sizes and colours. Then plant as above.

Once planted up, containers do not require complicated care although they do need regular checking. Look at them daily and remove dead or dying flowers, then poke a finger into the compost and water it if it feels dry. Feed the plant

Whatever shape it comes in, the traditional terracotta pot (above) is always pleasing to the eye. Check before you buy, though, as some terracotta pots are not frost-proof and may crack in severe weather.

Junk shops and market stalls can yield interesting finds for your garden, such as old washtubs or buckets. This unusual container (left) has been filled with a spring display of tulips and hyacinths.

regularly between spring and late summer with liquid or soluble plant feeds, following the manufacturer's instructions. Do not feed in winter. If tall plants need supports, push a few 45cm/18in green split canes in among them, and criss-cross between them with green garden twine.

Suitable plants

The range of plants that can be grown in containers is tremendous. Annuals are always popular. But as well as the well-known summer annuals, do not forget small, early flowering plants like polyanthus, and for autumn and winter, favourites like winter-flowering pansies and ivy. Bulbs – of which you can find spring-, summer- and autumn-flowering kinds – are usually treated as temporary residents and dug up after flowering when the foliage dies down, then stored somewhere cool, dark and dry to replant again later.

Out in the cold

Nowadays, though, people are increasingly interested in plants that can be put in containers and left out all year round. Evergreen shrubs and bamboos are useful here, but 'special' deciduous shrubs – especially the more compact kinds and small trees – also make good specimens for large pots. The pot tends to restrict the size of the plant, keeping it naturally dwarf.

Fruit trees such as patio peaches (a special dwarf kind), figs, a standard trained grape vine, or apples and pears grown on dwarfing rootstocks also make interesting container specimens, as do fruit bushes such as redcurrants. Or, for a strawberry pot, as an alternative to strawberries, try a collection of herbs, or several dwarf bush tomato plants like 'Totem'. And if you have space in a sunroom, greenhouse or conservatory in winter, why not try the new tender exotic shrubs and climbers. Compact plants like hardy ferns and many flowering perennials also make good permanent container plants.

Miniature garden

Finally if you want something special to enjoy in close detail, rock plants are interesting, with perhaps a dwarf conifer for contrast. With a few extras like granite chippings spread over the compost between the different plants and the odd architectural chunk of rock, you can create a perfect garden in miniature.

A blue-glazed Chinese pot (above) makes a very handsome holder for pink petunias and white alyssum. Containers like this are expensive, but you may find a similar but cheaper alternative in a second-hand shop. Most of these pots are not frost-proof.

This log container (below) is a perfect partner for the rustic wooden fence and stone wall in the background.

Composts & Soil Improvers

Few soils are perfect and when moving to a new home the garden you inherit is a matter of pot-luck. There are, however, ways to improve soils.

The easiest way to judge a soil's composition is to pick up a handful and to rub a sample between your thumb and first finger. If it creates a smooth, slippery, greasy surface, the sample contains clay. If rough and gritty, it is predominantly sand.

Another test is to slightly moisten some soil and roll it into a sausage, then curl this to form a ring. The smaller the ring – without breaking – the higher the clay content.

A further test is to fill a screw-top jar about a quarter full with soil, first removing any large stones. Fill the jar three-quarters full with cold water, screw on the lid and shake the jar vigorously for several minutes.

The mixture settles in layers – stones at the base, followed by coarse and light sand, then silt and clay. Organic material floats on the surface. The proportions will indicate the soil's nature.

Although not scientific, the 'boot' test usually says all one needs to know about clay soils. If, after walking over the soil – especially in winter – it sticks to your boots, you can be sure it is mainly clay.

A quick-growing crop such as mustard (left) can be dug into a bed to 'green manure' it. Plants grown next year will benefit.

Add compost to the bottom of the trench (top right) when double digging.

Waterlogged ground must be drained (bottom right) unless you want a boggy area.

Spread compost over the soil and fork it in (below) before sowing or planting.

GROWING TIPS

GREEN MANURING

This involves growing quick-maturing crops, such as annual lupins, mustard, Italian rye, Hungarian rye or red clover, and digging them into the soil before they flower and produce seeds. This introduces organic material into the soil and increases its fertility.

Green manuring is best reserved for vegetable plots, or perhaps large flower beds that are being replanned and will not be replanted for a year.

Taming the extremes

The dream garden has soil that is a balance between clay and sand – friable and light to

LIVING IMPROVERS

Go Organic!

Soil organisms such as fungi, algae, protozoa and bacteria are microscopic. They are vital for breaking down compounds in the soil for subsequent use by plants. Without these hidden warriors the soil would become dead and unable to grow plants.

Garden worms are frequently detested because they create worm casts on lawns. They are, however, valuable soil improvers, aerating and mixing the soil by their activities.

DOUBLE DIGGING

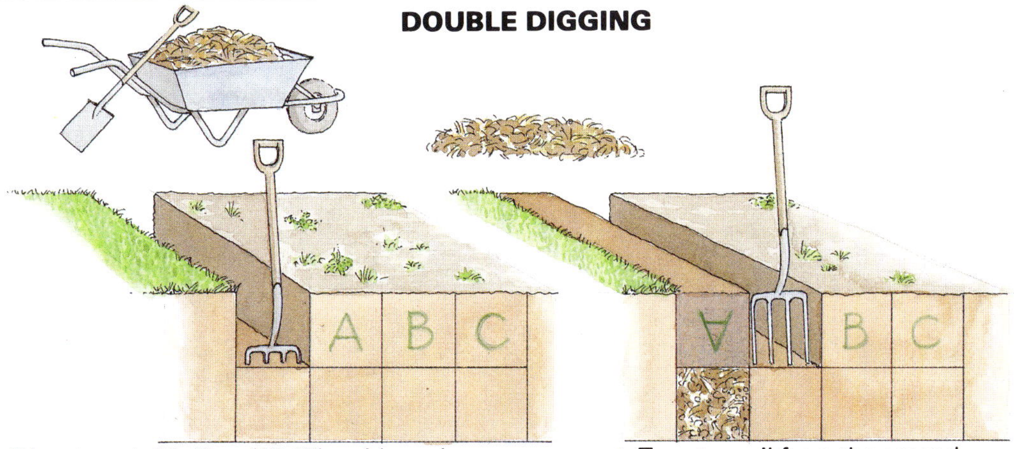

Dig a trench 30-45cm/12-18in wide and one spade's depth. Put the soil in a barrow. Fork over the bottom of the trench and add compost. Turn topsoil from the second trench into the first. Continue and fill the last trench with soil from the barrow.

Peter McHoy

handle, yet moisture-retentive and well aerated.

Gardening, however, can be a perverse hobby. Although neighbouring gardens may have a perfect loam, yours will be formed totally of heavy clay or entirely of sand. There are, however, ways to improve both of these extremes.

Clay soils are improved by digging in, during winter, as much bulky organic material as possible, especially farmyard and stable manure, garden compost, peat and spent mushroom compost.

Calcium compounds dusted over the surface are also beneficial. They encourage clay particles to form small groups and this improves drainage and aeration. The amount you should apply depends on the soil's acidity (see box).

You can help improve small areas by adding coarse sand or fine gravel. These physically open up the soil, improving drainage and aeration. However, to make a significant improvement you must add at least one or two buckets per square metre/square yard.

Shredded bark also opens up soil, but other than for the improvement of small areas its cost prohibits extensive use.

Putting in drains is essential if water remains on the surface in winter. It is pointless improving surface areas in clay soils if the underlying water is not drained. Modern slit drains are much less effort to install than traditional tile or rubble land drains.

Sandy soils need copious amounts of bulky organic material, such as farmyard manure and garden compost. Peat is ideal if the soil is alkaline, while spent mushroom compost is best if the area is acid.

Spent hops are ideal for improving sandy soils, but are difficult to obtain.

Because sandy soil is exceptionally well aerated, bulky organic materials soon decay. Therefore, be prepared to dig in these materials every year, as well as applying mulches in spring or early summer.

It is not without good reason that an old gardening adage says that sandy soils need a thunderstorm every month and a load of manure every other month!

Apply general balanced fertilizers every spring and install a hose sprinkler system for important areas such as vegetable plots, summer flower beds and lawns.

Silts are best treated in the same way as clay soils, as they tend to have an acid nature.

A to Z of improving soil

- **Bracken** when chopped up makes a good mulch, but beware of its sharp stems which can cut your hands.

TYPES OF COMPOST

GARDEN NOTES

The term 'compost' has several meanings and is often used confusingly.

- **Potting composts** are either loam-based or peat-based. The loam-based type is a mixture of loam, peat, sharp sand and fertilizers. Peat-based (loam-less) composts are mainly formed of peat. Peat substitute composts are now available. Plants are transferred into these composts when too large for their previous containers, whether a seed-tray where they were sown, or a small pot.
- **Seed composts** are similar to potting composts, but they are formulated for the sowing of seeds.
- **Garden compost** is decayed vegetative material, created in a compost heap from kitchen waste and garden plants. It is either dug into the soil or used to create a mulch on the soil's surface. Details of how to make a compost heap were in part 2.

Dry, sandy soils will absorb and benefit from large amounts of organic material such as garden compost (left). It will improve their fertility and their ability to hold water.

If you can get large amounts of well-rotted farmyard manure (above right) it can be used in many parts of the garden. Here, it has been heaped on an artichoke trench. Riding stables are a good source of horse manure.

A mulch (right) will keep the soil moist and will also feed it as the organic material gradually decomposes.

ALKALINE OR ACID?

SHORT CUTS

Clay soils can be improved by dusting the surface with lime, which makes soil particles clump together, but first it is essential to know how acid the soil is. The higher the soil acidity, the more lime can be used. Incidentally, sandy soils can also be acid, although it is usually peaty soils that are acid.

Judging the soil's pH (acidity or alkalinity) is easy. There are proprietary kits where a sample of soil is mixed with water then matched with a colour-coded strip that indicates the pH. More expensive are testers with probes that are inserted into the soil. The pH is indicated on a dial.

The cheapest test is with a piece of chemically-treated card. This is inserted into a soil and water mixture, and the resulting colour is compared with a colour code that indicates the pH.

- **Digging** ground in winter is the traditional way to aerate soil, improve drainage, incorporate bulky organic materials and to bury annual weeds. Also, many soil pests become exposed to winter weather and birds, and this helps to reduce their numbers.
- **Farmyard manure** is a legendary soil improver. Never use fresh manure, as during its subsequent breakdown in the soil it absorbs nitrogen, causing temporary starvation around plants. Also, roots and stems are scorched by fresh manure. Use well-rotted manure, digging it into the ground during winter.

After delivery, keep manure covered until it is dug in – rain leaches nutrients from it.

Do not apply manure and lime at the same time, as the nitrogen will be lost into the atmosphere in the form of ammonia. If manure is dug into the soil in early winter, wait until mid-winter before applying a dusting of lime.

- **Garden compost** is formed from soft-tissued, pest- and disease-free plants that have been encouraged to decay until they become crumbly. This usually takes about six months; decomposition speeds

Autumn leaves (above) will break down into rich leaf mould, as on this fork. Leaves must be composted, either on their own if you have enough of them, or you can add them to your compost heap.

MAKING YOUR SOIL LESS ACID

The amount of lime needed to counteract acidity depends on the pH of the soil, the type of soil and the form in which the lime is applied.

As a guide, the following amounts of lime will reduce acidity by about 1.0 pH.

Soil	Hydrated lime	Ground limestone
Clay	425g/sq m (18oz/sq yd)	575g/sq m (24oz/sq yd)
Loam	285g/sq m (12oz/sq yd)	380g/sq m (16oz/sq yd)
Sand	140g/sq m (6oz/sq yd	190g/sq m (8oz/sq yd)

Remember:

- Apply only sufficient lime to bring the pH to 6.5.
- The pH figure should only be taken as a guide. On dry soils (especially when assessed by a probe) the reading may indicate that the soil is more acid than it really is. Conversely, readings taken in late winter can indicate too high alkalinity.
- Avoid excessive liming as it leads to deficiencies of iron and manganese.
- Apply lime after digging the soil in early winter, dusting it over the surface so that subsequently rain will wash it into the ground; surface lime damages plants.

up in wet, warm summers.

Compost can be dug into the soil in winter or used to form a mulch on the surface during spring and early summer.

Do not compost thick, woody stems, perennial weeds or plants that have been treated with weedkillers.

- **Hay** forms a mulch, as well as keeping strawberry fruits off the ground and preventing them from being damaged by rain splashing off the soil during torrential storms.
- **Hoeing** is a routine job, creating a tilth on the surface of the soil, reducing water loss and removing weeds.
- **Leafmould** is created from decayed leaves and is used as a mulch or for digging into the soil in winter.
- **Mulching** is an excellent way to prevent the growth of weeds. It keeps the soil cool during summer, feeds it and assists in moisture retention.

Mulches are applied in late spring and early summer, as soon as the soil has warmed up. Water the soil well first.

Mulches of 7.5-10cm/3-4in are best, using well-rotted manure, compost, peat, shredded bark, chopped bracken, sawdust, straw, hay or leafmould.

Newspapers and corrugated cardboard can also be used, but need topping with something like pulverized bark to improve the appearance and prevent them blowing about.

Plastic sheeting is used, but this does not rot down and improve the soil's texture.

- **Peat** has long been used as a mulch and is often added to the soil when planting. However, it is a limited natural resource and its continuing use destroys many acres of peat beds each year.
- **Sand and fine gravel** open up clay soils, but need to be applied generously.
- **Sawdust** is a useful mulch, especially around gooseberries and currant bushes.
- **Seaweed** contains potash and trace elements and is superb for digging into sandy soils in early winter, as it is slow to rot. Do not use it in large amounts as a mulch.

Potatoes and tomatoes grow especially well on land where seaweed has been dug in.

Unfortunately, it may be contaminated with oil and, on the west coast of Britain, is said to be slightly radioactive. Unless you live in a coastal area its transportation is prohibitively expensive.

- **Shredded bark** forms an attractive mulch. Garden shredders can be used to turn stiff-stemmed garden waste into a mulch material.
- **Spent mushroom compost,** which contains lime, is ideal for digging into acid soil.
- **Spent hops** are ideal for digging into sandy soils, and for creating a good mulch. Unfortunately, they are difficult to obtain.
- **Straw** is useful as a mulch around soft fruits, though it does encourage slugs.

Fertilizers

Keeping your soil nourished with the right feed is vital for healthy, attractive plants. Find out what kind of soil you have, and what fertilizer it needs most.

A dressing of organic bone meal on a freshly dug vegetable plot in autumn. It needs to be forked in to the soil.

Fertilizers will help to make your garden soil more fertile and productive. They improve sandy and peaty soils which are not very fertile. They also replace nutrients where constant cropping has robbed the soil of the plant waste that would otherwise have been returned to the ground to rot down (thus recycling the nutrients).

Using fertilizers is just as important in your fruit and vegetable garden, where you remove all or part of a plant, as it is on farmland.

Modern methods

When you prune or harvest a plant, you are removing some of its food reserves, and these have to be replaced. Fertilizers are also useful on your lawn, if you always remove the dead grass clippings.

Fertilizers were originally applied in the form of animal dung, garden compost, seaweed or crushed, quarried minerals that were rich in certain nutrients.

WHICH FERTILIZER?

Fertilizer	Uses	Source	Features
Nitrogen (N)	When the whole plant appears weak and the lower, older leaves are yellow, small and curling, and the plant flowers and fruits poorly.	Urea Blood Hoof and horn Soot (old) Seaweed Ammonium sulphate Nitrates (various)	Organic, fast, acidic Organic, fast, acidic Organic, fast, acidic Organic, fast, neutral Organic, steady, neutral Inorganic, fast, acidic Inorganic, fast, most neutral
Phosphorus (P)	If older leaves have red or purple margins, and are small, drop prematurely and the plant is dark green and stunted.	Bone meal Seaweed Basic slag Mineral phosphate Super-phosphate	Organic, slow, alkaline Organic, steady, neutral Inorganic, slow, alkaline Inorganic, steady, alkaline Inorganic, steady, neutral
Potassium (K)	When older leaf margins are scorched and there are small spots of dead tissue at the leaf tip and between the veins	Wood ashes *Potassium sulphate *Potassium nitrate	Organic, fast, alkaline Inorganic, steady, acidic Inorganic, fast, alkaline

*Potassium sulphate is also known as sulphate of potash
*Potassium nitrate is also known as nitrate of potash

Nowadays most fertilizers used in agriculture and horticulture are manufactured synthetically. These are known as inorganic fertilizers, because they are not produced from once-living matter.

Restoring soil

Plants and flowers require many chemicals in small amounts for healthy growth. Some, especially nitrogen, which is required for leaf growth, are absorbed from the soil in greater quantities than others, quickly exhausting the supply.

Those elements required in the greatest quantity – nitrogen, potassium and phosphorus – are known as major nutrients. Other chemicals in the soil, known as minor nutrients, are also necessary to plants but are used in such small quantities that there is rarely a deficiency of them.

Plants in containers can also exhaust the soil's nutrients, major and minor, and need to be fed with fertilizers for good growth.

If you do not use fertilizer the plants will grow less well and be far more likely to succumb to pests and diseases. The exceptions are some culinary herbs, which thrive on poor soils, and should not be fed with fertilizers.

After aerating the lawn in autumn apply a sedge peat dressing and brush it into the holes to improve the soil (right). Then apply an autumn lawn fertilizer that is low in nitrogen and high in phosphorus to encourage root growth.

Fertilizer	Uses	Source	Features
Calcium (Ca)	If newer leaves and tips of shoots are turned inward, ragged, scorched or even dead. But first look for caterpillars and aphids, which cause curling on leaves	Calcium compounds Lime/chalk Gypsum	Inorganic, fast, alkaline Organic, slow, alkaline Inorganic, slow, acidic
Magnesium (Mg)	When older leaves are mottled with spots of dead tissue and the leaf margins curl upwards and have slender stalks. But these symptoms may also be the result of excessive potassium fertilizer.	Kieserite/ dolomitic limestone Epsom salts/ magnesium sulphate	Organic, slow, alkaline Inorganic, steady, alkaline
Iron (Fe)	If newer leaves are yellow or bleached, with the veins remaining green, and the plant is growing poorly.	Iron sulphate Sequestrene	Inorganic, steady, acidic Inorganic, steady, neutral Cures iron deficiency.

Choice of food

Whatever soil and type of garden you have, you need to supply a balanced diet to your plants. Bulky fertilizers such as stable or farmyard manure mixed with straw should contain a little of everything, and will improve the drainage of sticky soils, while helping dry soils to retain moisture for longer than usual. Manures should be stacked for a few months before they are used.

Many people, especially those living in towns, have no access to manure and use peat instead. But peat does not contain any nutrients.

For town dwellers, the main alternative to manure is garden compost. This can provide the whole range of nutrients in the same way that manure and straw do.

Lawn mowings make a good base for composting and, when mixed with shredded paper and kitchen waste, should allow you to produce enough compost for the vegetable garden and also some to place in

> **DON'T FORGET!**
>
> **TESTING THE SOIL**
>
> - A simple test kit will show if your soil lacks vital nutrients, and will tell you whether the soil is acid or alkaline.
> - Test the soil in spring and you will know what to expect in the coming season. You will also learn what the soil is lacking and, therefore, what you must add.
> - Foliage plants such as lettuce and grass may need plenty of nitrogen. A plant grown for its flowers or fruits could need more potassium. Root growth is stimulated by phosphorus.
> - General fertilizers benefit all plants. Apply a single element fertilizer only if the soil is low in one nutrient.

planting holes for ornamental plants. If you have no space for a compost heap you can buy bagged up manure-based composts.

Bulky manures supply the complete range of nutrients, albeit in very small amounts. But some plants need more of some elements than manure or garden compost can provide. You will have to add these extra elements in the form of concentrates.

Strike a balance between your use of fertilizers and farmyard manure or garden compost. Use manure or compost for the value of their physical bulk and use fertilizers to feed your plants.

Organic gardens

It is important to give plants the exact nutrients they need. So consider whether or not you want to use organic methods.

Organic growing is based on the long-term health of the soil. It uses bulky manures and nutrients that feed the soil organisms as well as the plants. These nutrients are supplied by organic fertilizers, which means that they have been produced from once-living matter, such as bone meal or compost.

Limestone, formed from the shells of ancient sea creatures, is an organic fertilizer, and quarried rock phosphate and potash (potassium) are also used by organic growers.

Organic fertilizers usually have to be broken down by organisms in the soil before their chemicals take a form which can be used by the plant. So, usually, they have a steady or slow effect on the plants, though this is not always the case. The exceptions are blood, urea and wood ashes.

Fast action

Inorganic fertilizers provide the same chemicals to the plants but in a soluble form with a fast effect. Their solubility means that some of these manufactured fertilizers can be quickly washed away from the root zone.

To counter this, firms have developed controlled, or slow-release, fertilizers for lawns, flower beds and pot plants. The particles of fertilizer are bound with a substance which either allows the nutrients to pass through gradually when wetted, or needs bacterial action to break down the coating. These coated particles are those often mistaken for slugs' eggs in the potting compost of purchased plants.

Choosing with care

Fertilizers are sold as straights, compounds and soil improvers. Straights are those which contain one nutrient, such as superphosphate, which provides phosphorus, or ammonium sulphate (sulphate of ammonia), which provides nitrogen.

Compounds are a mixture of materials which give a variety of nutrients in a certain ratio. You will find this ratio printed on the package.

The items are always listed in the order of nitrogen, phosphorus and potassium (often referred to as N:P:K, the abbrevations used by chemists), followed by other components.

For example, when you see a ratio described as 7:7:7, this shows an equal amount of nitrogen, phosphorus and potassium. The figures 10:0:6 would indicate that no phosphorus is contained in this particular compound.

Those without access to farmyard manure and without space for a compost heap can buy bags of concentrated organic manure (top). Though not cheap, it is convenient. Fertilizers are best applied to seed beds before planting (above).

The actual figures used refer to the percentage of each nutrient. So 7:7:7 shows that each component forms seven per cent of the compound.

You also find that the package shows the proportions of other nutrients in the overall weight of the compound. So 10g/kg means that 10 grammes of the nutrient is present in every kilogramme, or 1000 grammes, of the fertilizer, which works out at one per cent. This is handy to know when comparing brands.

Special treatment

Fertilizers are often sold for specialist uses. These include tomato fertilizer, chrysanthemum feed and spring or summer lawn dressing. If you look at the ratio given on the package, you will see that many are similar.

Tomato fertilizer, for example, which is only used once the fruit sets, contains a high proportion of potash which is required by the developing

Foliar feeds (above) are sprayed onto a plant's leaves. Here one is being applied to perk up a weak rhododendron. Add lime (below) to a lawn if a soil test shows the soil to be very acid. This is a rare problem as most grasses tolerate acidity.

fruits. It can be used for most flowering plants if necessary. Foliage plants, however, prefer fertilizers high in nitrogen.

Liquid or dry

Fertilizers can be applied as liquids or as dry granules or powders. Dry fertilizer is scattered over the surface of the soil and raked in before sowing or planting. This process is called base dressing. When applied to growing plants, it is known as top dressing.

Handling and storage

Dry fertilizer has to be weighed out for accurate dosing and can blow into your eyes during use on all but the stillest day. Lawn fertilizer spreaders are sold which help you to apply the material evenly. Take care not to overlap or miss strips as you apply it, or you will have stripes of different greens on the lawn.

These dry fertilizers must be stored in a dry place. If they get wet they will set rock hard in their packs and be extremely difficult to use. The packs are easily damaged and can leak the material everywhere. Fertilizer is also very corrosive to metals so keep it well away from your car.

Special dry mix fertilizers can be bought to add to other ingredients, such as loam, peat, perlite and sand, to make your own potting compost.

Keeping stocks

Some dry fertilizers can be diluted with water and kept as concentrated stock solution, to be diluted further when required. You can also buy liquid fertilizers that are ready to dilute; these can be kept in a damp place.

Liquid feeds can often be applied to leaves, and not just the soil, and can be used in a hose-end dilutor to spray the material to the far corners of flower borders and beds.

Hose-end dilutors also make feeding the lawn easy, with no danger of leaving stripes, and save you carrying watering cans across the garden. Some hose-end dilutors are designed to take tablet fertilizers.

Correct timing

It is important to apply fertilizer at the correct time. The fast-acting types will soon be washed from the soil, beyond the reach of the plants, so apply them at the appropriate stage of growth, which is usually the spring.

Slow-acting types can be effective for a year or more, so the timing is less critical, especially if you apply them annually or more often to ensure a continual supply to your valuable plants.

It is better to apply dry material to growing plants with dry leaves. If the leaves are wet from dew or rain, the material can stick to the leaves and scorch them.

If you are foliar feeding, do so on a dry day so that the nutrients stay on the leaves where the plants can quickly take them up. If washed off onto the soil, the effect may be slower.

Nitrogen encourages soft, leafy growth, so avoid applying it after mid-summer, or new growths could be damaged by the first frosts and cold winds.

GARDEN NOTES

FEEDING PLANTS

- The way your plants grow tells you what nutrients are lacking and need replacement.
- Some plants take up a nutrient early in the growing season and quickly exhaust the supply.
- Look out for signs of deficiency in the growing season, not in autumn when the leaves change colour and die.
- General purpose fertilizers supply a balance of the major nutrients. For specific nutrients, choose one that is readily available to you.

SOILS THAT 'LOCK UP' FERTILIZERS

Some plants find it difficult to absorb certain nutrients – particularly iron – from neutral or acid soils. Acid-loving plants, in particular, such as rhododendrons, camellias, skimmias and most heathers, find that the nutrients are 'locked up' chemically.

Using fertilizers that make the soil more acid (sulphate of ammonia instead of Nitro-chalk if you want a nitrogenous fertilizer, for example) may help over time, but can never be an adequate solution on a very chalky soil.

For more immediate results you can use a product called Sequestrene, which provides the necessary nutrients in a form that acid-loving plants can absorb even on ordinary soils.

Sequestrene is available as a powder or granules, so it can be diluted and watered on the soil or added dry and left for the rain to wash in.

Compost

Improve your soil while reducing waste by making your own garden compost. It is easy to do and very satisfying.

Making your own compost is perhaps the ultimate in recycling. There is nothing magical about composting: all plant and animal material will rot down eventually. By making a compost heap, you are just speeding up the process, concentrating it in one place.

In the past, garden compost was used both to enrich the soil and for growing seedlings and pot plants. There is now no point in using it as a growing medium as the widely available specialist composts produce much better results.

The nutrient value of your compost will depend on what has gone into it, but the main function of all garden compost is to contribute to the creation and maintenance of a healthy soil by nourishing the micro-organisms that live within it. These micro-organisms in turn release nutrients that will benefit your growing plants.

Better texture

Like all bulky organic material, including farmyard manure, compost helps free-draining sandy soils to retain moisture and conversely opens up sticky clay soils and helps them drain. Used regularly and fairly generously, this organic material helps to make the soil more workable and more able to support a wide range of plants.

Do not, however, expect instant results: feeding the soil is a slow, steady process and it takes time to see the benefits of continually adding compost.

Some experts manage to make compost-making sound very complicated. It need not be so. Garden compost is simply free organic matter and need not take hours of your

TIPS FOR SUCCESSFUL COMPOST

A cube- or cylinder-shaped bin is best as the contents will then heat up well and kill weeds and diseases. Your bin should be at least $1m^3/3ft^3$.

Make sure you can get easy access to your compost: a cube-shaped bin should have a removable side; lids should be easy to lift on and off.

Cover your heap to keep heat in and rain out.

Keep a bucket in the kitchen and empty your vegetable waste into it instead of just throwing it out. You can use anything from egg shells to cabbage leaves, apple cores to leftover carrots – it will all make excellent compost. Once you have filled the bucket (left) tip the contents onto the compost heap where it will soon decompose. Do not mix it. Remove compost from the bottom of the heap at regular intervals.

A good compost heap should not be completely air-tight. Turning your heap will help to introduce air.

A compost bin does not have to be made of wood: any good insulant will do.

Site on soil so that worms, fungi and bacteria have access and can speed up decomposition.

time to produce. Likewise, choosing what to add to your heap is not difficult. Suitable composting materials are anything that once lived, so do not restrict yourself to garden waste. Think about what you throw in the dustbin now: tea leaves, egg shells, vegetable peelings, for example.

How much to make

You do not need to make vast amounts of compost for it to be worthwhile. If you are keen to produce your own food, especially organically, you will need to feed your garden a lot and will probably want to make as much compost as possible. Use everything you can, from the garden, the house and even what you can beg from the neighbours.

You can almost never overdo the amount of compost you add to the vegetable patch, especially where you intend to grow potatoes, peas, beans and other vegetables which need a lot of moisture in order to crop satisfactorily. Aim to dig in a full barrow-load for every square metre.

Using grass cuttings

If your garden is mainly ornamental, on the other hand, and you have a large lawn, the compost heap is a convenient way of dealing with all those mowings. Mowings on their own do not make a satisfactory compost – much more than 30 per cent of mowings will result in a slimy although still usable mess, and you will need other ingredients.

All the waste products from flower beds and borders will help, together with the various types of kitchen waste.

The compost you make can be used as a mulch on the borders, around individual plants, or dug into the soil when you are preparing the ground for planting or are lifting, dividing or moving plants.

A mulch of compost

If you decide to use your compost as a mulch – a layer of material laid on bare soil to suppress weeds and retain moisture – you will need a 5-8cm/2-3in deep layer for it to be effective. When you apply the mulch, first place it around precious plants which could suffer during droughts and hosepipe bans. If you have any left over, spread it around other plants next, and finally on any bare ground. Be careful not to let the mulch touch the stems or trunks of any plants, as it could kill them – these parts are meant to be above

SHORT CUTS

SPEED UP DECAY

Bag up weeds and accumulate kitchen waste until you next mow the lawn. Then add all these materials at the same time, so that the heat from the grass mowings can start work on the rest straight away.

Compost is a wonderful substance that can be used in a number of ways. In autumn it can be used as a feed. It will not only add valuable nutrients but it will also greatly improve the soil texture. It should be dug into the soil with a spade. This is especially useful for any vegetables you may be growing. Alternatively it can be used at any other time of the year as a mulch (right) or be forked into the soil around shrubs.

Compost bins can be bought in a wide variety of forms and work in slightly different ways, but the end product is invariably very similar. This wire mesh bin (left) is fairly inconspicuous and allows lots of air to circulate, ensuring rapid breakdown of the compostable material. For something that looks a bit more professional this twin bin (below) is made from strong steel tubes and rot proof material which allows the air to circulate. Fill the first bin and allow the compost to make while you fill up the second. The compost which is ready is easily removed from the base.

WHAT TO ADD TO A COMPOST HEAP

- plant material
- lawn mowings
- wood ash
- kitchen waste, including vegetable parings and tea bags
- newspaper and other waste paper
- sawdust and straw
- finger-thick woody prunings
- thorny prunings (wear gloves when handling compost – thorns stay intact)
- manure mixed with 'bedding' (for example, straw, shredded paper or sawdust)
- droppings from poultry, pigeons and farm animals

MAKING A COMPOST HEAP

You can use wood, mesh panels, a plastic dustbin or barrel or even straw bales. Make sure you incorporate enough ventilation when you are building, or drill holes in solid sides. If you use mesh, line your bin with cardboard or plastic sheeting to reduce some of the airflow. Make sure you can get easy access to the heap, for adding and removing material.

The first layer of the heap should be brushwood, thick woody prunings or tough stems (e.g. cabbage). Lay this directly on the soil to help ventilation.

Add your compostable material in 15-30cm/6-12in layers. Each layer should be a well-mixed combination of soft, sappy greenery (like mowings) and drier, coarser material (like dead flower stalks or woody prunings). Water this layer if necessary to make it moist but not sodden and fit the lid.

Start collecting material again until you have enough to add another layer and repeat the process. Once the container is full, leave it with the lid on until the contents have rotted and you need to use it. Keep the outer edges for adding to the new heap as they will not have rotted down completely.

ground, not buried!

There are three main options when choosing where to make compost: burying compostable material in a trench; placing it in a bought or home-made container; or simply building a heap.

Making a trench

Burying compostable material in a trench is an ideal method for use with bare ground where you intend to grow vegetables. It gets rid of the need for a heap or bin and once you have dug your trench, all you have to do is place mowings

WHAT WENT WRONG?

Q Last year I decided to make my own compost from lawn-mowings, but after 12 months all I have got is a slimy mess that smells frankly offensive.

A This happens when too many grass mowings are added, all at once. Your 'compost' can still be used – dig it into the ground or spread it as a mulch – but in future, mix dry and bulky material with the mowings and you will get better results.

This compost is unsuitable for use, in parts it has not decayed and in others it is too slimy.

Q The ingredients of my compost look just the same now as they did six months ago. Why should this be and what can I do?

A Your heap has not become hot enough to start decomposition. Re-build it, including a source of nitrogen – mowings, nettles, comfrey or urine – to help the bacteria to digest the heap. Prevent drying out by lining a bin with cardboard or cover a heap with polythene.

WHAT NOT TO ADD TO A COMPOST HEAP

- diseased plant material
- coal ash
- bones
- meat scraps (as these attract vermin)
- cardboard
- lumps of soil
- very thick prunings (unless shredded first)
- seeding weeds and roots of perennial weeds (unless the heap is very hot)
- dog and cat manure (unless the heap is very hot and compost is not to be used on food crops)
- tree leaves (make a separate leaf heap)

If you don't want to go out and buy a compost bin why not build your own? It doesn't have to be anything too complicated but a cube or cylindrical shape is best. This bin (above right) has been made from wood and the mesh front ensures there is plenty of ventilation. Easy access to the heap is important. This bin allows you to add material to the top and to slide the mesh panel up to enable you to remove compost from the bottom.

and other material into the base. When you have a fairly thick layer, cover it with soil and tread it down.

Waste composted in this way will not heat up much, so you will not be able to put perennial weeds and seedheads in the trench and you will also have to avoid adding anything which animals may want to dig up. Leave it to rot until the following spring, then plant your vegetables – especially moisture-loving runner beans – or potato tubers.

If you do not have enough bare ground to bury your waste, you will need a compost heap or bin. Your bin need not be large as mowings and other material sink down surprisingly quickly. Start with a small container and buy or make a second one if the first begins to overflow.

Natural allies

Whichever type you choose, place it directly on to the soil so that the fungi, bacteria and worms, which all contribute to the decomposition process, have access to it.

The commonest bins on sale are either plastic cylinder shapes or cubes made of wood slats or mesh panels. Slats and mesh can let in too much air, so you may have to line the sides with plastic to cut down on draughts. Neither type is very expensive, but you could easily make your own.

The right mixture

Provided you put in a good mixture of materials, ensure the right amount of air and keep the heap damp, you should be able to make good compost in any container.

If you think of a compost heap as similar in principle to a fire, you will appreciate what is needed. Fuel, in the form of compostable material: air, to fan the flames but not put them out; and heat, which in turn helps more heat be generated, are all essential.

With a small compost heap, after the initial heat has diminished, mix up or 'turn' the contents, so that the material that was formerly on the outside is on the inside. This process adds more air to the remaining uncomposted material and re-kindles the 'fire'. To avoid doing this manually, you can buy tumbler bins which you regularly turn on their axis to re-mix the contents, but this can be hard work as the bin gets fuller.

SPECIAL TREATMENT

BRIGHT IDEAS

- Chop or shred dry materials such as straw and paper, then soak in water
- Shred or chop woody prunings of more than finger thickness to help them rot more quickly
- Use mowings from a lawn recently treated with weedkiller only if the compost is not used for 12 months (check weedkiller instructions for details)
- Compost leaves separately

GREEN FEED

omfrey leaves or stinging nettles on compost heap will add nutrients and oeed up decay.

A compost heap is the basis of good organic gardening and is also a productive way of re-cycling various materials. Do not limit yourself to re-cycling your garden waste; save your kitchen waste too (in a covered bucket). Use natural or recycled materials to construct your bin and mowings, nettles, comfrey or urine as a nitrogen source to speed decay. For true organic gardening use ingredients from organic gardens and farms only.

Coping with a Dry Soil

A dry soil need not be a problem – it can even have its advantages. Get the best out of yours, whether it's naturally dry or has become so in a drought.

If your soil is permanently dry, do not despair. There is plenty you can do to improve it and all the solutions are easy, if a little time-consuming. Most apply not only to naturally dry soils but also to those which lack moisture in a long, hot summer when there is no rain forecast and hosepipe bans make watering difficult.

The good and the bad

You may have to water a dry soil more often than one that retains water and you may have to add large quantities of compost, but dry soils can have their advantages, too.

For instance, many tender plants require especially good drainage to get them through a cold winter and a dry soil can offer this. Dry, light soils warm up quickly in spring, too, to give you a slightly longer growing season.

No one wants to have to water the garden any more than is really necessary – and water is an increasingly valuable resource. To reduce watering you need to increase the soil's ability to hold the water it receives naturally. To do this it needs extra organic matter – lots and lots of compost, manure, leaf mould or other bulky, fibrous additives.

Hungry soil

Dry soils tend to be free-draining, which means that they lose nutrients. A dry soil is therefore also a hungry soil. For this reason, when adding bulk to your soil, manure or a good, rich compost will be much more beneficial than peat, which holds water but has no nutritional value.

A lush, green lawn is every gardener's dream, and a careful programme of feeding, weeding and watering is the way to achieve it. Using a lawn sprinkler (above) is the ideal way to give your lawn a good soak – important in a long, dry spell or when a new lawn has just been laid. Do not forget to move the sprinkler occasionally during watering so that the spray can reach every corner of the lawn and no part risks becoming waterlogged.

For best results, incorporate your compost into the top two spits of soil (that is, to a depth of about 50cm/20in) before you plant. In a new border this is easy to do but in an established border you will have to treat small areas.

Marvellous mulching

A good mulch of compost around plants will not only seal moisture into the soil by insulating it from wind and sun, it will also provide a banquet for the worms; they will draw it down into the topsoil, taking all the extra nutrients down with it.

A 7.5cm/3in layer of compost in spring is the best start a plant can have on a dry soil. If you are short of compost use leaf mould or well-rotted manure. Spent hops and old mushroom compost are also useful and easy to apply. Bark mulch will help to insulate the soil but it has no nutritional value, while, conversely, concentrated manures, available in bags from garden centres, are full of nutrients but lack the sheer bulk that is needed to enrich a poor, dry soil.

Sandy soils especially need this bulk to improve texture. When such soils have been well composted over a number of years they can be wonderfully deep and fertile.

Chalk and gravel

Soils of mainly chalk or gravel are more difficult and slower to improve. You may have to literally build up a good soil depth over a number of years by adding more and more mulch each spring. There are no short cuts but after a few years you will be pleasantly surprised: your efforts will be rewarded by a richer and more manageable soil. Do not stop mulching, however, or the soil will revert and your efforts will have been wasted.

To keep soil well insulated, plant ground-covering plants. This does not mean crowding shrubs together but it does

WHAT IS DRY SOIL?

A naturally dry soil is any soil with a light texture, containing insufficient organic matter to retain enough moisture. But even a soil that is normally moisture-retentive can become dry during a long hot summer when there is very little rain.

Typical dry soils include:

- **sandy soils** which can be good for many different plants but are often very hungry and may also be acidic
- **chalk soils** which tend to be stony, are very alkaline and need regular generous dressings of compost to improve their fertility

Mulching is one way of conserving moisture around established plants – and, as an extra bonus, it will also help to smother weeds and so cut down on the amount of work you have to do in the garden. Here (right), an Elaeagnus × ebbingei 'Limelight' has been mulched with a layer of shredded bark. Unlike manure or compost, however, bark will not feed the soil at all.

It is very important that young plants like this viburnum (above) receive adequate water. Watering well with a can directly around the base of the plant ensures that the roots are thoroughly moistened.

If you have a new plot or unplanted border, you can really get to grips with improving the soil. Working across the plot, digging a series of trenches which you then fill with manure a number of years (below), is an excellent way of building up a more fertile soil.

IMPROVING DRY SOIL

- Add organic matter to increase the soil's ability to hold moisture naturally. Compost or manure will add valuable nutrients as well as hold water.
- Spread a mulch – a layer of organic matter – around plants to seal moisture into the soil. Again, compost or manure is best as earthworms will gradually draw this down into the soil.
- Grow ground-cover plants to shade the soil.
- Water thoroughly to promote good, deep root growth. Watering little and often will encourage shallow roots, which will be more vulnerable to moisture loss near the surface.

GARDEN NOTES

WALLS AND CONTAINERS

Plants growing at the foot of a wall need extra care as soil here tends to be dry. No matter in which direction a wall faces, it is likely to cast its own 'rain shadow'.

Plants in pots and containers also need frequent watering and feeding as they are often kept in a fairly sheltered spot or under house eaves where rain cannot reach them. So don't neglect your window boxes and hanging baskets, especially when there is a drought.

Whether your soil is permanently dry, or you are preparing for a dry summer, apply a mulch to a well-watered soil (above). Pay special attention to watering plants close to a wall as these receive less rain.

A seepage hose (below) delivers a small, steady flow of water through tiny holes. Devices are available which control the flow so you can go out without worrying that you will return to a flooded garden. Evening is the best time to water.

GROWING TIPS

GOOD FOOD GUIDE

Q Should I add artificial fertilizers to my naturally dry soil?

A No. A dry soil is not necessarily an infertile one and in any case artificial fertilizers will not help your plants as much as the addition of a rich garden compost. Composts and mulches serve a dual purpose: they help the soil to hold water as well as feeding it.

mean never leaving large expanses of bare soil.

Choose plants that positively enjoy dry conditions. A plant which is at home on your soil will always look better than one that is visibly struggling to survive.

There is a wider choice of plants for sunny spots in dry soil than there are plants suitable for dry shade.

Chemical remedies

Desperate circumstances do sometimes require quite desperate remedies and there is a substance available to provide a reservoir of water in the soil. Polymer gels, available in granular form from some garden centres, can be an excellent aid in establishing trees and shrubs on dry soils and means they need less watering.

You simply have to mix the dry granules into the bottom of the planting hole. When you water in your new plant the granules swell – like wallpaper paste – and form tiny pockets of moist gel. These act as reservoirs in the soil, from which thirsty roots can obtain water in times of drought.

Heatwaves

There are times when every garden is dry. In a summer heatwave it is frustrating to watch the beauty you have worked to create and nurture frying to a crisp in the hot sun.

The best advice is to be prepared for a sudden change in the weather. Use mulches just as you would in a permanently dry garden. Even in midsummer, a good mulch put down over well-soaked soil will help to keep the soil quite cool and moist. Do not, however, put a mulch onto a parched soil as it will then act like a sponge, soaking up the first rain before it reaches the plants' roots.

When you do water your garden, do it generously but sensibly. Use a watering can to top up thirsty plants like clematis once a week, whatever the weather. This keeps the plants strong enough to cope during dry spells.

A hand-held hose is usually more effective than a sprinkler, except on lawns. A soil that has only had its surface dampened by a sprinkler will draw up the thirsty roots. Sprinklers can also cause

If you have a dry soil or live in an area which is prone to seasonal drought it is wise to select plants which thrive in these conditions. Prunus laurocerasus (above) is ideal for a shady spot while Cytisus nigricans (below) is perfect if you want to fill a sunny area with vibrant colour.

PLANT CHOICE

For sunny spots with dry soil pick from the following:-

- **Shrubs**: brooms (cytisus and genista), cotton lavender (santolina), smoke bush (cotinus), spotted laurel (aucuba), rock rose (helianthemum), senecio, yucca, lavender, rosemary, halimium, hebe, sun rose (cistus).
- **Herbaceous plants**: bearded iris, bear's breeches (acanthus), sea holly (eryngium), cranesbill (geranium), ice plant (sedum), snow-in-summer (cerastium), penstemon, sempervivum, carnations and pinks (dianthus).

For shady spots in dry soil, any of the following plants are a good choice.

- **Shrubs**: spotted laurel (aucuba), box (buxus), *Daphne pontica,* false castor oil plants (fatsia), ivies, rose of Sharon *(Hypericum calycinum),* holly (ilex), privet (ligustrum), *Mahonia aquifolium,* cherry laurel *(Prunus laurocerasus)* and snowberry (symphoricarpos).
- **Herbaceous plants**: bergenia, brunnera, foxglove (digitalis), honesty (lunaria), Solomon's seal (polygonatum), lungwort (pulmonaria), comfrey (symphytum), periwinkle *(Vinca minor)*, waldsteinia, *Euphorbia robbiae* and *Iris foetidissima*.

leaves to burn when the hot sun shines on them. It is much better to use a hosepipe, directing a gentle flow of water at the root of each thirsty plant. In this way you will channel the water where it is most needed.

Slow but steady

As an alternative to a hand-held hose, a seep hose is effective for watering a border. Like a leaky pipe, a seep hose will deliver a small but steady supply of water through a series of tiny holes. Devices are available to switch off the water when the required volume has been delivered.

Water your garden in the evening, after the heat of the day has passed, and less water will be lost to evaporation. The plants can then take a long, cool drink to build themselves up for another hot day.

Lawns obviously need water but in the early stages of a drought the best advice is to give the available water to your border plants and shrubs.

When you do come to water your lawn, give it a really good soak. This will ensure that the roots are drawn downwards rather than towards the surface. In a drought, let the grass grow to at least 2.5cm/1in long. It will endure the dry conditions much better and can be close mown later on.

Some spots in the garden are inevitably drier than others. Steps or paved areas are usually very free draining and so a broom like the Genista pilosa (top) makes an ideal choice.

Not all plants which thrive on dry soil are shrubby. Honesty, Lunaria biennis (above) is a pretty herbaceous plant which prefers a shady part of the garden. Delicate white or purple flowers disguise the fact that it is particularly robust and can withstand dry conditions. The silvery seed pods make beautiful additions to flower arrangements.

Limy Soils

Many of the country's best gardens are on limy soil. You can grow wonderful plants, so long as you bear in mind a few limitations and garden accordingly.

Limy soils are usually found in areas where the rock beneath the surface is composed of chalk or limestone. However, certain sands, especially near coastal areas, are also alkaline; this is because they contain the remnants of sea shells which, like chalk, are composed mainly of calcium. Because calcium produces an alkaline reaction, such soils are generally referred to as 'alkaline' soils.

In limy areas you may, nevertheless, find pockets of topsoil that are neutral or even acid, especially at the bottom of a valley where the depth of soil is usually greater than on the hills.

The alkalinity or acidity of the soil determines which plants grow well and which

DON'T FORGET!

PLANTS TO AVOID

Some plants become chemically starved when grown in a limy soil, and quickly turn yellow and die. They include:

Rhododendrons
Azaleas
Camellias
Pieris
Heathers, including
Calluna vulgaris
Erica cinerea
Erica arborea
Daboecia cantabrica
and their varieties
Kalmia
Lithospermum
Perenettya
Gaultheria
Cornus kousa
Enkianthus

Whether your soil is thin or, as here, deep and rich, it pays to dig in humus (above). Organic material will make clay easier to work and will increase the depth of thin soil.

Junipers (opposite) will cope with a variety of soils. Some thrive on thin chalky soils.

languish unhappily. Fortunately, though, the majority of garden plants will grow well in both acid and alkaline soils.

Lime and plants

An excessively alkaline soil interferes with the ability of certain plants to take up nutrients. Even though an element like iron, vital for the production of chlorophyll, may be present in the soil, it becomes 'locked' in a form unavailable to some plants.

Those plants that cannot extract the necessary nutrients for healthy growth are called 'calcifuge', or lime-hating, plants. Rhododendrons and pieris, which are adapted to growing on acid soils, are well known lime-haters.

Many plants, such as lilac and carnations, however, have evolved so that they can make the most of the available nutrients. These lime-loving plants are known as 'calcicoles'.

Although most plants will grow well on most soils, they may struggle in very acid or very alkaline conditions. If you have a chalky soil it makes sense to grow plants that thrive in alkaline soils.

Limy soils vary greatly in quality, irrespective of their liminess. There are rich, deep, alluvial, limy soils which grow superb crops and support marvellous gardens. In England, for instance, there are also the cold, limy clays of Kent and Cambridgeshire, the thinner upland soils of the Yorkshire Dales, which lie over limestone hills, and the meagre scraping of stony soil over the chalk Downs. Some are difficult to garden on, but not just because they are limy. It is more to do with the type of soil, its depth and whether it is free-draining or wet.

Improving the soil

It is the poor, thin, limy soils which are the hardest to garden on. Often they are stony, and there is so much lime in the soil that the pH value is very high. It is not really possible to reduce the pH value significantly, and you must garden with it, rather than against it.

You can, though, improve the volume and quality of the soil by adding to it bulky, humus-rich soil conditioners. Compost and well-rotted man-

Short Cuts

MEASURING ALKALINITY

The pH scale, from 0-14, is a register of acidity and alkalinity. pH7 is chemically neutral, but 6.5 is regarded as neutral for most plants. pH test kits are available quite cheaply from all garden centres.

You must remember it is not a proportional scale. One step on the pH scale, say from pH6 to pH7, represents a ten-fold increase in alkalinity or acidity. Garden soils usually fall in the range 4-8.5.

If your soil has a pH value of 7.5 or above, your garden is alkaline enough to cause problems for some plants, so choose accordingly.

If you are new to an area and unsure of what type of soil awaits you, the best indicator is always to look at neighbouring gardens, to see what grows there. If the soil is acidic, someone is certain to be growing rhododendrons or heathers. If not, then the chances are you are on an area of limy soil, but test it to be sure.

HYDRANGEA COLOUR

The colour of the flowers of Hydrangea macrophylla *is altered by the pH of the soil. On acid soils (above left) the blooms are blue or purple. On neutral or alkaline soils with a pH greater than 5.5 the blooms will be pink or red (above right). The species shown here is* Hydrangea macrophylla *'Deutschland'. Adding colourants will make flowers bluer.*

GARDEN NOTES

PLANTS FOR THIN SOIL

The following plants grow well on thin soil over chalk:
Aucuba
Berberis
Buddleia
Buxus
Ceanothus
Cistus
Cotoneaster
Deutzia
Euonymus
Forsythia
Fuchsia
Hebe
Hypericum
Ligustrum
Lonicera
Mahonia
Philadelphus
Potentilla
Rosa
Rosmarinus
Sambucus
Senecio
Spartium
Syringa
Vinca
Weigela
Yucca

ure are best. If you can get them cheaply, rotted straw, spent mushroom compost, spent hops or anything similar will do. Spent mushroom compost, however, contains ground limestone, so it will not make your ground any less alkaline, though it well help to improve the soil structure.

Dig in generous amounts whenever you start a new border, or whenever you put in a new plant. And meanwhile, mulch regularly and thickly, letting the worms do the work of pulling the goodness down into the soil.

Mulching is important, too, because it helps keep the soil moist. Thin, stony soils dry out very quickly, which can be damaging to plants.

Growing calcifuges

It is possible to grow lime-hating plants, such as rhododendron and pieris, in limy areas by creating special conditions for them. Tubs or raised beds filled with acid soil or ericaceous compost will work up to a point, but there are problems with them.

In the case of raised beds, worms will eventually bring lime up from the natural underlying soil into your acidic soil. Tubs need an ample supply of soft, acid rainwater. Otherwise you will simply be watering lime onto them when you use alkaline tapwater.

Even if you garden on acid soil your tapwater may be alkaline because it has been piped from a limy area. If your kettle is full of scale, beware. Collect rainwater for your tubs and raised beds.

In time of drought, it is better to give limy water than no water at all. One or two small doses of limy water will not do any great harm.

Plants for limy soil

Rhododendrons and heathers may be non-starters on limy soil, but there are many other plants which grow best on lime. The only limitations will be the soil's other qualities, such as depth, fertility, moisture retentiveness and so on.

Most herbaceous plants do well on limy soil, and the choice there is endless.

Alpines do well, too. You can make a virtue of necessity and make a limestone scree garden, growing small cushion plants through white limestone chippings. Again the choice of plants is endless. You may already have a rockery made of weathered limestone. This will provide an interesting variety of situations for alpines and small perennials.

Most conifers grow happily enough on limy soil. This is true for full-sized specimens and dwarfs. Although you cannot make a traditional heather-and-conifer garden on lime, you can certainly make a collection of dwarf conifers and underplant them with lime-tolerant carpeters. Try using *Polygonum affine* (now more correctly called *Persicaria affine*), *Geum montanum*, *Dryas octopetala* and many others.

You can even grow several more lime-tolerant, winter-flowering heathers, such as *Erica carnea* (also sold as *E. herbacea*) and its varieties, so long as you are working with an open-textured soil.

A mulch of large river or seashore pebbles makes an attractive foil to the shapes of mixed conifers. Junipers are especially good on limy soil, and come in many habits, from

Senecio *'Sunshine' (above) is a bushy evergreen shrub with silvery-grey leaves that become dark green. It does well on poor limy soils. The yellow flowers appear in summer.*

Artemisia *'Powis Castle' (below) has finely cut silvery-grey foliage and insignificant yellowish-grey flowers.*

GARDEN NOTES

TREES TO GROW ON CHALK

Shallow soils over chalk can be difficult for trees, not just because of alkalinity, but because of the problems of stability. Not all trees will stand properly without a tap root into deep soil. The following trees are happy over solid chalk:

Ash
Beech
Hornbeam
Horse chestnut
Japanese flowering cherry
Norway maple
Sycamore
Hawthorn
Whitebeam

Rosemary (above right), a lovely Mediterranean shrub accustomed to growing on dry, impoverished soils, will thrive on thin soils over lime. Leaves can be used in the kitchen.

Japanese flowering cherries (below) cope with all but waterlogged soils. This weeping variety is Prunus 'Kiku-shidare Sakaru'.

tall and upright to dwarf and prostrate, and in colours ranging from green to blue.

Thin soils

Poor soils over lime are good for growing the slightly tender Mediterranean shrubs, such as lavender, rosemary, cistus, halimium and *Genista hispanica*. This can produce a wonderfully exotic effect in a poor, dry area which is also sunny and sheltered. Many of these plants have aromatic leaves, which will scent the air on warm evenings. They also flower generously in summer.

Grey plants can be mixed with them. Try growing the curry plant (*Helichrysum italicum*, often sold under the name *H. angustifolium*), which will really spice the air, even during the day. *Senecio* 'Sunshine' has yellow flowers over paddle-shaped grey leaves. Cotton lavender (*Santolina neapolitana*) has little, bright yellow, button flowers. The flowers are paler in the form 'Sulphurea'.

Euphorbia characias wulfenii, often sold simply as *E. wulfenii*, is an upright, shrubby spurge, with grey-green leaves and great cylinders of lime-green flowers.

Artemisia 'Powis Castle' will make a silvery mound of beautiful feathery foliage, 1m/3ft across. In a damper position, *Artemisia abrotanum*, or lad's love, can be used for its delightful aromatic foliage. Keep it by a path where you can pinch it as you pass. It will grow to 1.2m/4ft in height and produce yellow flowers.

Heavy soils

On a heavy alkaline soil roses of all kinds grow extremely well and appreciate some gutsy clay down below. Lilac enjoys an alkaline soil that is rich and heavy. A strong, well-fed lilac is as perfumed as any plant and picks beautifully.

Climbing and shrubby honeysuckles are at home on lime. So are the various species of clematis, as long as there is a good depth of soil.

Shrubs

Many shrubs are happy on lime. Philadelphus, deutzia and weigela all do well. The viburnums enjoy lime, and so do buddleia, pyracantha, box, spotted laurel, flowering currant, hazel, berberis, cotoneaster and hypericum.

Hydrangeas can be grown if the soil is not too limy, but it is difficult to achieve those marvellous blue colours. You will need to regularly use artificial colourants.

All the usual hedging plants are suitable for growing on limy soil. Yew, particularly, can be used with success on shallow chalky soils.

Gardening on Clay

Clay may seem like a serious problem, but properly treated, it can be very fertile. You will need to improve its structure and grow suitable plants.

Clay soils are characteristically cold, wet and muddy in winter. In summer, they set into hard rocky clods and wide cracks may appear in lawns. But they are easier to 'cure' than you might think.

Coping with clay soil needs a two-pronged attack. In the early stages, it is important to improve the soil; you will probably have to do this gradually in easy stages.

In time, there is no reason why you should not be able to grow almost anything. Improved clay is one of the best gardening soils you could possibly have. Plants growing in it rarely, if ever, suffer from drought – even in long, hot, sunny summers.

Clay's structure

Plants take in water, nutrients and air through their roots. In most soils, which are made up of different particle sizes, there are plenty of air spaces in the soil. But clay soil consists only of tiny particles, which have equally tiny air spaces between them.

This lack of aeration is one of the main reasons why plants have a problem growing in clay. The small particle size also makes clay soils muddy in wet weather; each individual particle is coated with a film of moisture when wet – so wet clay soil holds far more water than an equal volume of wet sandy soil.

Once wet, clay soil stays wet for a long time; water cannot drain away, due to lack of air spaces. To make matters worse, wet clay soil is soft, and is easily compressed if it is walked on, or if you run heavy equipment such as a barrow over it. As a result, plant roots find it difficult to penetrate the hard ground.

Worse still, compressed clay has fewer air spaces than ever, creating conditions in which roots have no oxygen, and rot very easily due to the presence of anaerobic bacteria.

The most frequent advice given for improving clay soils is to add lots of organic matter, such as well rotted manure or garden compost. Certainly clay soils do benefit from organic matter. But because it decomposes so fast, you must add more every year to

Gaping cracks often form in clay soil (below left) especially during the dry, hot summer months. In winter the reverse happens and muddy clods can occur. The 'cure' is to first break down the soil with grit. Plenty of bulky, organic compost (bottom left) can then be added to further improve its quality.

Plants that are especially intolerant of damp, wet clay, such as alpines, will thrive in a raised bed (below).

Ribes laurifolium *(below right), which grows well on clay, can benefit from an annual mulching, to conserve surface moisture in summer.*

maintain the improvement.

The very best improver for clay soil is coarse gritty sand. (Ask for washed horticultural grit – this can be bought by the bag from garden centres, or, if you need it, in bulk from a builder's merchant.)

Because grit does not break down in the soil one 'treatment' should do. Use about two barrows full of grit per square metre/yard. Spread this roughly over the soil, and dig it in to the top 'spit' (the depth of the blade of a spade).

Once this has been done, any organic matter you can add to the soil will be a further benefit, but you will have definitely made a lasting improvement to the overall physical structure of the soil.

Do not go to enormous efforts trying to dig clay soil. Once you have dug in enough gritty sand to open up the texture, you need never dig it again unless the soil gets firmly compacted.

Improving clay

Organic matter can be added as a mulch (in a layer 2.5-5cm/1-2in deep) spread round plants in the spring. This will be pulled down into the soil by worms. By replenishing the mulch every spring, the organic level in the soil will rise without effort on your part.

Hoeing, planting and pulling out old plants all help to incorporate organic matter into the soil without digging.

Clay soils are best cultivated fairly shallowly – certainly never more than a spit deep – due to the presence of infertile subsoil below the surface. If you dig a hole you will often see greasy blue or yellowish clay. This should never be brought to the surface as nothing will grow in it for many years, even if it is mixed with grit and organic matter.

If you take on a new garden where subsoil has been turned up by building work, it is best removed. Buy in good topsoil rather than try to work with clay subsoil.

Trees and shrubs

When planting trees or shrubs, do not just dig a deep hole and put compost at the bottom, as you would on lighter soils. If you do, the planting hole acts as a sump, filling up with water and drowning the plant roots.

Instead, improve the soil over the whole bed by digging in a mixture of grit and organic matter to one spade's depth. This encourages plants to form

GARDEN NOTES

DIGGING CLAY

Avoid digging clay soil when it is either very hard and cloddy in summer or too wet and muddy in winter. Not only is it hard work, but you risk damaging the soil structure.

There is a short time when clay is in a workable condition in autumn, shortly after the first serious rain. If you do not dig then, sowing and planting will be delayed, as clay soils are slow to dry out in spring.

Cover the ground with cloches or sheets of black polythene for two to three weeks before sowing or planting. This gives the soil a chance to dry out and warm up. It is vital for early sowings, as seed often rots if conditions are poor.

Always work from a plank when sowing or planting, to avoid compacting the soil.

a wide ranging root system which has a mixture of both shallow and deep roots.

Mulch trees and shrubs every spring, especially notoriously shallow rooting kinds such as rhododendron. This not only adds organic matter to the soil, but also conserves moisture near the surface in summer, preventing soil from cracking. (As soil shrinks, it strips off the fine root hairs and this can cause serious problems.) Mulching also insulates roots from heat and cold.

Beds and borders

Improve surface drainage by building beds up slightly above the level of the surrounding lawn. Use low retaining walls if necessary. In this way, plants grow in well drained soil, but their roots will be able to reach moisture reserves held by clay situated further down.

Plants that particularly need well drained conditions, such as Mediterranean plants, pinks and those with silver leaves, will need extra grit mixed with the soil, to prevent roots rotting in winter.

Always mulch between border plants each spring to retain moisture and maintain soil improvement. And as a precaution against rotting on unimproved clay, be sure to work a few handfuls of grit in among the crowns of herbaceous plants in autumn.

Fruit

Most fruit trees and bushes need reasonably well drained soil. Only blackcurrants and blackberries tolerate unimproved clay. Other soft fruit do best in the vegetable garden in raised beds.

Fruit trees are best trained as fans, cordons or espaliers and grown up against a wall – this soaks up some of the surplus moisture in winter. Mulch plants well in spring to retain as much soil moisture as possible in summer.

Most books recommend

PLANTS THAT THRIVE ON CLAY

Trees
Acer
Amelanchier lamarckii
Birches
Eucalyptus
Hawthorn
Laburnum
Malus
Prunus
Salix
Sorbus

Shrubs
Aucuba
Berberis
Chaenomeles
Choisya ternata
Cornus alba
Corylus avellana 'Contorta'
Cotoneaster
Escallonia
Forsythia
Hypericum
Kerria japonica
Philadelphus
Pyracantha
Rhododendron
Ribes
Roses
Spiraea
Symphoricarpos
Syringa
Weigela

Climbers
Clematis
Jasminum nudiflorum (winter jasmine)
Lonicera (honeysuckle)

Hedging
Hawthorn
Hornbeam
Privet

Herbaceous
Alchemilla mollis (lady's mantle)
Anemone japonica (Japanese anemone)
Artemisia absinthium 'Lambrook Silver'
Bergenia
Epimedium perralderianum, *E.* × *rubrum*
Geranium species
Hosta
Ligularia
Lysimachia nummularia
Kniphofia
Peony
Polygonatum × *hybridum* (Solomon's seal)
Pulmonaria (lungwort)
Ranunculus acris 'Flore Pleno', *R. repens* 'Flore Pleno' (double buttercups)
Thalictrum aquilegiifolium, *T. dipterocarpum* 'Hewitt's Double'
Tricyrtis (toad lily)

Grasses and ferns
Adianthum venustum (hardy maidenhair fern)
Asplenium scolopendrium (hart's tongue fern)
Miscanthus sacchariflorus, *M. sinensis*
Phalaris arundinacea 'Picta'

Flowers
Euphorbia characias wulfenii
Gentiana acaulis, *G. septemfida*
Helleborus orientalis, *H. foetidus*
Iris foetidissima
Liriope muscari
Polyanthus
Primroses
Verbascum bombyciferum

Bulbs
Allium sphaerocephalon
A. cernuum, *A. siculum*
Cyclamen hederifolium
Daffodils/narcissi
Lilium martagon, *L. pyrenaicum*
Snowdrops

Very popular for its aromatic and silvery-grey foliage, the **Eucalyptus gunnii** *(left) grows well on clay soils but requires shelter from strong winds in winter.*

The striking **Tricyrtis stoloniferia** *(toad lily) needs humus-rich, moist soil to flourish (above right) and brings late summer or autumn colour to the garden.*

Add a flash of colour with these unusually blue flowers (above far right) of the hardy gentian **(Gentiana acaulis)**. *It is an excellent choice for clay beds.*

This hardy, summer-flowering bulb, **Allium sphaerocephalon** *(right) also prefers to grow in clay and in a good year may produce as many as 40 ball-shaped, pinkish to purple coloured flowers.*

installing land drains before laying a lawn on clay soil. But this is far too expensive for most people. It is also no use unless the water has somewhere to drain away.

Lawns

A more practical solution is to dig in plenty of grit and organic matter when preparing the soil before sowing or turfing a lawn. If you can raise the level of the ground up even an inch or two above that of the surrounding land, you will have enough surface drainage to make the difference between a good and bad lawn.

If the grass is already established, you can still improve the soil beneath it. Every autumn, top dress the whole lawn with horticultural grit, or a mixture of grit and topsoil or sieved garden compost. Spike the lawn and work the top dressing into the grass with a stiff brush or the back of a rake.

If the lawn cracks open in dry spells in summer, take the opportunity to brush more of the grit mixture into the fissures. As the soil structure improves, it stops cracking.

Bulbs

Few bulbs grow really happily in wet, heavy, clay soils. Daffodils and narcissi are probably the most tolerant.

On clay, bulbs are best grown in a shrub border. The shrubs draw all the available moisture from the soil in summer, when the bulbs need to be dry. Even so, it is a good idea to plant them on top of a few handfuls of grit, for extra drainage in winter.

If you want to grow bulbs that are distinctly intolerant of winter wet – such as tulips or lilies – choose a raised bed in a sunny part of the garden. Crown Imperials, which have hollow tops to their bulbs, should be planted lying on their sides, so water cannot gather in them and make them rot.

Alternatively, plant difficult bulbs in pots. Keep them in a cold frame or unheated greenhouse in winter to protect them from damp, and plunge the pots in the garden in spring, when the soil is drier.

Rock plants

Alpines are the most difficult plants of all to grow on clay, as they easily rot in wet soil – especially in winter.

Raised beds are essential. In place of a conventional rockery, you could however grow them on a bank, or in a scree bed (basically a raised bed filled with a very open gritty soil, covered by gravel).

Using one of these three alternatives, your plants, many of which send roots long distances in search of moisture, will be able to reach water without sitting in it.

Types of Lawn

A lawn does not have to be made of grass. If space permits, a lawn scattered with wildflowers or one solely of herbs or flowers is delightful.

Lawns are to gardens what carpets are to living rooms. Like carpets, lawns vary and need choosing carefully and looking after properly if they are to look good, wear well and last a long time.

British gardens are famous for their lush green lawns. In the past, it was traditional to have large rolling expanses of perfectly maintained turf, closely cropped and elegantly striped, surrounded by well-tended herbaceous borders.

Today's gardens are much smaller, flowers grow in island beds and the lawn may not be grass at all, but a wildflower lawn or a herb or flower lawn.

Grass lawns

Each type of lawn has its advantages and disadvantages – so look at the options before deciding which is best for you. The basic choice, whether you choose turf or seed, is between 'utility' and 'fine' grass.

Utility lawns, traditionally used for back gardens, are now often used all round the house. The addition of ryegrass makes this type of lawn hard-wearing and easy to look after. It is ideal for family gardens.

Fine lawns, once used for front gardens, are more likely to be the choice of enthusiasts

A petrol-run cylinder mower (left) gives a firm, flat cut but, unlike the versatile rotary mower, its roller will always create a striped effect.

Well-placed patches of uncut grass (below) add depth and contrast, while a wild flower lawn (bottom) blends nicely with a well- tended brick path.

who prefer the superior finish and want to spend time and money looking after their lawn all the year round.

What is involved?

Utility lawns need little care or special equipment. An inexpensive hover or rotary mower is quite adequate, and can be used on wet grass although it is always better to cut grass when dry. Hover mowers can be used sideways to negotiate

GRASS SPECIES

Ryegrass A coarse, hard-wearing species in utility lawn mixtures. The flowerheads are tough and spring back up after mowing. Modern strains, such as 'Hunter' or 'Barclay', are sometimes recommended for sowing on their own. They are slower growing, finer and have better winter colour than traditional ryegrass. They are more tolerant than fine grasses of wet, heavy soils.

Fescues Fine grasses with a dense habit. They are slow-growing and drought tolerant but have poor winter colour. Chewings fescue is used with browntop bent as the basis of fine lawn seed mixtures. Creeping red fescue is usually used in utility mixtures as it does not stand close mowing.

Bents Fine grasses. Browntop bent is a very fine, dense grass which is mixed with chewings fescue to form the basis of fine lawn mixtures. It is very tolerant of close mowing.

Creeping bent is a strong creeping grass popular in utility mixtures.

Smooth-stalked meadow grass A drought-resistant, hard-wearing grass. It does not take close mowing, and is used in utility mixtures.

Crested dog's tail A hard-wearing grass with good winter colour. It is tolerant of low soil fertility, so is useful in wildflower lawn mixtures and utility lawns.

curves. They also let you cut up to the edge of the lawn, which makes tidying edges easier afterwards.

With a utility lawn, it is not essential to use a grass box provided you cut before the grass is very long; this too saves a lot of time. And one or two feed and weed treatments each year will keep a utility lawn looking good.

Fine lawns take more work and cost more to maintain. Most owners prefer a cylinder mower, with a roller and grass box, to give the traditional smooth finish and zebra stripes. This sort of mower must only be used when the grass is dry, to avoid tearing. To keep fine lawns at their best, it is advisable to follow a year-round care programme.

Selecting grass

When you buy turf, you do not usually get a choice of grass species. Even with seed, you are normally only offered mixtures of grass seed – for utility or fine lawns, or to suit dry soil or shady sites.

This is because, by growing a mixture of species, you stand the best chance of getting a good lawn. The most successful grasses will thrive and if the rest die out you still have nice grassy turf. If you choose a single species and it turns out not to suit your conditions, you will have a poor lawn.

There are, however, some single species which grow well under most conditions and have much finer leaves than the old ryegrass. Examples are the new strains of ryegrass, such as 'Hunter' and 'Barclay'. They have the durable growing quality of ryegrass but stay much greener in winter.

Wildflower lawns

As the name suggests, wildflower lawns look wild. Unless you live in a remote country cottage, a wildflower lawn is best kept to one end of the garden, with a conventional lawn round the house.

The commonly held idea that a wildflower lawn is just an ordinary one that is allowed to run to weeds, and is never fed and hardly ever cut, is wrong. A proper wildflower lawn is best grown by sowing a mixture of grass seed and selected wildflower seeds. Sow it in spring or late summer, as you would a normal lawn.

Several mixtures are available, including special blends for acid or chalky soil, sandy or clay soil, and shade. Or you can buy the grass seed separately and mix in the wildflower seeds of your choice.

You can also plant bulbs of bluebells or wild daffodils in 'drifts' among grass for spring colour before the main wildflower season gets under way.

Do not try to turn a normal lawn into a wildflower lawn by scattering wildflower seed over it – it does not work. If you have to convert an existing lawn, remove some squares of turf, fork over the soil and either sow seed or plant wildflowers there.

Once they are established and shed seed, those species will slowly spread over the lawn. Very fresh seed, shed naturally in large quantities, often succeeds where tiny portions of packeted seed fail.

Improving the soil

You may have to make changes to your soil to allow wildflowers to thrive. Poor drainage can be eased by laying pipes to a soakaway. If you cannot improve drainage, perhaps because there is a high water table in your region, there are still many wild flowers which will grow well in thick, moist soil, such as meadow-rue (*Thalictrum flavum*) and summer snowflake (*Leucojum aestivum*). On a heavy clay soil, add lime.

Wildflower lawns should never be fed – wildflowers grow better in slightly impoverished conditions. Nor will a

GO ORGANIC!

A CLOVER LAWN

A clover lawn grows better than grass in a drought, and never needs mowing. Buy seed of Kentish wild clover, or a mixture of this and other clover-like species for a variety of flower sizes and colour. These mixtures are available from specialist seedsmen.

Mix the seed with sand as it is so small, and sow on ground prepared as for sowing a normal grass lawn. Bees love it.

Clover lawns (above) provide rich, sprawling cover and, once established, do not turn brown even in constant sunlight and the driest soil. They will not flower thickly, but will need mowing once or twice a year after the flowers appear.

A subtly-toned chamomile lawn (above right) adds luxury to a small area, perhaps at the far end of a garden. This is* Anthemis nobilis *'Treneague', a popular choice. It needs little clipping or mowing but, in winter, sheds many leaves, giving the lawn an untidy look.

The cheerful flowers of* Anthemis nobilis *'Flore Pleno' (right), so reminiscent of daisies, contrast sharply with its fern-like leaves and, for lawns, its abundant flowering makes it less suitable than non-flowering varieties of chamomile.

CUTTING A WILDFLOWER LAWN

In its first year, the grass should be cut every two months to prevent it overtaking the wild flowers and smothering them out.

From them on, cut once in early spring before the wild flowers start to grow. Apart from mowing a few paths through the area, so you can enjoy the flowers without walking on them, do not cut the grass again until after all the flowers have shed their seed in late summer or early autumn. By then the grass may be a foot or more high, so cut it down in several stages with a hand or rotary scythe.

In winter, the wildflower lawn will look very much like a normal lawn but a bit longer and shaggier. Avoid cutting it shorter than 7.5cm/3in or it will lose its essential charm.

wildflower lawn need watering, unless there is a dry spell immediately after sowing it.

Weeding should be carried out by hand, since chemical weedkillers do not differentiate between wildflowers and weeds. Remove nettles, ground elder, thistles, brambles, docks and other invasive or undesirable species.

Flower and herb lawns

Herb and flower lawns are beautiful, but much more specialist than even a wildflower lawn. As they do not stand much wear, they are best kept to a small part of the garden.

The best known alternative is the chamomile lawn. For this, a non-flowering strain called 'Treneague' is usually chosen, although you could use the normal Roman chamomile, which has white daisy-like flowers in summer.

Creeping thymes look superb, especially when they are in flower in early summer. Either plant one species or a mixture of species in random shapes. Choose evergreen varieties for year-round appeal.

An alpine lawn

Alpine lawns are made of a mixture of flowers, to recreate the look of an alpine meadow. Choose robust, spreading flowers, the sort that become a

BRIGHT IDEAS

A LAWN FROM ANNUALS

There is no reason why you should not make a flower lawn from annuals (hardy annuals are best). These could be sown in early spring but, if the soil contains a lot of weed seeds, you would be better advised to raise them in trays and plant them out in the usual way about 7.5-10cm/3-4in apart.

Choose low-growing species like alyssum, *Convolvulus minor*, bedding echium and leptosiphon.

A sumptuous thyme lawn (above), though set in spacious grounds, reveals how even a thin strip of herbal lawn can transform your garden. The aroma matches its rich colour and thyme needs only one clip each year, after flowering.

Herbal lawns can serve as a base for weaves of colour when combined with hardy perennials, such as aubrieta (right). They are seldom substitutes for common grass lawns.

bit invasive in a rockery, such as snow-in-summer, aubrieta, mossy saxifrages, a few creeping thymes, *Alyssum saxatile, Geranium sanguineum lancastriense* and *G. cinereum* 'Ballerina'. Add drifts of dwarf bulbs, such as miniature narcissi, for the spring.

Groundcover lawns make excellent neighbours to bright borders. This mossy saxifrage (above), alongside white border plants, looks fresh and makes a good surround for trees and taller plants.* Dryas octopetala *and alpine geraniums (right) give even small lawns the look of a meadow.

The right conditions

For both herb and alpine lawns, good drainage and a sunny location are essential. Dig in plenty of coarse sand or gravel before planting.

To improve drainage further, raise the whole area up a few inches with a low retaining wall of bricks round the edge. Add a 5cm/2in layer of gravel through which the plants can be grown. This also acts as a mulch, preventing weed seeds from germinating.

Herb and flower lawns are rarely grown from seed since seedlings are slow-growing and get swamped by weeds. (Chamomile 'Treneague' does not produce seed, and can be grown only from cuttings.)

Pot-grown plants are best as they establish faster and can be planted at any time of the year. Rooted cuttings are more economical, however; these usually establish best in spring or autumn.

To minimize wear, it is a good idea to lay a path or stepping stones through the lawn.

Maintenance

Care is simple, but time-consuming. Herb and flower lawns are not mown like a conventional lawn. They are naturally low-growing and to keep them tidy they should only be clipped with shears after flowering. A light feed of Growmore could be given in mid-spring, but little feeding is necessary.

Weeding should be done frequently. Weed by hand since normal lawn weedkillers will kill the wrong plants – grass is itself a weed in a herb or flower lawn. Weeding by hand takes longer, but the end result of a fine, aromatic lawn makes it worthwhile.

Lawn Care

Whatever the present state of your lawn, the right treatment will quickly restore its condition and keep it looking its best throughout the year.

MOWING TIPS

- Reduce the height of long grass in several stages, rather than all at once, or the lawn will go brown.
- Let long grass dry before cutting, or it will look ragged.
- Always use a grass box when mowing fine lawns; this is not essential on hard-wearing lawns, provided you cut before the grass gets too long – short clippings soon vanish.
- Use grass clippings as a mulch under mature trees and shrubs or add them to the compost heap. For best compost results, use alternate 15cm/6in layers of grass clippings and kitchen waste or similar.

DON'T FORGET!

A lawn is like a large outdoor carpet. The big difference is that lawns are alive. Each square metre contains hundreds of tiny plants, each of which needs food and water. The lawn is regularly mowed and trampled on and, though few plants would put up with such punishment, grass thrives on it. Even so, lawns require regular attention if they are to look their best.

Types of grass

There are two basic types of lawn. Fine lawns are made up of narrow-leaved grasses which give a soft velvety texture, but need a lot of care and attention. They do not stand up to much wear, and have been traditionally used for front gardens.

Hard-wearing utility lawns are made of coarser grasses which grow fast and so stand up well to family use.

Families with small gardens are just as likely to have hard-wearing lawns everywhere, for ease of maintenance and low cost. Garden enthusiasts, particularly older people whose families have left home, often prefer fine lawns front and back for their better finish.

Mowing

Grass needs cutting regularly all the time it is growing – even in winter if the weather is mild. Rather than mowing once a week regardless, cut the grass when it actually needs it. Mow hard-wearing lawns when the grass reaches 5-6cm/2-2½in, and fine lawns when the grass is 2.5-3cm/1-1¼in high.

In late spring, when growing conditions are good, this

CHOOSING MOWERS

GARDEN NOTES

Electric Cylinder and rotary types available. Cheapest to buy and no regular servicing needed; sharpen or replace blades each year.
Motor Cylinder and rotary types available. Expensive to buy and need regular servicing each winter; costly unless you do it yourself.
Hand Small 'push' cylinder mowers are still available new. Cheap to buy and produce a good finish; ideal for a small fine lawn.
Rotary mowers (including hover types). Can cut wet grass but, for safety reasons electric models should not be used in the wet. Hover types are useful for awkward areas like banks. Rotary mowers with a roller will produce a striped effect.
Cylinder mowers Best for fine lawns. Give a closer cut and will produce zebra stripes if you mow up and down the lawn in alternate directions in neat parallel lines. (The stripes are caused by grass in alternate rows lying in opposite directions after the mower's roller has passed over it).
Width of cut Wider mowers make less work of cutting big lawns; narrower mowers are easier to manoeuvre round fiddly beds.

There is something satisfying about trimming lawn edges in a straight line. If doing it manually you will need a pair of long-handled edging shears (above).

For an even effect all over, apply lawn feed and weedkiller with a fertilizer spreader (below).

A fine lawn (left) is the perfect complement to bright borders of flowers. Neat edges complete the effect. A good petrol mower with a roller (below) will produce alternate stripes. A grass box saves you the unnecessary chore of having to rake up the lawn clippings.

may mean cutting twice a week. In late autumn, once every three to four weeks may be enough. Hard-wearing lawns should not be cut too closely – leave the grass at least 2.5cm/1in high. Fine lawns can be mown more closely, but not shorter than 1.25cm/½in.

Leave grass slightly longer in spring and autumn and whenever growing conditions are poor (during a summer drought, for instance) to avoid over-stressing it. Set the mower blades 6-13mm/¼-½in higher. Longer grass can look greener during a drought.

Edging lawns

After mowing, use a pair of long-handled shears to neaten the edges of the lawn. Nylon-line trimmers are handy for tidying up grass along walls and around trees. An electric lawn-edger is a labour-saving device for trimming the grass along the edges of beds. It only works properly if your lawn has well-made edges.

To make a neat lawn edge, use a half-moon edger (also called an edging iron or edging knife) to cut along a garden line marking the correct position of the edge of a flower bed. Make the cut vertically, about 5cm/2in deep, turning the turf forward into the bed as if digging. Lawn edges may need remaking every few years. To avoid beds getting bigger and the lawn smaller, use hard edging strips.

Feeding

Lawns need feeding regularly, especially if you use a mower with a grass box. (By removing clippings you are also removing nutrients that would otherwise find their way back into the soil to improve it).

LAWN CARE PROGRAMME

GARDEN NOTES

Early spring
Start cutting when grass starts growing; set the blades high.
Mid spring
Apply lawn feed; if moss or weeds are a problem use a treatment combined with a feed. Continue to feed at 6-8 week intervals during the summer, unless you used a slow release feed (one application only will be needed). Reduce height of cut to 1.25cm/½in for fine lawns and 2.5cm/1in for utility lawns.
Summer
Avoid feeding lawns during drought, as grass may be scorched. Mow twice weekly when the grass is growing fast.
Early autumn
Rake lawn hard to remove moss and organic debris. Spike lawns on heavy soil or those which get a lot of wear. Apply sieved topsoil, peat and sharp sand at one bucketful per square metre as a top dressing on fine lawns. Apply an autumn lawn feed. Raise mower blades.
Autumn/Winter
Continue cutting until grass stops growing. Rake up fallen leaves. Avoid walking on the lawn when it is either wet or muddy as this can damage it.

Utility lawns will survive on one feed a year; this should be given at the start of the growing season, in mid spring. Instead of expensive lawn feed, you could use a product such as Growmore which thickens the grass without making it greener or grow too fast (but all fertilizers will speed up growth). Fine lawns must be regularly fed to keep them looking their best.

Any lawn which is poor, starved or patchy, can be quickly restored by regular feeding. Choose a spring and summer lawn feed (high in nitrogen to promote leafy growth) for use from mid spring to late summer, or a slow release lawn feed (one application in spring will last all summer too).

In early autumn, use an autumn formulation that is high in phosphates to promote strong healthy roots; one application is enough.

Lawn feeds come as granules or liquids. Granules can be broadcast by hand, though irregular spreading can give patchy results. Liquid lawn feeds should be watered on with a watering can and some can be applied using a hose-end diluter.

Weeds and moss

If the lawn contains weeds or moss, use a weedkiller or a mosskiller that is combined with a lawn feed. Apply this in mid spring in place of a plain feed. If you prefer to use a liquid mosskiller or weedkiller, apply it about three weeks after using a feed. Several applications may be needed for persistent, established weeds.

If you dislike using chemicals, you can remove moss with a spring-tined rake (one with long springy tines) or a powered lawn raker. Weeds can be dug out manually using a daisy grubber.

Utility lawns are relatively

LAWN PROBLEMS

Weeds
Cause: thin, patchy grass, lack of feeding. Remedy: feed regularly, treat with liquid weedkiller or with weedkiller plus feed in spring.

Moss
Cause: thin, patchy, underfed grass; poor surface drainage; shade. Remedy: apply mosskiller in spring and rake out dead moss; feed regularly; rake and spike in autumn and top dress with sharp sand (one bucket per square metre). In shade where moss is a regular problem, use a shade tolerant grass mixture.

Green slime
(algae and liverworts) Cause: as for moss. Remedy: apply lawn sand or liquid mosskiller, follow lawn care programme as for moss.

Fungi
Cause: occasional fungi in autumn are due to organic matter in the soil plus the damp weather. Persistent fairy rings are permanent unless treated – grass inside the ring is yellow and stunted due to removal of nitrogen by the fungi. Remedy: autumn fungi soon go, or can be removed by hand. Fairy rings should be excavated to a foot deep and a foot beyond the ring, and the soil disposed of away from the garden. Refill with new topsoil and reseed.

Bumps and hollows
Cause: poor preparation before sowing or turfing. Remedy: lift turf from affected area and either remove or add soil until the ground is level. Firm the soil and relay the turf. Slight hollows can be levelled by top dressing.

A twiggy birch besom is the perfect tool for brushing in a good top dressing (above). On fine lawns this only needs to be done once a year in autumn. Top dressing is also a good way to level out any shallow hollows and can be done every few months on all types of lawn.

A fairy ring (left) will kill the grass and spoil the look of your lawn. Removing the visible fungi is not enough, as the underground thread-like hyphae – a type of root – spread out year by year to find fresh nutrients, having exhausted those within the ring. You will need to dig up the soil, replace it and reseed the area.

Lawns need watering during hot, dry spells (left). If there is no ban on hoses and sprinklers, give the grass a good soaking.

This picture (below) shows how effective a selective weedkiller can be if you have a problem with daisies and white clover. The central strip was sprayed ten days before the photograph was taken and is virtually clear of all weeds.

drought tolerant, and usually survive dry summers with little or no watering. Even if they go brown, they quickly green up again when the rain comes in autumn. Fine lawns are quicker to show signs of stress, and really need watering regularly in dry spells. If you cannot water, bare patches may need reseeding in autumn.

Avoiding drought

You can 'drought-proof' a lawn to a considerable degree by adding lots of organic matter before sowing or turfing, and then following a good lawn care programme (see box) which encourages deep rooting and builds up organic matter.

If you have to water a lawn, the golden rule is 'do it thoroughly'. Stand a dish under the sprinkler. When the dish holds 4cm/1½in of water, the lawn is well watered.

Scarifying

Over a period of time, a lot of decomposed lawn clippings, dead moss and creeping grass stems build up in a lawn. This occasionally needs clearing out, to make way for fresh new growth. Scarifying, as it is called, is done in autumn.

Mow the lawn as usual, then run over it with the lawn raker in the opposite direction to that of the mower. Repeat both mowing and raking at 90 degrees to the original angle, then apply autumn lawn feed.

Fine lawns need scarifying every year, and utility lawns benefit from it every two years or so.

In the past, scarifying had to be done by hand with a spring-tined rake. But now there are relatively cheap electric lawn raking machines which make light work of it. Larger petrol-driven machines can be hired.

Top dressing

Top dressing is used regularly for maintaining fine lawns, and is also useful for filling small depressions in a utility lawn. Make up a mixture of equal parts good topsoil, with peat, cocopeat or garden compost and sharp sand. Sieve it to remove any lumps.

Spread it in a layer 1.25cm/½in deep over the whole lawn (if treating a fine lawn), or in any shallow depression in a utility lawn. Work the mixture into the grass with the back of a rake. The grass should show through the dressing and not be smothered by it.

One top dressing a year, in autumn, is enough for fine lawns. If you are filling hollows in utility lawns, you can top dress every few months until the hollow is level with the rest of the lawn. This works fine so long as the grass is allowed to grow through the dressing and never smothered by it (which would kill it).

SAFETY FIRST

USING CHEMICALS

- Always read and understand instructions before using products.
- After using weedkiller on the lawn, keep the first 2-3 weeks' clippings in a separate heap. They can be used for mulching or as garden compost after they have been composted for at least six months. Do not use them earlier as weedkiller residues may remain in them.
- Keep neat lawn feeds, weedkillers and other chemicals away from pets and children. When used as directed, children and pets can be allowed on to lawns, though it is a good idea to wait until liquid products have dried. Grazing pets like guinea pigs and rabbits are best kept off a lawn for several weeks after weedkiller treatment.
- If spreading dry lawn feed by hand practise first, spreading sheets of newspaper on the garage floor, until you can apply the fertilizer evenly. Or use a speader; these can be hired from tool hire shops.
- Never apply dry lawn fertilizers during drought, as they may scorch the grass. Wait until after heavy rain, or water the lawn first then use a properly diluted liquid lawn feed.

Stocking a Pond

Although not essential to creating a natural balance, fish and other aquatic creatures add life to a pond, giving you something to watch in peaceful surroundings.

Beautiful golden-orange fish and a wide variety of water and marginal plants (above) all help to make this pond a peaceful retreat from the stresses and strains of modern life.

Watching fish is a soothing pastime for adults, and youngsters find pond life fascinating. Your pond will provide a valuable habitat for many wild creatures that spend all or part of their time in water.

Pond life can be beneficial in other ways, too. Fish will eat several unpleasant pond pests, such as mosquito larvae. These are the small squiggly creatures found just under the surface of the water in summer. Adult mosquitoes visit the pond to breed, but linger in gardens and cause nasty bites. Fish also take water plant pests such as aphids and water lily beetles.

Fish excreta provides a natural fertilizer for water plants. And the carbon dioxide fish exhale when they breathe is used by submerged plants in photosynthesis.

Frogs, toads and newts visit the water to breed. The adults benefit gardeners by feeding on slugs, snails and beetles in the garden.

Water snails help the pond, keeping the water clean by feeding on algae, while freshwater mussels act as living water filters.

Buying fish

Fish can be bought from water garden departments of garden centres, fish farms or, by post, from mail order water garden specialists. (See ads in gardening magazines).

Where possible, choose your own fish so you can be sure of getting healthy specimens. Healthy fish move quickly and have a good colour. Avoid sluggish fish or those with disease spots and obvious injuries.

Do not buy more fish than your pond can support. As a rough guide allow one square metre of pond surface to each 15cm of fish (about 11 square feet for a 6-inch fish). Stock the pond first at a quarter this rate, to allow for the fish growing.

The ultimate size that fish will reach is determined by the size of the pond and the amount of oxygen in the water. Adding a fountain or waterfall helps oxygenate the pond, especially in warm weather when the water holds a great deal less oxygen.

When stocking the pond, select fish of roughly the same size, otherwise large fish may bully the smaller ones.

Types of fish

Goldfish, shubunkin and golden orfe are probably the best choice for a small garden pond. These are all colourful fish which show up well, and swim close to the surface where they

A relative of the goldfish, the shubunkin (left) is a popular choice of fish for a garden pond. Easy to care for, its bright colours and habit of swimming close to the surface give it considerable ornamental appeal.

The freshwater winkle (below) is a valuable addition to a pond because it helps to control the spread of algae by scraping it off underwater stones and plants.

BREEDING FISH

Goldfish and shubunkins readily breed in garden ponds. The eggs hatch out to produce hundreds of minute transparent 'fry'. Unfortunately, both these and fish eggs are eaten – often by the parents themselves – so very few live to become adults.

If you want fish to breed successfully, it is essential to provide plenty of water weeds in which the fry can take cover.

can be seen and admired.

Avoid catfish and tench, which are bottom feeders and stir up the mud, making the water murky. Catfish are also aggressive; they bully other fish and, unfortunately, can often cause serious injuries.

Koi carp need a large pond which should be 1-1.2m/3-4ft deep, ideally with moving water. Where possible, install a pump with an external filter through which the water is pumped, perhaps feeding a waterfall.

Koi live mainly at the bottom of the pond, where they root around, stirring up mud and dislodging water plants. So take extra care to bed oxygenating plants under a heavy rock and use large planting baskets for water lilies.

GROWING TIPS

FEEDING FISH

Various types of pond fish foods are available. The flaked type is most suitable for young fish, as it breaks up into tiny fragments that even the smallest fish can swallow. Floating pellets are often used for larger fish, particularly koi, which can otherwise be difficult to persuade up to the surface.

Feed fish daily from mid spring to late autumn, giving them as much as they can finish within ten minutes. High protein foods, such as daphnia and tubifex worms (normally bought dry but sometimes live), are recommended for feeding in spring and autumn, when fish need building up either side of their winter rest.

If you always feed fish at the same time and the same place, they will come to associate you with food and may eat out of your hand. Koi carp, particularly, are easy to 'tame'. During winter, fish scarcely feed and any food in the water may go bad.

Introducing fish

Do not be in too much of a hurry to add fish after making your pond. If the pond is concrete, change the water a couple of times over the next two weeks or buy a product from your pond supplier that neutralizes the lime in the concrete immediately. Modern butyl, plastic or glass fibre liners can be filled and planted as soon as they are put in. But allow about a week for the water to warm up and any chlorine to disappear before adding fish.

With established ponds, most people think about adding fish in spring. But you can do so in summer, if the kinds you want are available.

Fish are normally supplied in large polythene bags which have been inflated and tied at the neck. This prevents water

The ever popular goldfish (below) will thrive even in the smallest pond.

FISH AND OTHER WILDLIFE FOR A POND

Goldfish Chunky orange fish, many variants available with bulging eyes, long flowing fins and tails, etc; of these only long-tailed comets are really suitable outdoors.
Shubunkin Colourful goldfish relative, with blue, purple, red or orange markings on a lighter body. Strong colours most sought after.
Golden orfe Slim, pencil-shaped orange fish that swims in shoals and darts about close to the surface. Can reach 38cm/15in in a large pond. Rarely breeds in temperate ponds.
Koi carp Spectacularly coloured fish in a variety of colours and patterns (koi enthusiasts have Japanese names to describe fish with particular markings). Long-lived fish, easily tamed to feed from the hand; can grow very big in a large pond.
Common frog Adult: smooth moist skin, moves by hopping; breeds from late winter to mid spring. Spawn: large jelly-like masses floating near surface of water; it hatches in a few weeks. Tadpoles: black or dark brown tadpoles, rounded tips to tails, swimming in shallow water near pond edge.
Common toad Adult: rough, dry, warty skin, walks rather than hops. Breeds in mid spring. Spawn: long double strands which sink to the bottom of the pond and tangle in water weeds; hatches in a few weeks. Tadpoles: dark brown, tails have pointed tips and goldish speckles.
Newts Several species, like lizards but with broad, paddle-like tails. Breed in mid spring. Eggs: individual, stuck to underside of water plants. Tadpoles: big feathery gills protrude from sides of head. Slow to mature, they don't become young newts until early autumn.
Freshwater whelk Whelk-shaped, feeds on submerged water plants; inadvisable.
Ramshorn snails Shells shaped like Catherine wheels, black or reddish; beneficial.
Freshwater winkle Winkle-like snail; beneficial.
Dragonflies Large, vividly coloured insects that dart over ponds; lay eggs on water plants. These hatch into ferocious larvae that feed on water insects etc; take a year to develop.
Water boatman and pond skaters Fast-moving insects that shoot back and forth across the water on warm days. Pond skaters are harmless but water boatmen may attack small fish.

slopping about in the car, and ensures the fish are safe.

When you get them home, float the bag, still tied at the neck, in the pond. This allows the fish to acclimatize to the temperature of the water. After at least an hour, untie the neck of the bag and allow it to slowly fill with water.

Make sure the neck is wide open, so that the fish can swim out when they are ready. Avoid tipping or handling them, as they are easily damaged, and injured fish usually die.

Amphibians

Amphibious animals – frogs, toads and newts – are delightful to have in and around a pond. Adults return to the pond they hatched out in to breed, if necessary crossing miles of inhospitable countryside to do so.

A good way to ensure a crop of tadpoles each year is to introduce spawn in the first place. These can sometimes be obtained from friends, through wildlife trusts or from schools. Young tadpoles are preyed on by fish, so provide plenty of pondweed to give them somewhere to hide.

By midsummer, when tadpoles are growing their front legs, they will need to get out of the water occasionally. Give them a large stone as an 'island', or provide a ramp if the pond does not have any

The tiny water boatman (above right) can sometimes be seen skimming across the water on warm, summer days. Unfortunately, it can attack small fish and pond owners should keep an eye out for it.

Frogs are one of the most delightful amphibians to encourage in and around ponds (right). Often they will appear of their own accord; otherwise, introduce frog spawn, obtainable through wildlife trusts or from schools.

gently shelving sides.

Water snails are valuable in ponds as they help to control some algae.

Molluscs

The best kind are ramshorn snails (which have shells shaped like Catherine wheels). Freshwater winkles are also useful. Both feed by scraping algae from underwater stones and plants.

The snail often sold for ponds, however, is the freshwater whelk. These feed on water plants, especially the oxygenators, so should not be introduced. They can be caught by floating a cabbage or lettuce leaf on the water, and removing the snails that gather under it daily.

All water snails are hermaphrodites and breed fast. Their eggs and young are readily snapped up by fish.

The other useful pond mollusc is the swan mussel, which lives by filtering water through its large shell. This helps to keep the water clear. Swan mussels grow 10-13cm/4-5in long. They are rarely seen, as they lie on the floor of the pond and hardly move, though they can shuffle about.

When feeding, the mussel extends a whitish tube through the slightly open shell and sucks water through it. Like snails, the mussel's young form part of the diet of fish. Enough young survive to replace the parents.

The pond habitat

A well set up pond should provide shade, protection from predators and food. For shade, grow water lilies and floating plants such as azolla, plus clumps of tall marginal plants round the edge – water irises, lythrum, primulas, arrowhead and others.

Predators of pond life include herons, hedgehogs, foxes and domestic cats. Herons visit early in the morning. An artificial heron standing close to the pond may deter them, but is not always successful.

Since herons wade into the pond rather than flying into it, they can be put off by stretching a nylon line (such as thick fishing line) 10-15cm/4-6in high round the pond edge.

A line may also help deter hedgehogs, foxes and cats. If these are a regular nuisance, it may be worth trying several lines at various heights. But in really bad cases, cover the pond with a net that is well secured round the edge.

Mosquito larvae, water fleas (daphnia) and other insects, including flies, which settle on the water will all be taken by fish, tadpoles and adult amphibians. So, too, will the jelly-like egg masses of water snails, which are laid on the under surface of lily leaves and on weeds.

Given a large enough pond, there will be enough natural food. But in small ornamental ponds a certain amount of extra feeding is necessary (see box on page 1097).

Spectacular ornamental koi carp (above) need a large, deep pond with moving water in order to flourish. With patience, some of them can become tame enough to eat out of your hand.

Canadian pondweed (below) helps keep pond water oxygenated. In winter, when other plants have died down, it gives protection to fish; in summer, it provides deep shade.

GO ORGANIC!

ESSENTIAL OXYGENATOR

Canadian pondweed (*Elodea canadensis*) should be in every pond stocked with fish. It is an evergreen oxygenating plant, so it keeps on working, even in winter when other oxygenators have died down.

Besides giving off vital oxygen all year round, it provides valuable cover for fish, giving them somewhere to hide from herons and other predators in winter. In summer, it provides deep shade where fish can escape from the sun, and allows tiny fish fry to hide from larger fish.

Buy it in unrooted bunches. Anchor three clumps to stones or plant in proper planting baskets, and sink close together in the middle of the pond.

First Steps to Pruning

Knowing why and when to prune is the essence of good gardening. Learn the basic needs of plants and you will soon cut with confidence.

Are your roses rambling when they are not really meant to and your small shrubs beginning to form an untidy thicket? Then it is time to master the art of pruning.

Don't panic – pruning is not always the difficult and technical business it is sometimes made out to be. No plant is going to die simply because it has not been pruned, but without a bit of careful cutting the plant may not flower as well as it might or can become overgrown and shapeless.

Best results

Pruning really is just a matter of encouraging the best from your plants. It can help them to grow more efficiently and bear as much fruit and as many flowers as they can – for as many years as possible.

Pruning is easy to carry out at the right time once you have a grasp of the special needs of different groups of plants.

Keep them blooming

One important use of pruning is to induce plants to make flowers rather than leaves. Fruit trees require this kind of pruning so that a sensible balance is achieved between fruit production and the foliage which feeds the tree.

Often, however, pruning serves two purposes at once: while encouraging flowering shoots, at the same time it allows light to reach the fruit or flowers. Rambler roses and mock orange (philadelphus) have the older flowered shoots cut out to improve the chances of the new ones.

Pruned to perfection, the splendid yellow rose bush (above) shows how a little work pays dividends. Cut back growth to 20cm/8in from the base in early spring.

Also as shrubs grow older, there is a tendency for the stems to become too congested, and one use of pruning is to keep an open shape for those plants which need light and air to reach the centre. Roses and gooseberries are both best kept with a simple framework and an open centre.

When pruning any plant, a vital consideration is whether

The red-stemmed dogwood, Cornus alba 'Sibirica' (right) is grown for its attractive bark rather than its flowers and so it should be pruned to encourage plenty of young stems. Old stems can be cut almost to ground level in the spring and they will grow to 1.2m/4ft.

The sumptuous, rich magenta flower heads on the butterfly bush (left) have been produced in late summer on the same season's growth. The plant should be cut back to within 5-7cm/2-3in every spring. Weak growth can be cut out entirely.

Hydrangea macrophylla (below) suffers from hard pruning in spring. This is because it flowers on last year's wood. For the first few years it requires only cosmetic pruning.

PLANTS WHICH NEED NO PRUNING

Some plants are better not pruned unless it is absolutely necessary. If they are planted with space to develop fully they may never need any pruning. This does not mean that they cannot be cut, say, for flower arrangements in your home. These plants, if left to themselves, provided they are planted in the correct position, will maintain a good shape.

Some care is needed when cutting from conifers, however (firs, pines, cypresses and Leylandii). Cuts made into older wood will not sprout again, and caution is needed to avoid making a gap in the foliage.

- Japanese maple (*Acer palmatum*)
- camellia
- conifers (especially dwarf and low-growing kinds)
- daphne
- witch hazel (*Hamamelis mollis*)
- hebe
- calico bush (*Kalmia latifolia*)
- magnolia
- osmanthus
- pieris
- rhododendron

it flowers on the previous or the new season's growth. If you prune a plant which flowers on last year's wood in spring, then you are effectively cutting off this year's flowers. So always check before you start to snip away.

Buddleia, the butterfly bush, can be cut hard down to a framework each spring. Its flowers are then produced at the end of the current season's growth, in late summer. Hydrangeas, on the other hand, flower on the wood they

GARDEN NOTES

WHEN TO PRUNE

Timing is important. You must understand the growing habits of a tree or shrub before you begin to prune it. Many established plants are pruned according to flowering habits, while young shrubs and fruit trees or ornamental trees are often pruned hard at the time of planting. If in doubt, check before you cut.

make in the previous year so prune after flowering. But this is not vital. If left until spring the old flower heads protect the new buds from harsh weather.

Fancy foliage

Sometimes plants are pruned to encourage leaf shoots to grow, rather than flower shoots. This is done where the bark or stems are more attractive than the flowers; they may have vibrant autumn foliage or winter colour. The red-stemmed dogwood, *Cornus alba* 'Sibirica', is pruned this way. The old stems can be cut off just above ground level every spring, and new shoots rise up 90-120cm/3-4ft. (In winter these scarlet wands are ideal for flower arranging.) The same method is also used for purple or white stemmed willows.

The holly tree (above) has acquired its present shape after good pruning over several years. Two basic techniques have been used. Side shoots have been systematically removed to keep one single stem encouraging it into a standard shape. It has also been trimmed into an attractive bushed outline.

Shrubs which do not have a central trunk should have their stems shortened after planting, to encourage a generous bush with plenty of stems. For instance, newly planted roses are cut down hard to coax lots of low shoots and give the roots time to establish before the bush becomes top heavy.

Heathers are much better looking in later life if the leading shoots have had the tops nipped out from the first year.

Waves of luscious heather bring warmth and texture to a garden (above). Heathers do not need to be pruned but without a bit of skilful snipping they can look very scraggy.

Dead-head all varieties of heather after flowering by trimming with shears. This will encourage more compact, bushy growth.

PRUNE IN SPRING BEFORE FLOWERING

- lad's love (*Artemisia abrotanum*)
- barberry, if necessary
- butterfly bush (*Buddleia davidii*)
- common heather (*Calluna vulgaris*)
- clematis (late-flowering species and hybrids: *C. orientalis or 'Etoile Rose'*)
- caryopteris
- red-stemmed dogwood (*Cornus alba*)
- bell heather (*Erica cinerea*)
- Cornish heath (*Erica vagans*)
- fuchsia
- hypericum 'Hidcote'
- bay (*Laurus nobilis*)
- tree mallow (*Lavatera olbia*)
- flowering nutmeg (*Leycesteria*)
- honeysuckle varieties
- Russian sage (*Perovskia atriplicifolia*)
- Jerusalem sage (*Phlomis fruticosa*)
- Cape figwort (*Phygelius capensis*)
- potentilla
- roses (hybrid tea and floribunda types)
- rue (*Ruta graveolens*)
- sage (*Salvia officinalis*)
- elder (*Sambucus*)
- cotton lavender

A tidy trim

The natural growth of many plants may not be as tidy and attractive as you would like. Pruning can correct this.

Heathers, again, are a good example of plants which are 'prettier' when pruned. If the old flower shoots, which can be as long as 25cm/10in, are cut in early spring, they need

CUTTING QUESTIONS

Q I am just back from holiday and it is the middle of spring. Am I too late to prune my hybrid tea and floribunda roses?

A No, you're not. Seasonal pruning is always better done late than not at all. This applies to spring and summer pruning. In the case of the roses, the flowers may be a little delayed by late pruning, but the bushes will at least retain their shape and vigour.

Q I have just moved into a house with an overgrown and neglected garden. How drastically can I prune to tidy it up?

A Some plants are better not pruned if you can avoid it (see list on p.79). Those which can be pruned will probably stand very drastic pruning indeed – even cutting off at ground level. To stop the garden looking too bare, try doing a section at a time. Spare a thought for your garden wildlife, too.

Q What is meant by 'new wood'?

A It is simply a term to describe this year's stem growth. Past growth is known as 'old wood'. Plants that flower early in the season tend to produce their flowers on the previous year's growth.

PRUNE AFTER FLOWERING

- *Clematis montana*
- broom (*Cytisus species*)
- deutzia
- escallonia
- forsythia
- Spanish broom (*Genista hispanica*)
- rock rose
- winter-flowering jasmine (*Jasminum nudiflorum*)
- Jew's mallow (*Kerria japonica*)
- mock orange (*Philadelphus species*)
- cherries, plums
- roses (ramblers and old-fashioned shrubs)
- weigela
- hydrangea
- *Buddleia alternifolia*

This cider gum, Eucalyptus gunnii (above) has an abundance of healthy new growth. Coppicing is the best method of keeping it in check for a small garden and encourages plenty of attractive young foliage growth. Cut the whole stem down to ground level each spring.

The cherry laurel, Prunus laurocerasus does not require regular pruning, but can be cut right back if it becomes too large. Prune into the old wood after flowering. Left to its own devices, this unsightly specimen (right) has become overgrown.

The vibrant rhododendron 'Blue Ensign' (left) requires the absolute minimum of pruning. The shrub is naturally bushy and forms a neat, compact shape. Flowers and seeds are produced abundantly. To encourage good, strong shoots, however, dead-heading is advisable.

A stately pair of common yew trees (Taxus baccata) create an imposing look for the front of a grand house (below). Yew has a neat, tidy growing habit and requires only cosmetic pruning. If the tree grows out of control it can be cut back. Dead, diseased and damaged growth can be removed at any time of year.

never become straggly. Any large-flowered, vigorous clematis such as *C. orientalis* is also pruned hard in early spring, to relieve it of a mass of old tangled growth. The flowers will appear in due course on the new shoots. If they are not pruned in spring they begin to grow from where they flowered the year before. Soon the plant will become bare at the base with flowers at the top only.

There are, of course, times when a mass of congested shoots looks right. This effect is achieved by clipping.

All shapes and sizes

Naturally dense bushes, like hebe, can have any long rogue shoots cut back to maintain the rounded form. It is worthwhile noting that not all shrubs grow at a regular rate, one section may be more vigorous than another and the result is an asymmetrical shape. To rectify this the weak shoots require hard pruning and the stronger shoots a light touch; this is because hard pruning stimulates growth.

Often, pruning is simply used to limit the size of a plant. For instance, many which have become just too large for their situation can, of course, be cut right down to start again. This is true of roses, mock orange, hydrangeas, holly, laurel, yew and many others.

A healthy garden

Pruning helps to keep plants strong and healthy, preventing disease as well as curing many ailments. It is vitally important that all dead, damaged or diseased shoots are removed from the plant as soon as they are spotted. They should be burned immediately and should never be added to the compost heap.

The shoots should then be cut back into the healthy wood, to a bud if possible, as this will provide strong, healthy new growth.

A special pruning saw has no back to it and therefore can be used in very tight corners or in dense growth as pictured here (right).

Anvil-style secateurs are used (below right) to prune a mass of dense honeysuckle. This is an ideal tool for rough work. The most important consideration when buying secateurs is that they are comfortable in your hand.

There are several different groups of clematis which require pruning in different ways. The intense purple hybrid 'Perle d'Azur' (top) flowers in summer and autumn on the growth it has produced in the same season. In late January or early February the whole of the previous year's growth should be cut back. If this is not done it will rapidly become bare at the base. C. m. rubens (above) is from the spring flowering group. It blooms on growth developed the previous summer and so it should not be pruned until after it has flowered.

SAWS FOR PRUNING

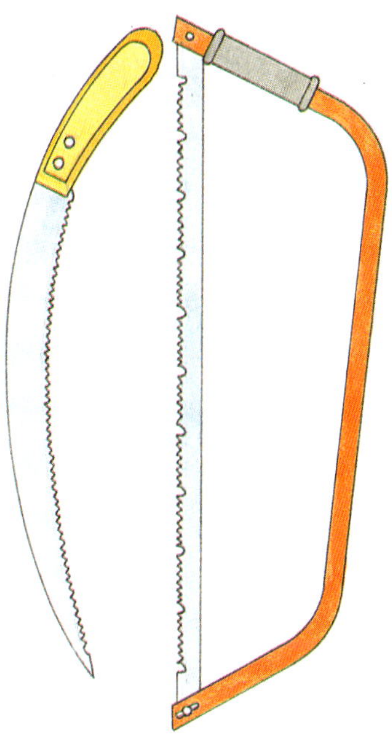

For smaller cuts in hard-to-get-at places a pruning saw is ideal. It cuts on the pull-stroke only.

For larger branches you will need a bow saw. An excellent choice is a small bow saw with a pointed nose to get into smaller spaces. The blades are easily replaced and inexpensive.

Though long-handled pruners (loppers) are useful where more leverage is needed, a saw is often just as easy, much cheaper and generally more useful.

Use a saw to cut branches thicker than a broom handle. Choose from a Grecian saw (far left) or a bow saw.

SECATEURS

In the anvil type, the blade is brought down onto a fixed block opposite. Beware though, as blunt blades will crush the stems or fail to cut right through.

In the scissor type (sometimes known as 'by-pass' secateurs), two blades move together. They must be hinged as tightly as possible but still with free movement, if they are to cut cleanly. They are often more expensive, but serve a wider purpose.

When choosing secateurs, go for the simplest-looking mechanism (with safety lock and hinge) and buy the best quality you can afford. A good pair of secateurs, with no gimmickry should last a lifetime.

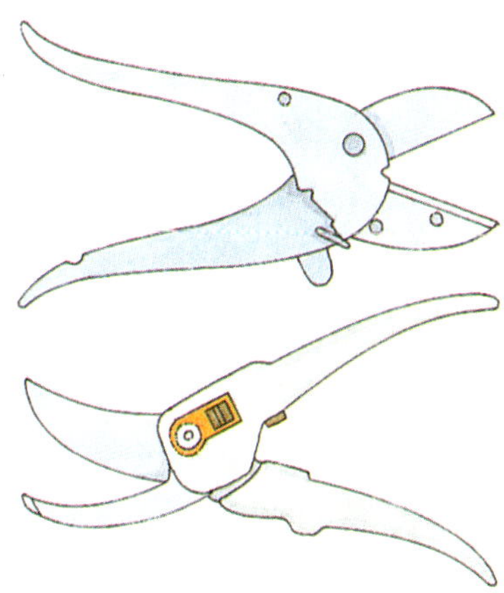

Choose secateurs which are comfortable in your hand and keep them as sharp as possible.

Stem Cuttings

Taking cuttings is the most cost-effective way of increasing your stock of garden plants – and it's so simple, too. Just follow these basic guidelines.

When you are in a friend's garden and you see a plant you would like to have in your own garden ask if you can take a stem cutting (above) you can guarantee that if it is successful it will look exactly like its parent plant. As this chart (right) shows there are a few basic seasons for taking cuttings. Softwood cuttings taken in spring are ideal for delphinimums chrysanthemums and dahlias. Take semi-ripe cuttings in late summer with a 'heel' of older wood.

Have you ever seen a plant in a friend's garden you would love to have and don't know where to find? Have you a particularly successful specimen in your own garden that you would like more of? In fact, it is really quite easy to make more of them – all you need to do is learn the simple art of taking cuttings.

When you take a stem cutting you remove a stem from a plant and encourage it to form roots to support itself as a new and separate plant.

There is nothing difficult about stem cuttings as the basic operation is really very straightforward. What you do need to remember is that there are right and wrong times to take a cutting, depending on the plant. A cutting taken at the best time will always stand a much greater chance of succeeding.

How and when

Some plants will root in a jar of water or straight into the ground. Others need more controlled conditions. Some cuttings need to be taken when the plant is in full leaf and growth, and need careful attention to tide them over that critical period before the formation of new roots. Others can be taken when the plant is dormant, making the process less stressful for the cutting. Different plants respond differently to different methods.

One thing about stem cuttings is certain: they are a very cheap way of obtaining new plants. Often from the purchase of a single plant you can make dozens of cuttings several times a season. Young plants from cuttings can make an interesting and lucrative stall at a bazaar – you will find yoghurt cartons are usually quite acceptable as plant pots.

Plant clones

Unlike a plant grown from seed, a cutting has the advantage of being identical to its parent plant. So if you take a liking to a plant variety in a friend's garden, a cutting will give you the same specimen. Plants produced in this way are said to be of the same clone, which simply means that they all stem from identical genetic material.

This is especially useful where uniformity is needed in the garden. For instance, a yew or cypress hedge made from cuttings from one particular plant will give you a hedge of even greenness and density of habit. Hedges from seed-grown plants will always show individual colour and density variation; growth rates will vary, too.

When it comes to cuttings, as with so much else, you get the best from the best. Good strong healthy shoots always produce better plants and root more easily. Of course, you will not want to disfigure a favourite plant or spoil its shape, but spare a little of it for cuttings as it will pay off later. It is no surprise that in nurseries cuttings are taken from carefully grown stock plants trained to produce ideal cutting material even if they have a poor shape.

SHORT CUTS

EASY OPTIONS

Some plants are very easy to grow from cuttings. Geraniums or fuchsias will root at almost any time during the growing season. Busy Lizzies and willow will root in a jar of water on a window sill. Roses are worth trying as hardwood cuttings, any time between late summer and the middle of winter.

Collecting cuttings

When a plant is in leaf and growing strongly, it is best to take cuttings when it is as full of sap as possible – so avoid midday or very hot weather. The day after a heavy rain storm is ideal, as the plants will have had a good long drink. Early morning is another good time, before the heat of the day reduces the moisture level within the leaves.

If you are collecting cuttings from the garden, cut a slightly

GARDEN NOTES

HEEL CUTTINGS

Semi-ripe cuttings are often taken with a heel of older wood attached. By pulling rather than cutting off a side shoot, a little of the older wood on the main stem comes away with the cutting. Using a very sharp knife, trim it clean of any damaged tissue (without removing the heel), before rooting it.

Some plants such as the buzy Lizzie (above) are so keen to propagate that they need practically no encouragement. All you have to do is cut off a piece, strip off the bottom leaves and stick it in a jar of water.

To propagate thuja take semi-ripe cuttings with a heel. Instead of cutting through the stem pull off a side shoot taking a little old wood with you (below).

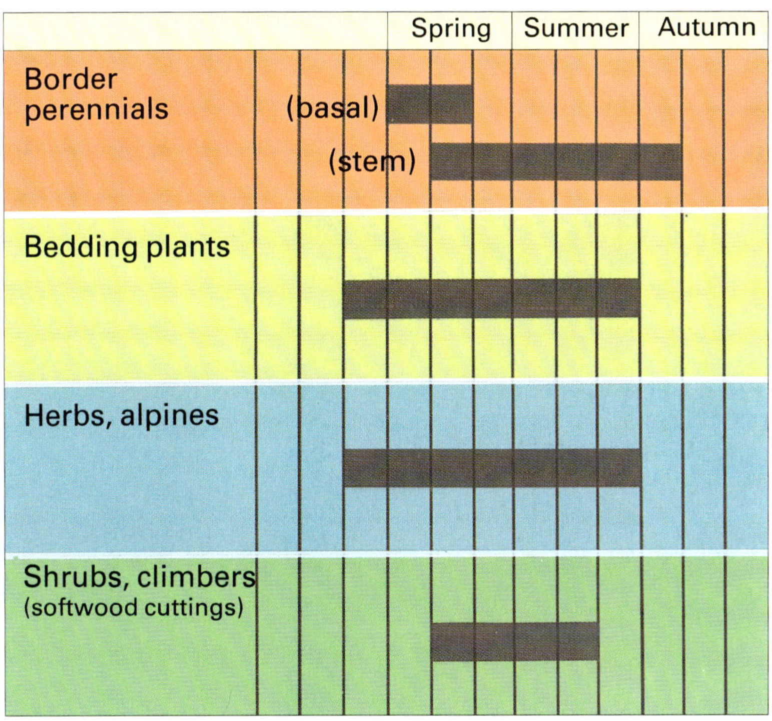

LAVENDER FROM CUTTINGS

Lavender is easy to propagate from cuttings, and you can easily make a hedge of it from cuttings taken the previous season. Follow these easy steps to make your hedge. The cuttings will take about three weeks to root. Once this has happened, remove the polythene and gradually reaccustom your plantlets to full sun. Keep them indoors on a cold window sill (or in a cold frame) over winter. In the early spring, pot up the plants individually into 8cm/3in pots and plant them out about two months later, after hardening off. In well-drained soils, lavender flowers from mid-summer to autumn.

1 *In late summer collect lavender cuttings 7.5cm/3in long. These should be the tips of non-flowering shoots.*

2 *Use a sharp knife to cut through the base just below a leaf joint, remove the leaves from lower third.*

3 *Dip the cuttings in a fungicide solution and shake off the excess. Dip stem in rooting powder.*

4 *Fill with an equal mixture of peat and sand. Make holes 2.5cm deep. Push the cuttings into the holes and firm in*

5 *Cover with well-ventilated polythene and put in a warm, light place. Turn the polythene inside out regularly.*

GROWING TIPS

HORMONE ROOTING POWDER

Hormone rooting powder is best used in the season of purchase. Many plants root perfectly well without it if the timing is right. The process may be slower without rooting powder, but do not let that put you off.

If you only want to produce one plant then experiment with timing, too. It is surprising how often you will succeed with a chance cutting offered by a friend on the spur of the moment.

longer length than you need. You can then trim them up properly on a table indoors. Always keep your cuttings in a closed plastic bag in the shade until you are ready to deal with them, to prevent wilting. Remember to collect a few extra cuttings, too, to allow for a few failures.

Sharp, clean secateurs are best for collecting all cuttings and are perfectly adequate for making the final trimming up of woody cuttings. Softer stems are best cut on a board, using a sharp craft knife.

Take semi-ripe cuttings with a heel and dip them into hormone rooting powder. Plant cuttings in individual pots filled with an equal part of peat and sand. Place the pots in a polythene bag tent to prevent the cuttings from wilting and keep them in a shady spot (below).

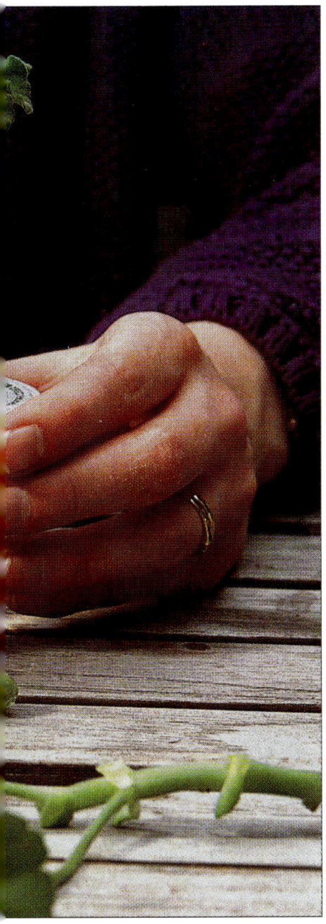

Cuttings from a pelargonium are inserted into a growing medium (above). Choose two or three good shoots and strip off bottom leaves.

Make sure cuttings have rooted before transplanting. Pull gently and if it resists it is rooted (below).

Cuttings have a language all of their own and this may initially be confusing but in the end it all boils down to a few basic seasons for cutting: softwood cuttings are taken in spring, semi-ripe in late summer and hardwood in autumn and winter.

Softwood cutting

Softwood cuttings are made from short sections of new growth in spring. Take them as soon as about 5-10cm/2-4in of stem have developed.

In early spring take cuttings of the new basal shoots of delphiniums, chrysanthemums, fuchsias, achillea, dahlia and perennial salvias. In early summer try tip cuttings (4-6.5cm/1½-2½in) of potentilla, deutzia and cistus.

Softwood cuttings should be cut cleanly to 6.5cm/2½in long at the leaf joint or 'node', using a sharp knife. Remove the lower few leaves by nipping them off with your fingernails or with a knife. Dip the whole cutting in a solution such as benomyl fungicide and shake off the excess. Then dip the bottom inch into hormone rooting powder and push the cuttings 2.5cm/1in into an equal mixture of peat and sand in a shallow plant pot. Water well. Cover with a clean plastic bag and seal with a rubber band. (Alternatively put the pot in a propagator with an electrically controlled bottom heat at 70°F.) Keep in a light place but out of direct sunlight. Most cuttings should take root within three weeks.

Turn the plastic bag inside out every few days to reduce condensation and so minimise the risk of moulds developing. It also helps if you cut off the corners of the bag, to give just a little ventilation.

Root resistance

To test a cutting to see if it is rooted, first look underneath to see if any roots are visible at the drainage holes. If not, pull the cutting gently. If it resists well, it is rooted.

As soon as the cuttings are rooted, take off the polythene (or remove from the propagator) and give them a few days to re-acclimatize before you pot them up individually.

Semi-ripe cuttings are taken in late summer, when growth is slowing down and the new shoots are slightly firmer. In midsummer try geraniums, heathers, deutzia, weigela, philadelphus, forsythia, potentilla, and dogwood (*Cornus alba*).

You can often just take a side shoot, and cut it off either at a suitable leaf joint or with a little 'heel'. This means that you pull off your new stem with a little piece of wood from the older stem still attached.

Semi-ripe cuttings are easier than softwood cuttings because the risks of disease are less. They are slower, though, and it will be next year before your new plantlets begin to grow. Side-shoots are taken from the parent plant, from 10-20cm/4-8in long (2.5cm/1in in the case of heathers). Remove the leaves from the lower 5cm/2in of stem which is cut cleanly at a leaf-joint or with a heel. Dip the lower part into hormone rooting powder, and insert the cuttings into a pot of an equal mixture of peat and sand or into soil in a cold frame. Water well.

Stop wilting

A polythene bag tent over the pots will prevent your cuttings wilting, but they will still need shading from bright sunshine. Pots kept indoors on a window sill should root in 3-5 weeks and can be overwintered in a cool garage after their leaves drop, ready for potting up in spring.

Cuttings in soil in pots or a cold frame may not root until well into the winter, and are often best left undisturbed until the following autumn.

Hardwood cuttings are very easy but not all plants can be propagated in this way. In autumn try willows, roses, currants and cypresses. Simply cut off 23cm/9in lengths of good vigorous stem, and insert them into the soil for three-quarters of their length. You can either grow them in their final position or in an unused corner to be transferred the following autumn. Rooting takes place in the spring.

WHAT WENT WRONG?

NO ROOTS

Q Last winter I took some cuttings to make a Leylandii hedge. Four months later they have not rooted. Is this right?

A Yes. Evergreens and conifers are slow to make roots. Just leave them alone in a cool place, out of direct sun, and wait. As long as they remain green, the chances are that they will root. Any that have gone black or brown should be removed. By next autumn the rest should have rooted. Because of their slowness, a cold frame is the best place for evergreeens, where they can remain until rooted.

Propagation by Layering

For beginners and experts alike, layering is a method of propagation which is almost guaranteed to provide plenty of plants for the garden or indoors.

It is easy to propagate strawberries by potting up runners while they are still attached to the plant. When roots have formed, the runner can be severed. Plants in strawberry barrels (above) will produce runners at a variety of heights, so pots often need to be propped up on bricks.

Layering involves rooting a shoot or stem while it is still attached to the parent plant. Unlike the alternative of taking cuttings, there is little risk of the shoot dying before it has formed roots. As the process requires only simple preparation and aftercare, this makes layering one of the easiest and most reliable methods of plant propagation for the newcomer to gardening.

It is one of nature's own methods of propagation. Shoots of brambles, for instance, root into the soil at their tips. The branches of some trees, such as beech, will often take root where they sweep to the ground, and stems of rhododendron will root and form new plants at the point where they come into contact with the soil.

Why layer?

There are many good reasons for layering. The main one is that some shrubs and trees are very difficult to propagate by other means, such as cuttings, but prove easy from layers. Examples include rhododendrons, magnolias, witch hazel (*Hamamelis*), camellias, pieris, elaeagnus and hollies (*Ilex*).

With certain plants, such as strawberries, this is perhaps the only practical way to propagate new stock.

Layering requires very little equipment or expertise and needs no artificial heat (except when layering houseplants).

The usual method for shrubs is simple layering. This is suitable not only for those which are difficult to propagate from cuttings, but also for virtually any shrub or climber whose stems can be brought into contact with the soil.

Carry out layering during the growing season, ideally between mid-spring and late summer. Use young shoots produced in the current or previous season, as old woody ones will fail to root, or will do so only over a long time. If desired, several shoots from each shrub can be layered.

How to layer

First, the surrounding soil should be prepared by digging or forking it over to a depth of

Growing Tips

ENSURING CLEAN CUTS

The success of layers where a cut has been made in the stem depends on clean cuts, as opposed to ragged ones.

Ideally, you should use a proper horticultural knife, such as a budding or grafting knife. The best ones have a non-stainless steel blade which should be kept really sharp on an oilstone.

Try to make a continuous cut, as this will ensure really smooth surfaces to the tongue, which is then more liable to form roots. Jerky cuts result in ragged tongues which may not then produce roots.

30cm/12in. Mix in some coarse horticultural sand and moist sphagnum peat or coconut fibre. Break the soil down as finely as possible.

The shoot is prepared about 30cm/12in from its tip by first stripping off some leaves to make a clear section of stem. Then, in this area, cut a tongue about 5cm/2in in length by drawing a knife halfway through the stem. Make the cut through a leaf joint (also known as a 'node').

Wedge the tongue open with a small piece of wood or a stone and dust the surface of the cut with a proprietary hormone rooting powder.

The prepared part of the stem is then pegged down into a 15cm/6in deep, saucer-shaped hole in the prepared soil. Hold it in place with a piece of thick galvanized wire bent to the shape of a hairpin, and make sure the cut is still open. The top part of the shoot beyond the cut should be tied vertically to a short bamboo cane so it grows upwards.

Cover the pegged part of the stem with a 15cm/6in layer of soil and firm it lightly. The soil around layered stems should be kept moist until they have formed a good root system.

Gradual growth

Rooting will take place where the cut was made in the stem. Layers should not be lifted until a substantial root system has formed. This process may take as little as a year with some shrubs, such as forsythia, but can take 18 to 24 months with some of the more difficult shrubs. If you lift a layer and find that it has not rooted, replant it straight away and firm it in.

Lift the layers in autumn or early spring carefully, using a garden fork. If well rooted, cut away from the parent plant just beyond the roots. Rooted layers of shrubs should be immediately replanted elsewhere in the garden. Either put them in their permanent positions or, if you have the space, in a nursery bed to grow on to a larger size.

Another technique

Tip layering is even easier and is used for blackberries and loganberries and for other similar hybrid berrying fruits that have long stems.

It is carried out in mid- to late summer, using the current year's stems. Soil preparation is precisely the same as for simple layering.

Simply bury the tip of the stem about 8cm/3in in the soil. If necessary, keep it in place with a wire peg.

Alternatively, tips can be rooted in 9cm/3½in pots containing a peat and sand mix. Sink the pots to their rims in the ground below each tip.

Tip layering a thornless blackberry (above). The tip of a stem has been buried in the soil and will soon root.

Rhododendrons (below) can be layered at any time. A small slit along the stem hastens rooting. Roots take two years to form.

What Went Wrong?

MY LAYERS FAILED TO ROOT

Q I layered a number of shrubs about two years ago but they have not rooted, although I closely followed all the 'text-book instructions'. Can you tell me where I have gone wrong?

A The most common cause of layers failing to root is the soil drying out.

The soil must be kept moist at all times. In spring and summer and perhaps in autumn, too, you will need to water as soon as the soil becomes dry on the surface.

Do not settle for a 'quick splash'. Apply enough water to penetrate the soil to a depth of at least 15cm/6in.

Using a watering can fitted with a rose, water on at least 27 litres per m^2/5 galls per sq. yd.

AIR LAYERING

Cut a slit 15-38cm/6-15in below the tip, between growth buds.

Dust the cut with hormone rooting powder. Pack with moss.

Enclose the cut with polythene, securing it at the bottom.

Pack the sleeve with more sphagnum moss and secure it at the top. Roots will grow into the moss. Tie stem to a cane.

In late autumn of the same year, when the tips have rooted, cut them away from the parent plant and plant them elsewhere in the garden. The best place is in a nursery bed where they can grow on.

Air layering

It is impossible to bring the stems of some shrubs and the branches of most trees down to ground level. These can be propagated by a technique known as air layering.

Prepare a young shoot as for simple layering, but hold the cut or tongue open by packing it with a wad of moist sphagnum moss, which you can buy from a florist.

Wrap more moss around the prepared part of the stem, holding it in place with a 'bandage' of clear polythene sheeting. Use waterproof tape to hold the polythene in place, making sure it is firmly attached to the shoot.

You should be able to see when roots have formed. Rooting will take one to two years. Treat rooted layers as already described. Remove the polythene but leave the moss in place; removing it will damage the brittle roots.

Border carnations

Many people are surprised to learn that border carnations can be layered. This is an easier and more reliable form of propagation than the alternative method of taking cuttings.

As the plants soon deteriorate, it is a good idea to propagate border carnations every couple of years or so.

The best time to layer carnations is in late summer, when flowering is over. For success, you must use the current year's shoots before they start to become woody. Several shoots can be pegged down around each plant.

First, lightly fork over the soil around the parent plants, using a hand fork. Then spread a 5cm/2in layer of John Innes potting compost evenly over the cultivated soil.

Using unflowered shoots, carefully cut off the leaves at the base of the shoots, where they will be pegged down. Then cut a 3.5cm/1½in tongue in each, using the technique described under simple layering. Make the cut through a leaf joint. There is no need to use hormone rooting powder.

Peg down each layer into the compost, keeping it in place with a wire hairpin-shaped peg. The tongue must be kept open. Cover this part of the stem with a 5cm/2in layer of

Air layering is the most successful way of propagating any Ficus *shrub. Taking cuttings is a chancy method, not least because they have to be propagated at a relatively high temperature, which can be difficult. Here (above) a cut has been made in a one or two-year-old stem in early to mid summer and rooting is taking place. The whole process, which is a little unsightly, may take two years.*

John Innes potting compost.

Keep the layers moist and they should root in about eight weeks. Cut them from the parent plants and leave them in the ground for a few days to recover from the 'shock'. Then lift them with a fork and replant them in permanent positions in the garden. These new plants will start to flower next year in mid summer.

Strawberries

Strawberries are propagated by layering the young plants which form on the ends of runners (creeping stems). Strawberry plants, like carnations, soon deteriorate and should be replaced by young plants about every three years to keep up crop yields.

If runners are not needed for propagation, remove them. Runners can be layered in early or mid summer. Always layer the first plantlet on a runner, removing any beyond it. Five to six runners can be layered around each plant.

Hold the plantlets in close contact with the soil by inserting a wire peg just behind each one. They can be rooted in the soil or in small pots of John Innes potting compost that have been sunk in the ground. Keep layers moist at all times.

When the plantlets are well rooted, in late summer or early autumn, cut them away from the parents and plant them in a newly dug strawberry bed. Flowering and fruiting will start the following year.

Indoor uses

Layering is not just a technique for garden plants. It is suitable, too, for some houseplants. Air layering can be used for woody or tree-like kinds, such as rubber plants and figs (*Ficus* species), crotons (*Codiaeum variegatum*), philodendrons, and dumb cane (*Dieffenbachia species*).

These are often air layered when they become too tall and need to be replaced with smaller specimens. You can do it in normal room conditions during the spring or summer.

Prepare a stem about 30cm/12in from its tip, as described for simple layering. The cut, which forms the tongue, is made in an upward direction. Dust with hormone rooting powder and then wrap the cut with moss covered by a protective polythene sleeve.

In warm conditions the stem should root in several weeks. Remove the polythene (but *not* the moss) and place the layer in a suitably sized pot, using soilless or soil-based potting compost. If possible, keep the young plants in warmer conditions for a few weeks.

If you wish, you can cut back the parent plant, by about half to two-thirds. It should then form side shoots and make a good bushy specimen.

SERPENTINE LAYERING OF CLIMBERS

Instead of obtaining only one plant per stem, you can ensure several from climbing plants by a technique known as serpentine layering.

Examples of climbers suited to this method are wisterias, clematis, honeysuckles (*Lonicera*), vines and jasmine (*Jasminum*).

This method is a variation on simple layering. Instead of rooting a stem in just one place, a long young stem is pegged down in several places along its length.

Climbers sometimes root more quickly than shrubs – often in as little as 12 months.

It is advisable to mark your layers with canes or plant labels so that you remember where they are. Make a note of the date so you know when to check them for roots.

1 *Take a young, pliable outer shoot of the climber – here it is honeysuckle – and lay it out on the ground where you want it to root.*

2 *With a sharp knife make slanting cuts 1-2.5cm/½-1in long in the stem. Make the cuts close to nodes. Several cuts can be made.*

3 *Having added humus and sand to the soil, peg down each cut with a staple of bent wire and cover it over with soil.*

4 *Shoots layered in early summer should form roots by early autumn. Sever the plants, pot them up and plant out in the spring.*

Bulbs, Corms, Rhizomes & Tubers

Bulbs, corms, rhizomes and tubers are types of food storage organs developed by plants for their survival from one growing season to the next.

Onions, daffodils, tulips and fritillarias all grow from bulbs. A bulb is a modified shoot, with its very short stem enclosed by layers of fleshy leaves.

In the first year of a bulbous plant, the food manufactured by the leaves is moved to the base of each leaf. These bases become the fleshy layers of the bulb. They are the part of the onion that we eat.

The following year, a bud within the bulb springs into life and produces new leaves, which in turn make food and store it in their bases.

Once the bulb is large enough (and the exact size depends on the plant) a flower bud is produced and this grows in the following year.

Corms

Corms are swollen stem bases. Examples are crocus, freesia and gladiolus. The first year's leaves make and then transport food down the stem to form a corm.

This lies dormant until the next growing period, when the terminal bud uses the stored food to grow. The roots then develop and flowers and leaves are produced.

More manufactured food is transported to the bottom of the stem where a new corm is formed on top of the old one, which eventually shrivels. Cormlets (small corms) are also produced. These can be separated from the parent corm and replanted.

Rhizomes

A rhizome is an underground stem which does not necessarily store food. Examples of food-storing rhizomes include iris

GARDEN NOTES

MAINTENANCE

Bulbs need moisture so they can elongate rapidly during their short growing season.

Keep the area where they are planted well mulched with leaves, leaf mould or garden compost. Or you can use a mulch of coir, bark or coco shells. Top the mulch up when the bulbs are dormant.

Resist the temptation to tidy up foliage by tying it off. The foliage is only present for a short time and has to manufacture food for storage underground.

The plant needs this food to send up next year's leaves and flowers.

Bulbs grown in lawns must be left until the foliage has yellowed before mowing.

You can help the leaves manufacture the maximum amount of food by applying a fertilizer. Spread or water on a general purpose fertilizer, or, better still, bone meal or another high phosphorus fertilizer. Then you will have a beautiful display, year after year.

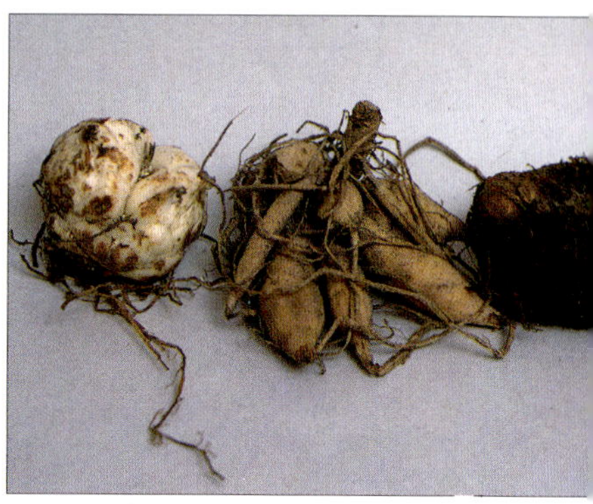

The white flowers of **Ornithogalum nutans** *(above) grow from bulbs.*

At near left is a bulb, then two tubers, three corms and two more tubers (right).

Bulbils (mini-bulbs) grow from the stems of lilies and the onion family (top).

and arum. The leaves manufacture food which is transported to the rhizome and to any lateral buds.

The main rhizome increases in length each year. One or more branches may develop off it and they, too, will grow longer. In spring, food is transferred to aerial shoots which develop into the plant's new leaves and flowers.

Tubers

A tuber is a thickened, fleshy underground root (as in the dahlia) or stem (a potato, for example), which helps the plant survive periods of cold or drought. Many popular plants have tubers, including arum lilies, dahlias and many types of begonias.

Once the plant is dormant, the tubers can be lifted and cut up, with at least one 'eye' or bud on each piece, which is then replanted.

Planting depth

As a rule of thumb, plant bulbs, corms and tubers at least twice as deep as their diameter. Gardening books give detailed information about particular species.

Some plants which are not completely frost-hardy have a better chance of survival if buried deeper than the rule of thumb suggests. Further insulation can be provided by mulching the ground.

Rhizomes are not usually planted as deep as bulbs and corms. Iris rhizomes are planted very shallowly, with their tops visible on the soil's surface, so that the sun can ripen each year's growth.

What to lift

You only need to dig up (lift) bulbs, corms, rhizomes or tubers if they are not winter-hardy. They should be brought into a frost-free place to ensure survival. The only other time to lift them is when dividing and replanting (see box).

However, garden tulips (but not species tulips) benefit from being lifted and moved to another part of the garden each year, in order to prevent disease problems.

The other situation where you may want to lift bulbs, corms, rhizomes or tubers is where you grow spring and summer bedding plants. When you pull up the spring bedding to make way for the summer plants, the bulb foliage may still be present, or the bulbs may be too near the surface for you to plant above them.

In this situation, you can lift all the bulbs, but you must replant them elsewhere straight away, so that they can complete their growth cycle and die back naturally. Otherwise the bulbs will not receive a top-up of nutrients and next year's flower bud may not form.

Bulbs, corms, rhizomes and tubers are liable to damage and drying out, so try to buy them as soon as they are delivered, healthy and intact, to the shop or garden centre.

Avoid shrivelled up material (but remember that corms are often very dry and shrivelled). Do not buy very soft, bruised or otherwise damaged material. Also to be avoided are those with shoots or roots.

Replanting

Bulbs, corms, rhizomes and tubers are sold in a dry state for convenience. You can, though, dig up and replant them while they are in leaf, providing that you do not allow the roots to dry out.

In fact, snowdrops are more successfully established 'in the green' – that is, with their leaves on. Specialist nurseries sell these by mail order or you can beg some from friends. Wait until the flowers are over, because the flowers will wilt if you move them and you will not have the pleasure of their display.

Snowdrop bulbs dry out too much indoors, which is why shop-bought bulbs are often unsuccessful. Grape hyacinth

GROWING TIPS

PROPAGATION

You can increase your stocks by digging up congested clumps, teasing the growth apart and replanting them at a better spacing. Bulbs should be teased apart, as should corms.

Rhizomes grow outwards, which leaves old growth in the middle of the clump. Dig up and chop off the outer pieces for replanting. Discard the central section.

If leaves are attached to new sections of rhizome, cut them down to half their original height, to prevent the wind dislodging the newly planted piece.

Propagate bulbs and corms once the foliage has died back; iris after flowering.

PLANTS FOR DRY SHADE

Name	Type	Flower
Chionodoxa luciliae	Bulb	Spring, blue
Colchicum speciosum Meadow saffron	Corm	Autumn, pink, purple, white
Corydalis solida	Tuber	Spring, purple
Crocus tommasinianus Crocus	Corm	Early spring, lilac
Cyclamen hederifolium Cyclamen	Tuber	Autumn, pink
Eranthis hyemalis Winter aconite	Tuber	Early spring, yellow
Galanthus nivalis Snowdrop	Bulb	Early spring, white
Hyacinthoides non-scriptus English bluebell	Bulb	Late spring, blue
Narcissus pseudonarcissus Wild daffodil	Bulb	Spring, yellow
Ornithogalum nutans	Bulb	Spring, white
Scilla bifolia Squill	Bulb	Spring, blue

PLANTS FOR VERY MOIST SOIL IN SHADE

Name	Type	Flower
Allium siculum	Bulb	Early summer, purple/green
Camassia leichtlinii Quamash	Bulb	Early summer, blue
Lilium pardalinum Panther lily	Bulb	Summer, red/orange
Lilium superbum Swamp lily	Bulb	Summer, red/orange
Trillium spp	Rhizome	Spring, various

(*Muscari* spp) bulbs are also prone to drying out so they should be bought soon after being delivered to the shop. These are not often sold 'in the green', but they are so common in gardens that you can probably beg some from a friend.

Growing conditions

Those bulbs, corms, rhizomes and tubers that need full sun require it in order to ripen and produce good growth and flowers the following year. Few will tolerate extremely dry soil, however.

Moisture is necessary to start them into growth and to help elongate the flower stalks of the taller types. You may have noticed how a clump of daffodils produces shorter flower stalks in dry years.

Our spring-flowering bulbs are adapted to grow in woods. They thrive because they complete their growth before the trees begin theirs. The trees are still dormant when the bulbs need moisture. Sun and rain can penetrate to the ground because the trees' leaves are not yet open. By the time the full leaf canopy is out, the ground level show is over.

A garden is less natural. It often has evergreen trees, hedges and shrubs, which are a barrier to sun and rain and are competing for moisture.

Several of our most popular spring flowers grow from bulbs. They include bluebells (left) and daffodils (below left).

Iris rhizomes (opposite bottom) are usually divided and planted out after flowering. They can take a time to become established and often do not flower until the second season.

After lifting in autumn these gladioli corms (below) must be dried out before being stored in a cool, frost-free place.

PLANTS FOR FULL SUN

Name	Type	Flower
Agapanthus African blue lily	Tuber	Summer, blue
Allium aflatunense	Bulb	Late spring, pink/ purple
Allium moly Golden garlic	Bulb	Late spring, yellow
Arum spp	Tuber	Spring, yellow or black
Brodiaea spp	Bulb	Late spring, blue/ violet
Gladioli Gladiolus	Corm	Summer, various
Hyacinth Hyacinth	Bulb	Spring, various
Iris spp Iris	Rhizome or bulb	Spring, summer, various
Nerine spp	Bulb	Autumn, pink
Oxalis spp (most) Sorrel	Rhizome or tuber	Late spring, various
Tulipa spp and hybrids Tulip	Bulb	Spring, various

To naturalize bulbs in grass or woods plant them in random groups and singly.

When planting in flower beds, plant them near other plants which will grow up and disguise the bulb foliage when it is dying back. You can also plant them beneath deciduous shrubs and among shrubs with a short flowering season, to brighten up a dull area.

Sources of bulbs

The demand for bulbs, corms, rhizomes and tubers from gardeners has resulted in wild populations of plants being robbed. Although garden hybrids are bred and grown by commercial nurseries, species such as cyclamen, snowdrop and snowflake may not be.

Unfortunately, once dug up from the wild, they are not kept for propagation, but sold. This is happening particularly in Turkey. If possible, buy stock from cultivated plants of endangered species such as cyclamen.

PLANTS TO LIFT BEFORE FROSTS

Name	Type
Agapanthus spp (hybrids are hardy) African blue lily	Tuber
Anomatheca laxa Lapeirousia	Corm
Caladium spp Angel's wings	Tuber
Chlidanthus fragrans Perfumed fairy lily	Bulb
Clivia spp Kaffir lily	Rhizome
Eucomis spp Pineapple lily	Bulb
Freesia spp Freesia	Corm
Gladioli Gladiolus	Corm
Haemanthus spp Blood lily	Bulb
Iris orchioides one of the Juno irises	Bulb
Sauromatum venosum Voodoo lily	Tuber
Sparaxis tricolor Harlequin flower	Corm
Tigridia pavonia Tiger flower	Bulb
Tritonia spp Tritonia	Corm
Watsonia spp Bugle lily	Corm
Zantedeschia spp Arum lily	Tuber

Make sure that the soil in which you plant the bulbs will be moist (but well-drained) at the critical growing time.

You may have to add garden compost to the planting area to increase moisture retention. Water the area well in order to encourage growth.

Many bulbs, corms, rhizomes and tubers, such as anemones, can be started off by soaking them before planting. If you soak the ground, too, they will have a good chance of becoming established.

Plant bulbs in clumps for a splash of colour, or plant them in drifts to flower through other plants or between rocks.

WHEN TO PLANT

Spring: summer-flowering bulbs.

Early autumn: madonna lilies, colchicums, autumn-flowering crocus, daffodils, winter aconites and snowdrops.

Late autumn: tulips.

Dead-heading and Disbudding

Dead-heading and disbudding are easy jobs, well worth doing. It pays to know which plants need this treatment and when and how you should do it.

You have probably disbudded plants without realizing it. It means removing, usually by pinching out, new growth buds. This allows the plant to concentrate all its energy on producing fewer, but showier flowers or better fruit.

New buds are produced at the leaf axil (where the leaf stalk is attached to the stem). They can grow into either a shoot or a flower, possibly followed by a fruit.

Controlled growth

In many plants, the development of buds lower down the stem is suppressed by the main growing point of their stem. So gardeners 'stop' plants, pinching out the growing point to enable lower buds to grow freely; this produces a much bushier plant.

Stopping a plant does just that – checking its growth for a while. But after a short delay, it starts into growth again.

You don't have to stop or disbud many plants in the garden; it all depends on your aims. If you are developing an interest in exhibiting blooms, then you will want to stop or disbud certain flowers.

Dead flower-heads are often removed for tidiness, but there are other reasons too.

Many early-flowering herbaceous perennials will give a fine second display if cut back. Other plants will give a display over a long period if the old, dead flowers are cut off and removed regularly.

In nature, plants flower in order to attract pollinators so that seed can be formed, to ensure the survival and spread of the species. But seed production takes a lot of energy. It should be prevented in the case of bulb, corm, rhizome and tuber-forming plants, because it will affect the following year's display of flowers.

Plants that can produce a continual display of flowers may do so only if you prevent them from setting seed. This stimulates them into eagerly producing more flowers, with the aim of eventually being able to set seed.

Some plants are good at setting seed and spreading themselves around your garden, so you must dead-head these promptly if you want to confine them to one place.

How to dead-head

Certain plants, including the heathers, lavender and herbs, produce flowers on long extension growths. Dead-head them to keep the plant vigorous and to prevent it becoming straggly and bare at the base.

Garden shears or one-handed shears are useful for

Dahlias need regular care. Three or four weeks after planting, you should stop them by neatly pinching out the main shoots. In time, fading flowers must be dead-headed (below left).

With rhododendrons (left), always dead-head with finger and thumb as secateurs may harm the tender shoots.

Calluna *heathers (right) flower in summer and autumn. Dead-heading tidies them up and encourages new growth.*

Cerastium *(below right) can be safely dead-headed with shears.*

trimming heathers and similar plants, and for removing dead flowers from some of the larger herbaceous perennials.

Plants such as pansies are easier to dead-head with finger and thumb. All-purpose scissors are useful for tougher plant stems, and secateurs are best for woody plants.

When dead-heading shrubs, cut back to where another bud arises, which is usually in a leaf axil. If a side-shoot has already begun to grow, cut back to that shoot.

Carnations While garden pinks are dead-headed to produce a long flowering season, greenhouse-grown, perpetual-flowering (florist's) carnations require more attention.

Spray carnations are stopped, but not disbudded. However, single-flowering and early-flowering sprays are not stopped, but are disbudded!

Stop spray carnations by removing the first small pair of leaves, a couple of weeks after planting. This encourages the production of many stems but delays flowering.

Carnation stems are jointed. The two or three joints at the base of the stem are disbudded on single-flowering carnations. Those part-way up the stem are left with buds. Once you can see the main flower bud, you should disbud the six joints which lie below it.

When you cut the main stem and its flower off, you should cut above the joint which still has a bud. You are effectively stopping the plant and the remaining buds will develop healthily into laterals bearing the second flush of flowers.

Chrysanthemums Annuals benefit from stopping as this produces bushy plants. They are often used for cut flowers; picking the blooms prolongs their display, which will be a colourful highlight in any border.

Hardy perennials just require dead-heading.

The tender chrysanthemums are classified according to flower type, size and season. Only large or medium flower types are disbudded. However, all types are stopped when the plant is about 15cm/6in tall, to induce branching.

You then remove one or two side-shoots from each stem every day, by snapping off the shoot with your fingers, until you have the number of shoots that you want. This is around six for garden or cut flowers, but you will need only two or three for exhibition.

The central bud is then removed, because it flowers earlier and is larger than the blooms on sideshoots. If the

GROWING TIPS

PLANTS BEST STOPPED

- Sweet peas.
- Garden pinks.
- Spray carnations.
- Florist's chrysanthemums.
- Fuchsias.
- Coleus.
- Anthirrhinum.
- Schizanthus.
- Wallflowers.
- Annuals of the *Compositae* family, e.g. pot marigold, ageratum and annual aster.

SECURING THE CENTRAL BUD

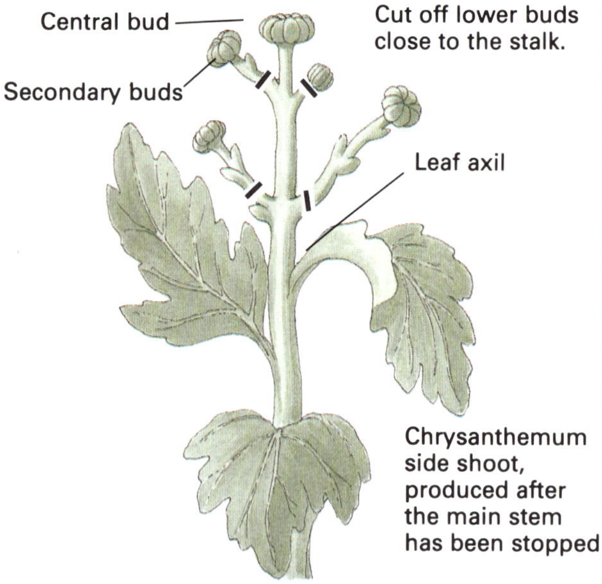

A chrysanthemum side shoot has a central bud with other buds beneath it. Remove the lower buds to produce one good bloom.

Dahlias Stop them about a month after planting outside, once strong shoots appear.

If you are growing them for exhibition, restrict the number of side-shoots which develop.

Dahlias are classified by flower form and size. Restrict Giants (over 25/10in) to 2-3 stems, Large (20cm-25cm/8-10in) to 3-4 stems, Medium (15-20cm/6-8in) to 5-7 stems, Small (10-15cm/4-6in) to 8-10 stems and Miniatures (up to 10cm/4in) to 10-12 stems.

In addition, if growing pompons, pinch out the side-shoots once they have two pairs of leaves. This will produce a mass of 5cm/2in blooms.

When dead-heading dahlias, cut down the stem to a developing side-shoot. This prevents the plants from becoming spindly and top-heavy.

central flower bud has not formed by early summer, the growing tip is pinched out anyway, or flowers on the side-shoots will be delayed.

The remaining flowering stems then produce their own side-shoots with flower buds. These are snapped off as soon as they can be handled so that there is only one flower left on each stem.

Other side-shoots on the flowering stem are also removed as they are produced. Snap off one or two each day.

If spray chrysanthemums, which are not disbudded, show signs of the crown bud (the terminal bud) developing ahead of the surrounding flower buds, then make sure you pinch out the crown bud.

Chrysanthemums (above right) are normally stopped before they reach full height. With a little practice and knowledge, they can be made to produce their best blooms by a certain date, which is invaluable for those who exhibit them.

Dead-heading (right) not only improves the look of a plant but often encourages more flowers.

The leading shoot of a standard fuchsia (far right) is allowed to grow until it reaches the required height. It is then pinched out. Stopping laterals at every second leaf will increase the number of blooms.

GROWING TIPS

PLANTS BEST DIS-BUDDED	PLANTS NOT DIS-BUDDED
Greenhouse perpetual-flowering (florist's) carnations. Dahlias for exhibition. Sweet peas for exhibition. Florist's chrysanthemums – types grown for large blooms.	Dahlias for garden display. Spray carnations and garden pinks. Spray, Korean, cascade and charm chrysanthemums. Annual and herbaceous perennial chrysanthemums. Most garden plants.

Roses Some roses tend to produce two or three buds at the site of a pruning cut and you should rub out these to leave only one bud. If all of them develop, they will grow into weak stems.

If exhibiting hybrid tea roses (now called large-flowered bush roses) you should look for extra flowers that may form on a single stem. Prune them out to leave one main bloom.

When dead-heading roses, prune to the first five-leaflet leaf below the bloom. When dead-heading floribunda roses (now called cluster-flowered roses), ensure that you remove the whole flower truss down to the first five-leaflet leaf on the main stem.

Because the dead-heading of repeat-flowering roses stimulates new growth, stop dead-heading in early autumn. Otherwise new soft growth can be killed by early frosts. The buds below the dead flowers are best left dormant so that they will grow the following spring.

GROWING TIPS

PLANTS TO DEAD-HEAD

Herbaceous perennials that flower before late summer and will put out a second display, e.g. avens (*Geum*), lungwort (*Pulmonaria*), delphinium and cranesbill (*Geranium*).
Sweet peas.
Garden pinks.
Bulb, corm, tuber and rhizome-forming plants.
Bedding plants such as bedding dahlias, African marigolds, nemesia, geranium (*Pelargonium*) and pansies. Roses which repeat flower.
Self-seeding plants, e.g. lady's mantle (*Achemilla*), ornamental onions (*Allium*) and columbines (*Aquilegia*).

PLANTS NOT TO DEAD-HEAD

Those plants with attractive dead-heads or seed or fruit, grown for flower arranging, e.g. honesty, hydrangea and poppy.
Most bedding plants.
Shrubs which only flower once a year, e.g. lilac, viburnum and mock orange.
Cold-sensitive plants in cold gardens, where the old flower-heads give some protection to buds below, e.g. hydrangea.
Plants grown for fruit for food, ornament or wildlife, for example firethorn (*Pyracantha*), quince (ornamental and edible types), cotoneaster and varieties of roses with ornamental fruit (hips).

Sweet peas These need stopping once they have two to four true leaves, because the first shoot usually turns out to be blind (flowerless) after growing about 1m/3ft tall.

If you pinch out the plant it will produce two shoots from the base and these will flower.

Daily care

If you want straight flower stalks and exhibition-quality blooms, you have to grow sweet peas carefully. Only allow one shoot per plant and tie this in to a support regularly. Snap off all side-shoots and tendrils to let the plant's energy go into the flower. You must do this daily for success.

Even if you are content to let your sweet peas scramble up supports with their own tendrils, you must dead-head regularly. Do not let the pods form, because this suppresses further flowering.

Common Garden Weeds

Docks or dandelions, nettles or thistles – whatever weeds have invaded your flower border, they are sure to be uninvited guests.

In this neglected garden (left) the weeds have taken over, leaving the roses looking very sorry for themselves.

In contrast, here is a well-tended garden (below) where weeds are obviously not welcome. A bark mulch around the healthy-looking hostas and potentilla supresses weed growth and looks neat and attractive.

Weeds are any unwelcome plants in your garden. They usually have lots of fairly small flowers, which make way for hundreds of seeds. The secret of their success is that they multiply so well that, if you did not keep them under control, they could quickly take over your whole garden. As the old saying goes – one year's seed produces seven years' weeds – so get on top of weeds as soon as you can.

You need to control them before they spread thickly, excluding light, water and nutrients from your expensive, more desirable garden plants. Some weeds also harbour pests such as aphids and diseases such as powdery mildew. Both can wipe out cherished flowers and vegetables.

Know your weeds

To deal with weeds you need to know a bit about them. Learn how to recognize weed seedlings from their leaves or flower buds and you can get rid of them before they cause trouble. If you wait until they flower, you might have left it too late as they may already have set their seeds.

There is an easy way to tell which weeds are annuals or have a very short life cycle. Basically, the quicker they come, the quicker they'll go. Those little weeds that come up, at almost any time of the year, with perky new leaves, are the easiest to hoe down or hand-weed and destroy! They are usually compact plants with shallow roots and many tiny flowers. The flowers are hardly open before the plant begins to set its countless seeds. Favoured with rustic-sounding common names such as chickweed, annual meadow-grass, shepherd's purse, cleavers and field speedwell, these are the annual invaders.

Old-timers

Long-lived or perennial weeds are more tricky as they usually have deep roots that are difficult to dig out. Some, such as bindweed and couch grass, have ribbon-like creeping underground stems. When you pull them they snap and new growth starts from the broken ends. Make sure you remove all the new white underground shoots as you fork them out. If not, they will spread again.

Celandine and oxalis both spread by means of masses of tiny bulbils: when you dig them up you have to be careful to remove all the bulbils. Creeping buttercup spreads by producing baby plants at the end of runners, much like a strawberry plant.

What went wrong?

You may be discouraged when new weed seedlings appear in a bed that you have cleared a few weeks before. Seeds can survive in the soil for many years. Digging brings them closer to the light and then they start to grow. Each wind or breeze brings with it countless weed seeds, all ready to spring into life given half the chance. So weeding is an ongoing event, but if you make it a regular activity it will not be an overwhelming task.

> **GO ORGANIC!**
>
> **MULCH MAGIC**
>
> Follow these simple mulching tips for suppressing weeds.
> - Mulch in late spring, when the soil is warm.
> - Spread compost or well-rotted manure approximately 7.5-15cm/3-6in deep.
> - To exclude light from weeds use old carpet, black polythene, a thick layer of newspaper cardboard or bark.

There are many methods of weeding and several useful tools to make it simpler. Chemical weed killers (herbicides) offer the quickest most effective results but their side-effects on the balance of nature in your garden may not always be desirable.

Chemical weapons

Use sparingly and follow the manufacturer's instructions. Chemical herbicides work in two main ways: they are taken into the plant through its leaves or are absorbed from the soil. Usually, they have to be applied with a sprayer.

When your onion bed has been invaded by thistles, a spot treatment may be the best answer. Here (above) the thistles are being painted with glyphosate.

Take care not to let spray drift onto the leaves of precious ornamental plants. Some herbicides, called spot weeders, can be applied to the leaves of individual weed plants.

Green weapons

Hand-pulling is the most successful and satisfying method for removing weeds from a small garden. Do this on a sunny day, when the soil is dry and you may even find it restful. Put the weeds into a box or garden bag as you work, making sure you do not scatter seed or tiny bits of bindwind root. Work systematically

If your soil is dry and heavy, you may find the best method of dealing with weeds is to lift them out with the help of a hand fork. Place weeds in a box or bag rather than on the lawn or soil, as this helps to prevent seeds spreading and multiplying your problems.

Chickweed is an abundant, self-seeding annual.

Lesser celandine (Ranunculus ficaria), one of the buttercup family, is at home in a wild garden, not in your flower bed.

Brambles produce blackberries, but they also form a tangled thicket.

Groundsel is a very common weed, which increases by self-seeding.

ANNUAL WEEDS

NAME	CHARACTERISTICS	REMOVAL
bittercress	spreads by countless seeds	hoe/hand-pull before flowering
chickweed	smothers as it spreads; also sets seed	hoe before the abundance of white flowers appear
shepherd's purse	seeds all year	hoe/hand-pull before flowers
groundsel	seeds all year	hoe or hand-pull before the yellow flowers appear
annual meadow-grass	seeds all year	be vigilant and hoe or hand-pull as soon as it appears
fat hen	seeds summer to early autumn	hoe or hand-pull as soon as it appears
sow thistle	seeds all through the summer, roots regrow. Harbours lettuce greenfly	make sure you dig out all the roots or the weed will quickly reappear.

Pull up shepherd's purse before these pretty white flowers appear, to prevent them from self-seeding.

from one end of a flower border to the other. Make sure you are comfortable: use a kneeler or pads to protect your knees. Loosen the soil around weeds with a hand fork, then pick out the individual weeds.

In vegetable gardens, hoeing is the best way to get rid of annual weeds as soon as they appear. Simply move the hoe along the row, chopping the tops off the weeds just as they appear above the soil level.

You can also use a sharp hoe to chop the tops off perennial weeds. Regularly hoeing off the top growth will prevent a plant from making its own food supply: eventually the roots will shrivel up. Always hoe in dry conditions, so that the chopped weeds do not re-root like cuttings. Perennial weeds with long tap roots must still be dug out.

Mulch magic

Block out a weed's light for long enough and you will kill it 'root and branch', though you will need to be patient as this method may take six months for a stubborn perennial. There are several mulching materials. They serve many purposes; controlling weeds, saving moisture and warming the soil. If the mulch is organic it will mix with the soil and improve its structure.

Choose a mulch of black polythene, an old carpet, a thick layer of newspaper or

Nettles are nasty in more ways than one, so handle with care.

Couch grass, sometimes called twitch, is a perennial with creeping roots and long, wiry rhizomes.

Dead-head thistles to prevent self-seeding.

PERENNIAL WEEDS

NAME	CHARACTERISTICS	REMOVAL
bindweed	creeping underground stems; roots from fragments	mulch to check weed growth, or use spot treatment
couchgrass	creeping underground stems; roots grow from fragments	dig up roots and underground stems or mulch
creeping buttercup	creeping surface stems root to form new plant; also sets seed	dig up runners with fork or mulch to prevent growth
lesser celandine	spreads with small bulbils; which are difficult to remove	dig up, taking care to remove all bulbils, or mulch
dandelion	tap root; fragments regrow; also sets seed	dig or hoe flowers and leaves, or mulch to prevent growth
dock	thick, long tap root sets seed	dig or hoe off seedlings
horsetail	creeping underground stems; fragments regrow	hoe or, for long-term success, mulch to prevent growth
stinging nettle	spreading roots; sets seed	mulch for best results

Dock leaves are a useful antidote to nettle stings – but are still weeds!

cardboard, weighted down with bricks or earth if you have a neglected, weed-infested patch to clear. Leave it on for up to six months and next season, remove the cover and rotovate or dig. Some weed seeds may grow, but they will be easy to hoe off.

In ornamental flower beds and borders use a 5cm/2in layer of bark chippings for the same effect. It looks better than old carpets or polythene. It is, however, expensive to use in large quantities.

One place in the garden where weeds look fairly harmless is round the base of young trees or shrubs, in a hedge or in the lawn, but they should still be discouraged. Remove all weeds and turf from around the plant's trunk, then stop new weeds finding light by placing a square of polythene on the soil surface. Cut a hole and slit in the plastic so it fits round the plant.

Water tips

Water the plant well before you cover the soil: the mulch will keep moisture in and fresh rain water will reach the plant from the hole cut in the plastic. The mulch's main purpose, though, is to keep down the weeds that would otherwise compete with the young tree or shrub for moisture and nutrients. If you find the black polythene mulch unsightly, cover it with a layer of bark

The dandelion, with its deep tap roots, is troublesome in lawns and difficult to remove.

APPLYING A HERBICIDE

Mix up the weedkiller according to the instructions on the packet. Do this out of doors.

A special attachment to fit your watering can is a good investment, as it ensures an even distribution.

The results: brown, withered weeds. This treatment is very extreme, so think carefully before spraying.

chippings to disguise it.

Mulch rows of strawberries with a layer of black polythene. This suppresses the weeds and keeps the fruit off the soil – so it is cleaner when you come to pick.

In a rock garden or alpine bed a layer of gravel keeps weeds under control and offers an authentic look of alpine scree to your planting. Any weeds that do grow through can easily be lifted as they are usually not very strong.

Dig that weed

Here-to-stay-until-you-get-rid-of-me weeds such as creeping buttercup, with its spreading side-shoots, or dandelions, with long tap roots, are best controlled by digging. Use a garden fork to lever the weeds out. Try to get as much of the root out as you can.

If the weeds are growing near established shrubs, it may be difficult to dig them out without damaging the roots of the shrubs. If so, knock the tops off with a hoe. This way you will prevent them flowering, seeding, and feeding up for future growth.

Clever planting

Plants that grow in hummocky clumps or spread to look like carpets are called ground cover. They include bugle *(Ajuga repens)*, lady's mantle *(Alchemilla mollis)* and elephant's ear *(Bergenia cordifolia)*. They

will make a living carpet or ground cover that excludes sunlight from weed plants as effectively as a mulch. In a weedy vegetable patch grow potatoes as a successful ground cover. Their leaves cover a wide area and will blot out light from the weeds. Close plantings of carrots, beetroot and lettuce will also reduce space for weeds.

Using ground cover as a control you will be able to remove annual weeds easily. In their weakened condition they put up little resistance to hand-pulling. Perennial weeds will still need special treatment, however, as only hard digging or a spot weedkiller will remove them from the border!

The best tool for weeding

SHORT CUTS

A CUNNING PLOY

Trick the weeds into growing before you plant your seeds. In spring prepare a seed bed in the usual way. Wait a few weeks and you will have a flush of green seedlings – but they will be weed seedlings. Hoe them off, rake the seed bed and make furrows for your seed sowing. You should not be troubled by weeds again until your seedlings are growing well.

Weeds love bare soil, but a low-growing, ground-covering plant will help to foil them. Here (left) the pretty Ajuga reptans 'Burgundy Glow' with its dark red-tinged leaves, forms an attractive carpet in a flower border.

By covering the soil in your flower bed with a sheet of plastic (above) plants such as these pelargoniums can be planted through holes cut in the plastic, but weeds simply will not get through. Add a thin layer of compost on top. If you don't fancy the look of plastic, however, a mulch of coconut waste material (left), available from garden centres, will do the same weed-supressing job.

Although they are unpopular with gardeners, weeds can be pretty. If you have enough space, why not confine them to a small area, creating a wild garden like this one (below), where symphytum, comfrey, dandelions and forget-me-nots provide a mini haven for wildlife, such as insects, birds and hedgehogs.

is a special type of hoe or 'swoe', that cuts on both the push and the pull strokes through the soil. It is much better for your back than an ordinary hoe, where the repetitive chopping action can be tiring or even damaging.

Take care of tools

A hand fork, a daisy grubber or a weeding fork are all useful hand tools. A good garden fork is best for dealing with perennial, deep-rooted weeds.

After using tools, scrub off soil, dry and oil them before storing in a dry place. The sharper and cleaner they are the better you can control weeds and the less chance there is that you will introduce infection to your garden plants.

Pros & Cons of Chemicals

Gardeners have increasingly been encouraged to use chemicals to improve yields, deter pests, control diseases and eradicate weeds – but is this wise?

When using pesticides or fungicides in spray form, it is wise to protect the nose and mouth from possible contact with the chemicals. This is especially important if you are spraying fruit trees (above) on even a slightly breezy day, when the liquid can easily blow back onto the face.

Using chemicals in gardens is not new. In the last century BC the Romans used the residue from olives – after the oil had been extracted – as a weedkiller. It was probably the high salt concentration in the mixture that was toxic to most of the plants.

The Romans also encouraged cuttings to root by dipping their bases in ox dung. Today, hormone rooting powders are used.

Ever since Man embarked upon a settled existence, the task of increasing crop yields and the problems of keeping pests and diseases at bay and of maintaining the fertility of the soil have been a challenge.

In recent decades, both farmers and gardeners have turned increasingly to chemicals to solve their problems. Today there is a vast armoury of chemical pesticides, fungicides, weedkillers, mosskillers and artifical fertilizers.

There are alternatives, however. The natural control of pests is an important alternative to spraying and is based on the fact that insects – as well as animals – prey upon each other.

For instance, ladybirds and their larvae are voracious eaters of aphids, scale insects, mealy bugs and thrips. The larvae of the two-spot ladybird eats 15 to 20 aphids a day, and up to 500 in the course of its larval life.

These and other beneficial insects can be bought, and are excellent alternatives to the use of chemicals. A future arti-

cle on 'Organic Pest and Disease Control' will look at the organic option in more detail.

Gardener's dilemma

The question for gardeners is when and to what extent can chemicals be safely used in gardens without becoming a risk to families, pets and wildlife and without contaminating the soil or water courses.

Some gardeners rely totally on 'natural' controls, while others believe in spraying as soon as trouble is seen. There is, however, a halfway measure and one that increasingly more gardeners are adopting.

This is to employ as many 'natural' ways as possible – rotating crops, using natural predators to kill pests and having a compost heap to improve the soil's fertility – and only to use chemicals when desperate measures are needed. Many gardeners use organic fertilizers nowadays.

Scientific developments

The introduction of pesticides and fungicides, other than those derived from plant extracts, dates largely from World War II. Chemical warfare research into poison gases, for instance, led to the development of pesticides such as malathion and parathion.

Home-made pesticides were once part of every gardener's arsenal but they are now illegal. Traditional recipes often relied on extracting nicotine from cigarette ends or boiling rhubarb leaves, but all pesticides now have to be approved by the Government.

Today's pesticides and fungicides are mainly reliant – but not entirely – on man-made chemicals. But whatever their derivation they must be handled with respect. Even insecticides derived from plants, such as pyrethrum and derris, though organic chemicals, are potentially dangerous. Derris, for instance, will kill fish if it gets into a water course.

Choosing the wrong weedkiller can result in near total devastation of vegetation, as here (above left).

Young lettuce plants (above) should be dusted with an insecticide to protect them against aphids.

Rooting powders (below) contain not only growth hormones but also a fungicide to prevent the rotting of the cuttings.

Why use chemicals?

It is all too easy to dismiss the use of chemicals to kill pests and control diseases as anti-environmental, and therefore to be avoided by the responsible gardener. They have, however, become part of convenience gardening and without them a great many plant problems would reach epidemic proportions.

Whenever plants of the same species are concentrated in one area it is inevitable that pests will breed rapidly and damage their host. If left unchecked, they reduce yields of vegetables and fruit, sometimes destroying them entirely. They also disfigure ornamental plants.

Insects that suck sap, such as aphids and thrips, are not only a pest but are fundamental in spreading a great many virus diseases.

Some diseases are particularly virulent on certain varieties. Apple canker, for in-

GROWING TIPS

FASTER ROOTING

Using a hormone rooting powder to encourage cuttings to develop roots is sensible. It works equally well for softwood, semi-hardwood and hardwood cuttings.

The quicker that cuttings can be encouraged to develop roots, the less chance there is of their bases decaying and of valuable cuttings being killed. If you are rooting softwood cuttings in a greenhouse, they will take up space and warmth for a shorter period if you use a hormone rooting powder.

SYMBOLS ON LABELS

To assist users of garden chemicals, EC law stipulates that, where applicable, warning signs must appear on containers and packaging.

These indicate those chemicals that are harmful or irritant, oxidizing, toxic, highly flammable, explosive, or corrosive. However, the only signs applicable to garden chemicals are harmful, irritant and oxidizing.

Chemicals that are highly flammable, toxic, explosive or corrosive cannot be supplied for use in home gardens.

SAFETY FIRST

Potato blight (left) can be treated with a fungicide containing mancozeb, a substance which is relatively environment friendly.

Scatter slug pellets among plants (below left) in places where the slugs will emerge at night to feed.

The damage caused by slugs to valuable plants such as tulips (right) can be devastating. Slugs and snails are probably the organic gardener's biggest headache; nothing seems to deter them except a pesticide containing the poison, metaldehyde.

Most liquid fertilizers (far right) are non-organic but in times of rapid growth, after a plant is well-established, can promote necessary health and vigour.

stance, affects the varieties 'James Grieve', 'Worcester Pearmain' and 'Cox's Orange Pippin'. As a way of reducing the need to spray with chemicals, grow those varieties that are not prone to infection.

Potato blight is especially harmful, but again there are varieties that are resistant to infection. Similarly, potato wart disease is damaging – but not common – and is usually kept under control by the use of immune varieties.

The decision to use a fungicide or pesticide is not an easy one, but for many gardeners the answer is to use them only as emergency measures. You can avoid many of the problems by selecting immune varieties, using 'natural' measures and by good garden hygiene, such as burning infected plants and thoroughly tidying up in autumn. Sensible techniques of cultivation, like not cramming seedlings and plants together so that air circulation is restricted, will also help keep disease at bay.

Herbicides

Controlling weeds in flower borders and vegetables plots is important. If left, weeds are an eyesore, likely to harbour pests and diseases, and they will suffocate your plants and use up their moisture and essential nutrients.

In lawns, weeds and moss are less critical but they can spoil the look of a good sward.

The easiest way to kill young weeds between vegetable crops, and broad-leaved types in lawns, is to use weedkillers. Some weedkillers, when applied to bare soil, will also prevent the emergence of weed seedlings.

Moss in a lawn is often due to poor cultivation and/or bad drainage. Even regular doses of mosskiller will have little effect unless the underlying problems are solved. Rake out

CAREFUL USE OF GARDEN CHEMICALS

Pesticides, fungicides and weedkillers are potentially dangerous to yourself and your family and to pets and wildlife. They can be quite safe, though, if you take sensible precautions.

- **Read labels** on the package before buying – and again before using. Make sure the product will control the problem.
- **Check the toxicity** when using chemicals on fruit or vegetables. Some chemicals render the crop unsuitable for eating within a specified period.
- **Keep all chemicals away from children.** Do not store chemicals in empty soft or fizzy drink bottles, from which children might unwittingly drink. Put all chemicals on a high shelf in a locked cupboard.
- **Do not put chemicals in greenhouses,** where extremes of temperature may affect them.
- **Do not use chemicals with labels that have faded** and cannot be read.
- **Do not get rid of chemicals by tipping them down drains** or into ditches. Put them in a secure bag or box and consult your local refuse disposal authority. Tell them exactly what the chemical ingredients are, and if the container has a warning symbol.
- **Do not transfer chemicals** into other containers.
- **Wear rubber gloves,** washing them after use. And after using chemicals, always wash your hands in warm, soapy water.
- **Seek medical advice** urgently if chemicals come into contact with eyes, are swallowed or irritate skin. Take along to the doctor the chemical and instructions packaged with it. Ensure that the manufacturer's name and address is also present, as they may need to be contacted.
- **Do not use the same equipment** for spraying

pesticides, fungicides and weedkillers. And thoroughly clean spraying equipment after use.

- **Do not experiment with the concentrations** of chemicals – it will not make them more effective.
- **Check that the chemical is not toxic to the plants being sprayed.** Some plants, such as cacti and other succulents, as well as insectivorous plants, are soon damaged by certain chemicals.
- **Keep rabbits, guinea pigs and other grazing pets away** from recently treated plants. Do not replace cages on lawns until the grass has been cut at least once after being sprayed.
- **Do not put slug pellets in heaps**. Instead, scatter them in places from which the slugs emerge at night. Pellets in heaps are more attractive to inquisitive dogs than when scattered. Since 1980, metaldehyde pellets and powders for use in domestic gardens have had a dog repellent incorporated in them.
- **Do not spray during windy weather,** as it may contaminate food crops or damage sensitive plants. It is also a waste of money.
- **Do not spray when pollinating and other beneficial insects are active.** In summer, spray during early morning (8 to 10am), in the late afternoon (4 to 5pm) or during the evening (6 to 8pm). Avoid spraying open flowers, as these are the prime attraction for pollinating insects.
- **Do not spray near ponds** as this is where toads, frogs and newts congregate.
- **Do not use rodent poisons where domestic animals might eat them.**
- **Do not mix more spray than you will need**, as it cannot be kept.
- **Do not spray plants when they are in full sun,** as they may become scorched.

dead grass and moss, spike the lawn, feed it, top dress it and cut back any shading trees or shrubs. These measures and a limited use of mosskiller should work, unless the area is so waterlogged that drains are needed.

Unless you are ridding a lawn of weeds – and many people like their sward peppered with bright-faced daises – or are gardening over a vast area, the use of a hoe or kneeling down and pulling up weeds is the best alternative to the use of weedkillers.

Feeding plants

When plants are grown intensively and in groups, regular applications of manure and fertilizers are needed.

The question, therefore, is not whether to apply plant foods, but in what form? And should they be natural and therefore termed 'organic', or man-made and known as 'artificial' or 'inorganic'?

Some organic types, such as manure, are bulky, while others are less bulky and are more concentrated.

The bulky types, provide plants with food *and* improve the soil's structure. These bulky materials include seaweed, spent hops and the farmyard manure of cows, pigs, chickens and horses.

Concentrated organic fertilizers include bone meal, dried blood, hoof and horn meal, fish meal and wood ashes.

Inorganic fertilizers, if used continually and in high concentrations, eventually create conditions toxic to plants. Additionally, water draining through land with high concentrations of inorganic fertilizers will contaminate ditches and other water courses, to the detriment of fish and other kinds of wildlife.

The environmental trend towards green and natural gardening has encouraged more gardeners to have a compost heap and to use organic fertilizers whenever possible – and only to use inorganic fertilizers in moderation.

Organic Pest & Disease Control

Make the most of the many environment-friendly methods available to keep pests and diseases at bay – and see how 'green' your garden will grow.

Organic controls work on the basis of encouraging plants to grow well while discouraging pests and diseases from developing. Common pests that affect the garden include insects, mites, birds, cats and dogs. Diseases are caused by viruses, bacteria or fungi. The methods used in organic or 'green' gardening avoid all-out war on life in the garden and work with nature instead of against it, relying on a mixture of preventive measures and environment-friendly cures.

Prevention

Strongly growing plants can fight off the effects of attack, so the first step in preventing many pests and diseases is to choose a healthy plant. If a plant is already struggling when you buy it, a pest or disease could be the last straw.

Look for plant varieties that are resistant to the problems in your garden. For example, if your neighbours have blackspot on their roses, choose varieties that have some resistance to the disease, such as the hybrid tea 'National Trust'. Avoid growing plants that are particularly susceptible to any pests or diseases

> **BRIGHT IDEAS**
>
> **CONTROL OF WHITEFLY**
>
> Whitefly are a nuisance in the greenhouse and are difficult to control. Even commercial growers, with access to many pesticides, struggle to keep this pest at bay. You can keep the greenhouse clean in winter, to prevent overwintering populations from starting an early infestation. A cordless vacuum cleaner is ideal for sucking up these flies. Just shake the plant and vacuum up the cloud of flies that will emerge.

Applying a generous mulch (above) of organic matter, such as chipped bark, has a dual benefit. In hot weather it keeps the plants' roots moist, which reduces the occurrence of powdery mildew.

TABLE OF PREDATORS TO USE IN THE GREENHOUSE

Pest	Predator
Aphids	*Aphidoletis aphidimyza* (a midge)
Caterpillars	*Bacillus thuringiensis* (a bacterium)
Leafminer	*Dacnusa sibirica* (a wasp)
Mealybug	*Cryptalemus montrouzieri* (a beetle)
Soft scale	*Metaphycus helvolus* (a wasp)
Thrips	*Amblyseius cucumeris* (a mite)
Red spider	*Phytoseuilus persimilis* (a mite)
Vine weevil	*Nemasys* (a nematode)
Whitefly	*Encarsia formosa* (a wasp)

This cunning collar (above) placed round a young cabbage or cauliflower provides a barrier against the often devastating effects of the cabbage root fly.

Simple but effective yellow sticky insect traps (right) catch any pest that dares sets foot on them.

Grease bands placed round the trunk of fruit trees (below) act as a natural deterrent to moths by preventing them from laying their eggs in the upper branches. They therefore reduce the numbers of these troublesome pests.

known to be prevalent in your area. For example, don't grow pyracanthus, if fireblight is a serious problem.

Diseases

Avoid bringing problems into your garden on a plant that you have been given or have purchased. Diseases may be visible on the foliage or lurking on the roots. Beware of wallflower plants and other brassicas (members of the cabbage family), as these are susceptible to clubroot, a soil-borne disease. Only bring them in if they have been grown in compost.

Garden hygiene is important. Wash flower pots before re-using them and clean out every nook and cranny in the greenhouse in late autumn, with a general disinfectant (if you do not mind using a few household chemicals), to ensure that nothing overwinters there. Sterilize secateurs frequently by holding them over a flame for a few seconds to prevent transmission of viruses from one plant to another. For the same reason, wash your hands before handling plants such as tomatoes, which are highly susceptible to viruses.

Infection from tools

Damage from tools such as pruning shears can allow disease to infect plants, so be careful when hoeing near woody plants. In the case of stone fruit trees (including ornamental cherries), prune only when necessary, because they are very susceptible to silver leaf, which kills the tree.

Unlike most woody plants, prune this group only in summer when it is growing well. An actively growing tree can heal pruning cuts quickly.

Pests

Simple barriers can sometimes keep pests off your plants just as effectively as pesticides.

Protect seedlings and young plants with a blanket of polypropylene fibre or fleece sold for crop protection. These let light and water through but protect the plants from most flying insects.

REPLANT DISEASE

If an area of the garden is replanted with the same species of plant, the new plant often sickens and dies. Roses, fruit and pansies are particularly prone to this. The answer is usually to replace the soil as well as the plant. In the case of pansies, the answer is crop rotation, where the same piece of land is used for different plants each year so that no build up of toxins, pests or diseases can occur.

This sticky trap (left) has been specially baited with a sex hormone to attract the male codling moth that preys on fruit. By reducing the number of males, the codling moth population – and the damage done to fruit trees – is lessened.

The poached egg plant (Limnanthes douglasii) is an easy to grow annual (right) favoured by the aphid-eating hoverfly (below). Cultivating it therefore encourages more hoverflies to dispose of larger quantities of aphids.

Hedgehogs (below bottom) are a useful natural predator as they eat slugs. Encourage them to stay by providing plenty of cover for them in the garden.

Erecting a simple barrier of polythene sheeting about 45cm/18in high around your carrots will protect them from carrot fly (the eggs laid in the young carrots hatch into maggots later). The flies keep close to the ground and will go round the barrier.

Cabbage root fly can devastate cabbages, cauliflowers and related crops, but a collar placed around the stem at ground level should provide protection. You can buy these from garden centres or make your own from circles or squares of carpet underlay. Cut a slit in the centre so that they can be placed around the plants.

Birds can usually be controlled by netting vulnerable plants, but this is usually only worthwhile to stop them eating your fruit. Black cotton stretched between pegs, a few centimetres above the ground will help protect vulnerable spring flowers such as yellow crocuses and polyanthus from being pecked.

Humming line (a blue plastic tape) is another useful way to frighten birds away, but it is only effective for a few weeks – then the birds get used to it. Bird scarers also work on their novelty value but this soon wears off. So only use these methods at the critical growing stage.

Some organic animal repellents will work against birds, and also stop cats fouling an area – the strongest smelling products, such as pepper dust, are the best. But they have to be renewed after rain. Grass seed is usually already treated with a substance to deter birds from eating it.

Apples, pears and plums can be damaged by various moth caterpillars, but there are some effective organic controls. Grease bands or a special glue can be placed around the tree trunk to trap the flightless females as they crawl up it to lay their eggs.

The codling moth does a great deal of harm to fruit but can be controlled with a sticky trap baited with a sex hormone (pheromone). This attracts the male moth to the trap and so reduces the number of males available for mating. Fewer eggs are laid and the codling moth population is reduced gradually.

Ordinary yellow sticky insect traps are also useful in the greenhouse. The yellow colour attracts flying and crawling pests and once they touch the trap they are stuck.

Slugs can be quite a problem during damp weather and to minimize their damage, keep the area around susceptible plants, such as hostas and delphiniums, clear of leaf litter. Encourage hedgehogs and toads (which eat slugs) by providing cover for them in odd corners of the garden.

Predators

Other natural enemies or predators of pests can be encouraged in order to keep numbers down. During winter, tits search for food, including aphid eggs that are found in and under bark. If you hang a small amount of fat or bacon

rind on a string near roses or soft fruit bushes, the tits that cannot find a place on the fat will search for aphid eggs.

Hoverflies should be encouraged. They look like wasps, with their yellow and black markings, and have a habit of hovering by open flowers, where they feed on nectar and pollen. They also feed on aphids – both adults and larvae eat huge numbers. By providing plants such as the poached egg plant (*Limnanthes douglasii*) that attract them, you can help increase the number of hoverflies in your garden.

In order to encourage a wide range of insects, avoid using tar oil winter washes. These are indiscriminate and kill many beneficial insects along with pests. Red spider mite became a serious pest as a result of the wide-spread use of this winter wash, which killed many of its predators.

Companion plantings or growing different plants together to prevent epidemics is often cited as an organic control. But while the general principle is sound, growing alternate rows of certain plants in the vegetable plot has not been proven to be beneficial.

Natural remedies

Preventive measures reduce the risks of problems occurring, but even so you will need to turn to organic pesticides and fungicides from time to time. Check plants regularly (weekly in the garden, daily in the greenhouse) for poor health, damaged leaves and pests on the underside of leaves. Arm yourself with an identification book to help you diagnose the symptoms correctly. Do not reach for a pesticide unless you know there really is a need for one.

If you have time, you can pick off the eggs of pests and caterpillars and you can always squash aphids. You can also pick off diseased leaves and collect up any that have fallen to the ground. Put all affected material into the dustbin, unless you are confident that your compost heap reaches 85°C which is necessary to kill the organisms.

Sprays and mulches

Sprays based on copper or sulphur are sometimes used by organic gardeners. These are not strictly organic in origin, but they are non-persistent and many organic gardeners use them in moderation.

The need for fungicides can be reduced by good cultivation. For example, if grey mould develops in the greenhouse, it is a sign of high humidity, so cut down the watering on cool days and pick off dead flowers and leaves.

Powdery mildew on outdoor plants is worse during hot, dry spells and can be reduced by keeping the roots of plants moist. Plant them with plenty of organic matter (leaf mould, garden compost, rotted manure), water well during the first year and mulch with more organic matter or grass mowings or black plastic, to keep the moisture in.

The organic way of controlling caterpillars uses harmless bacterial spores. For slugs, organic gardeners resort to aluminium sulphate, which is not a bait and is more environment- and pet-friendly than the usual slug pellets.

Greenhouse pests can be controlled by introducing specific predators that can be purchased from a number of specailist mail order suppliers.

VIRUS-FREE STOCK

Look for soft fruit stock which is certified free of virus. These plants will give good yields until they eventually succumb to viruses (transmitted by aphids, secateurs and so on). When this happens replace with new stock, rather than cuttings from your own or friends' stock, which may also be infected.

Safety First

Gardening is one of the safest hobbies, but accidents do happen from time to time. A little care is all it takes to avoid many common mishaps.

Compared to many activities of modern life, gardening rates very low as a potential hazard as the highest proportion of accidents happen inside the home. But even in the garden many injuries can be avoided by taking a few simple precautions.

The key to safe gardening is to plan ahead, use the correct equipment for the job, and maintain tools and equipment in good condition. Follow our guidelines, and you and your family can look forward to enjoying many happy hours out in your garden – safe and secure from harm.

Paving and steps

Fix uneven paving slabs and broken concrete; elderly people and small children fall easily, and this is a common problem in gardens.

Prevention is better than cure, so always use cordless powered tools when possible, such as this rotary trimmer (above). Protect yourself by wearing goggles to avoid dust and grit, as well as stout trousers and boots, to save legs and feet from being damaged by flying stones.

Hard surfaces can be slippery when wet, especially in autumn when dead leaves leave a greasy film. Keep steps and paths free of weeds, and brushed clean of loose stones and soil. Always scrape away algae and moss, and use warm water with a little detergent added to remove any remaining slipperiness.

In icy conditions, sprinkle steps and paths with sand – try to avoid using salt, which contaminates nearby soil and can kill plants.

Construct strong handrails above steep or narrow steps if elderly or disabled people use them. And put in outdoor lighting above potentially dangerous steps so they can be clearly seen after dark – this is especially important during the winter months.

Walls, fences and gates

Check periodically to see that walling blocks and bricks have not come loose where mortar has shrunk or cracked, and that fences are still properly secured, as both can damage plants, people or property.

Check too that all your fences and gates are secure,

DON'T FORGET!

TETANUS

Gardeners are advised to be vaccinated against tetanus, which is often present in soil. A booster shot is also recommended periodically as advised by your GP. If not vaccinated, go for a tetanus shot if you receive a cut or wound that punctures the skin.

COMMON POISONOUS PLANTS

Name	*Poisonous parts*
Garden flowers	
Monkshood (*Aconitum* sp.)	All parts
Meadow saffron (*Colchicum autumnale*)	All parts
Lily-of-the-valley (*Convallaria majalis*)	All parts
Foxglove (*Digitalis* sp.)	All parts
Lupins (*Lupinus* sp.)	All parts
Daffodil (*Narcissus*)	Bulbs
Shrubs and trees	
Daphne (*Daphne mezereum*)	All parts
Laburnum	All parts
Privet (*Ligustrum vulgaris*)	Leaves, berries
Rhododendron	Leaves, flowers
Yew (*Taxus baccata*)	Leaves, berries
Vegetables and fruit	
Rhubarb	Leaves
Potato	Stems, leaves
House/conservatory plants	
Dumb cane (*Dieffenbachia*)	All parts
Angel's trumpet (*Datura*)	All parts
Poinsettia (*Euphorbia*)	Sap
Mistletoe (*Viscum album*)	Berries
Weeds	
Buttercups (*Ranunculus* sp.)	Sap
Nightshades (*Solanum* sp.)	All parts

especially if you rely on them to keep pets and young children safely inside the garden.

Tools

Use cordless battery-powered tools wherever it is possible. Where this is not practical, be sure to plug mains-powered tools such as lawn-mowers, hedge cutters and rotary trimmers into a circuit breaker, also known as a Residual Current Device or RCD. (These cut off the power instantly should you cut through a cable, so preventing electric shocks.)

Always keep the cable well clear of the work in progress; thread it through a belt or special harness and carry out work in a direction away from the cable. Remember to disconnect electric tools from the mains power before adjusting, clearing blockages or cleaning. Store electrical equipment in a dry place, and don't use in wet conditions. Replace worn or damaged cables – don't try to repair them yourself.

Store garden tools, especially those with sharp prongs or blades, well away from children or pets. Avoid leaning rakes against a wall with teeth outermost, as many accidents are caused by people standing on the teeth and being struck by the handle. Always put hosepipes and watering cans safely away.

The attractive, black fruits of the privet (right) are poisonous.

Always store garden tools neatly away (below) where sharp prongs cannot cause injury.

Be sure to wear the right safety equipment when using garden machinery. Protect your eyes with goggles or a visor when using implements that produce a lot of dust or throw up grit (such as rotary trimmers), and protect ears with ear defenders when using machinery such as shredders.

Wear stout trousers rather than shorts to protect feet and legs from flying stones when using rotary trimmers. And put on strong boots whenever digging to avoid sticking prongs through the foot, another common accident. Strong boots are also essential when mowing, especially with a rotary or hover lawn-mower, in case you slip and your foot

USE OF CHEMICALS

DON'T FORGET!

- Read the label and follow the manufacturers' directions – do not use products that have lost their labels.
- Before spraying edible crops, check the interval between spraying and picking.
- When diluted and used as directed garden chemicals are safe, but store containers of 'neat' products away from food, and out of reach of pets and children.
- Place slug pellets, if used, inside a hollow pipe to prevent wildlife and pets taking them.
- Dispose of left over (diluted) spray by pouring on to bare soil or gravel paths in the garden; do not pour down drains or near water courses.
- Wash your hands well after using garden chemicals.

goes under the blade. Plastic blades are available for some rotary mowers which are much safer than metal ones as they claim not to harm feet.

If hiring a piece of garden equipment you have never used before, insist on being shown how to use it correctly, and that any necessary safety equipment is also provided. It is particularly advisable to have proper training before using a chainsaw.

Garden canes

Garden canes are one of the biggest causes of accidents. When used to support waist-high plants, people often bend over to work on or admire the plant and fail to notice the tip of the cane until too late.

Plastic or rubber cane toppers are available to prevent this sort of accident; these are specially useful for people with limited vision as they show up well. You can also push an old cork over the tip of thin canes, or nail a bottle top over the tip.

Otherwise use shorter canes that come well below the top of the plant, and tie the tip of the cane firmly flush to the stem, so it is not exposed. Alternatively, use link stakes or other types of support.

Glass

Nowadays many conservatories are constructed of special safety glass (made by sandwiching a sheet of polythene between two layers of glass, which prevents shattering if the glass is broken). If this is not provided as a standard feature, it is usually available as an optional extra.

Greenhouses, frames and cloches are less likely to shatter if constructed from thicker glass than normal. Use plastic cloches where possible.

Pets

Both dogs and cats carry toxicara, a parasite spread via their droppings, which is believed to be a health hazard to humans, especially children. Always keep gardens clear of pet droppings and teach children to wash hands after playing in the garden. And worm your pets regularly.

Poisonous plants

In practice, most 'poisonous' plants need to be eaten in large quantities to cause death, but many can make you very ill. Since many of them are unpalatable, this is not easily done. But it always makes sense to teach young children not to put any plants, berries or seeds into their mouths, and it is advisable to avoid growing plants known to be toxic. (See box on page 1193).

While very few of the many hundreds of toadstools are poisonous, it is advisable not to pick and eat those that may

Before mixing any garden chemicals such as fungicide (right) read the label and follow the manufacturer's instructions to the letter. Wash your hands well after you have finished the application.

Larger pieces of garden equipment can usually be hired when you need them. A small powered rotovator (below) is useful in the early stages of garden construction but insist on proper training before you start to use one.

Mains-powered tools will be far safer if they are plugged into a circuit breaker (above left). It will cut off the power at once and thereby prevent electric shock, should you be so unlucky as to cut through the cable of, say, a lawn-mower.

BRIGHT IDEAS

BONFIRE CONTROL

A proper bonfire container (which looks like a dustbin complete with lid, but has legs and holes in the side) is the safest way to keep a fire under control. Never use petrol for starting a fire. Always have a hosepipe standing by, and do not start a fire in the middle of a tinder-dry patch of dead weeds in summer. If you use creosote to treat a wooden fence or shed, keep bonfires well away from them for several months after treating because creosote is highly inflammable.

Plastic cloches (above) are far safer and cheaper than their glass equivalents.

occur in the garden unless you know how to identify them correctly. In case a plant or fungus has been eaten, contact your GP immediately. If possible take a sample with you. (This also applies to garden chemicals.)

Fountains and ponds

By far the safest type of water feature to have in a garden where there are young children is a fountain, perhaps playing from an ornamental statue or a low 'splash' coming up through the centre of a millstone. In both cases the water runs away through a gravel bed before being recycled via the fountain, so there is no open water for children to fall into. (Water features of this type are available from many mail order water garden specialists).

Conventional ponds can be temporarily screened off with tall canes and netting if small children visit the garden. Wildlife can also be at risk in ponds, and it is advisable to make at least part of the pond edge into a gentle shelf so that hedgehogs and other animals can climb out should they fall in. Otherwise a wooden ramp can be provided.

If young children play in the garden, a low fountain (below) which drains away through a gravel bed is far preferable to a pond into which they can easily fall.

Play equipment

Check swings, climbing frames, tree houses, tyres suspended from trees on ropes, and any other play equipment regularly for signs of wear, sharp edges, protruding nails, or anything that may have worked loose. Prevent children from using the equipment until it has been repaired.

BRIGHT IDEAS

FALLING BRANCHES

Old trees which have been badly affected by drought or disease, can become unsafe as their dead branches may eventually fall. Always remove such branches, and any trees that die entirely.

Where large trees are concerned it is best to call in a tree surgeon who has the necessary skills and equipment to do this job safely. Check that the surgeon is qualified and properly insured.

Garden Tools

A well-chosen hand tool lasts and becomes an old friend, so it is well worth selecting tools carefully.

The range and quality of all gardening tools has widened and improved in recent years. Wooden handles have largely been replaced by plastic or plastic-covered ones, which are long-lasting, easy to maintain and comfortable to hold, while the quality of metals used has made lighter and stronger tools possible.

At the same time there is increasing mechanization in the garden, and some of the hand tools once considered essential, even to simple gardening, have now been replaced by power tools. But even though nylon line trimmers (trade name 'strimmer') and electric hedge clippers make using hand shears seem like hard work, a few hand tools are still indispensable.

No gardener could be without a hand fork and trowel, and secateurs, too, are vital, as well as loppers if large, woody and old shrubs need pruning. Saws may also be essential, especially when renovating an old garden full of established trees, and a sharp knife is always a necessity. The best thing to do is to buy tools as you find you need them, rather than investing money on tools you may not use. You will soon find this approach has repaid you many times over.

Dibbers

You will find the simple dibber essential in the garden and greenhouse. This is a rod-shaped tool with which you make holes when transplanting young plants and seedlings. Small plastic dibbers – 13-15cm/5-6in long and 6-12mm/¼-½in in diameter – are useful for forming holes in potting compost so that the roots of young seedlings can be suspended in them and then firmed in. Outdoors, a more robust dibber, with a firm handle, is needed for transplanting vegetables.

Traditionally, dibbers were the re-cycled broken shafts of spades and forks, cut off to leave the handle and 20-38cm/8-15in of stem, with a neatly tapered end. Nowadays, they are sold ready-made, with plastic or metal handles and shafts made either of wood,

Dibbers are useful and inexpensive items in the garden or greenhouse. The small plastic variety is invaluable for forming the small holes in potting compost so that soft cuttings can be easily and safely inserted.

Garden snips (1) are an optional tool but are useful for cutting garden wire and plastic netting and will save you blunting secateurs. Secateurs come in various designs and sizes.

These (2, 3) are both of the bypass type but have different grips. They are medium pruners that will fit in a pocket and are suitable for most cutting and pruning jobs. Larger ones are

VALUE FOR MONEY

The quality of materials and workmanship in gardening tools varies and is usually reflected in their cost. Tools with a cutting edge must be made from high quality steel as they have to be sharpened repeatedly.

Small tools which are used to disturb or move soil – such as hand forks and trowels – range widely in quality, from light ones that are 'pressed' into shape to 'forged' types where heat and pressure have created the tool's shape. Those at the top-of-the-range are also made from stainless steel.

Stainless steel tools do not rust, and have a smooth surface so that they are easily pushed into soil, and easily cleaned. However, they cost three times as much as similar tools in the middle of the range, and four or five times as much as those at the bottom end, so decide if you need them.

The amount of use a tool will get often influences the quality bought, but this can be a false economy as subsequently its inherent disadvantages become apparent, and it bends, corrodes or falls apart, especially if not cleaned.

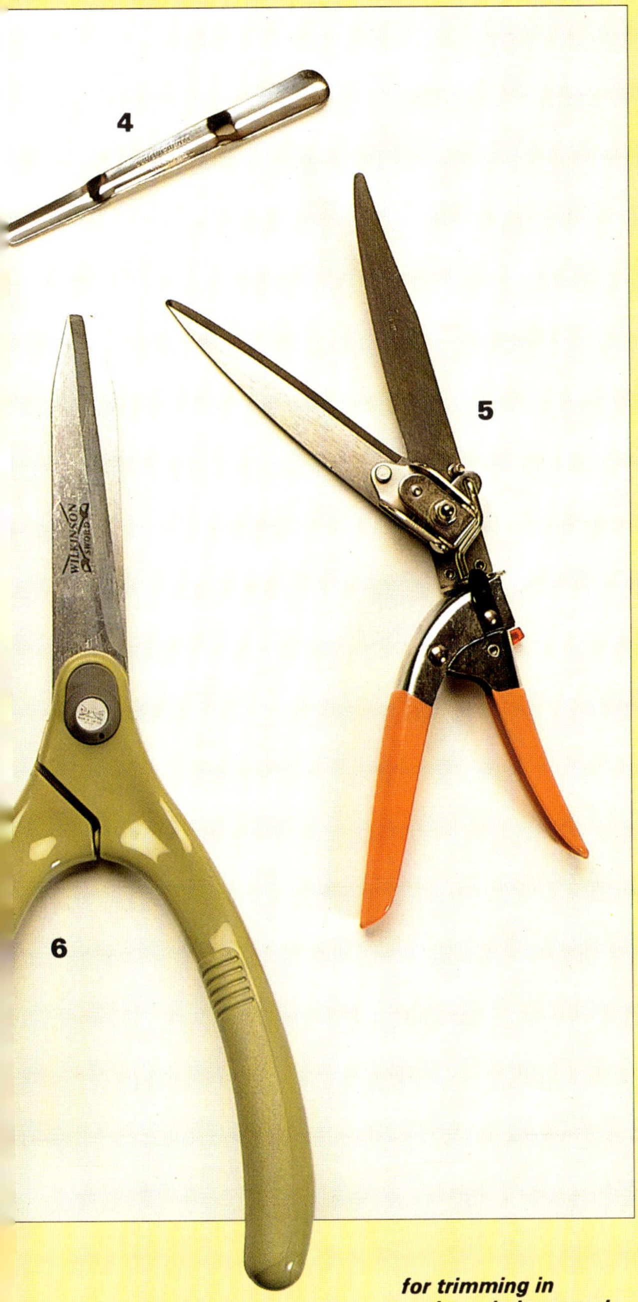

best for woody pruning. A metal widger (4) is a simple, durable tool for making holes to drop seedlings into. Hand shears (5-7) are ideal for trimming in awkward places and for trimming hedges and shrubs. The single-handed shear (5) is useful for small jobs. Hand shears usually have plastic handles (6) or wooden ones (7).

wood with a metal tip, or totally of metal. Metal or metal-tipped dibbers have a longer life than wooden ones, especially in abrasive, sandy soil that is hard on tools.

What to look for: For a garden dibber an easily gripped handle that enables the shaft to be pushed 13cm/5in into the soil is essential. If the dibber is metal-tipped, check that the metal is well secured to the wood.

Secateurs

There are two types of secateurs. One has a scissor-like action and cuts when one blade passes over the other. This is known as the 'bypass' type. The other is the 'anvil' type, which has one blade that cuts against a flat surface called the anvil. Both types have their devotees, but the anvil-type is sometimes preferred by professionals because, at least for some makes, replacement anvils are available. Size for size both types cost about the same.

Anvil secateurs are more robust and are therefore better able to survive neglect and being strained by attempted cuts through stems that are too large and hard.

Both types are sold in a range of sizes to suit the job, from cutting flower stems for vases to pruning roses and fruit trees. Apart from lightweight secateurs for flower stems, most types cut wood 15mm/⅝in thick, and large, heavy-duty types can tackle 25mm/1in stems.

Left-handed versions are available from some makers.

What to look for: Choose secateurs of the correct size for your hand, with good grips and jaws that move freely but are firm and do not buckle.

Hand shears

Garden shears are like over-large scissors, and are used mainly to cut hedges and the edges of lawns where they abut paths at the same level, and for trimming bushy plants such as heathers. They are ideal for cutting small stems up to the size of privet shoots, so can be used to trim most hedges. Some have a notch to enable thicker wood to be cut, but this can damage them.

What to look for: Shears should be strong, light, well-balanced and easy to use. Always handle shears when choosing them to check they feel comfortable, and don't buy shears that are heavy as handling them will tire you. This is important, as you may be using them to cut hedges 1.8m/6ft high. They should also open and close without undue effort. Rubber-clad handles absorb some of the juddering strain created by repeatedly closing and opening the blades, and some shears have adjustable pivot bolts to ensure the blades cut perfectly.

Single-handed shears

These miniature hand shears have 12cm/4½in-long blades. They are spring-assisted and operated by one hand, so are ideal for trimming grass around trees and other edges. Some also have an enclosed grip that prevents hands being scraped on hard surfaces.

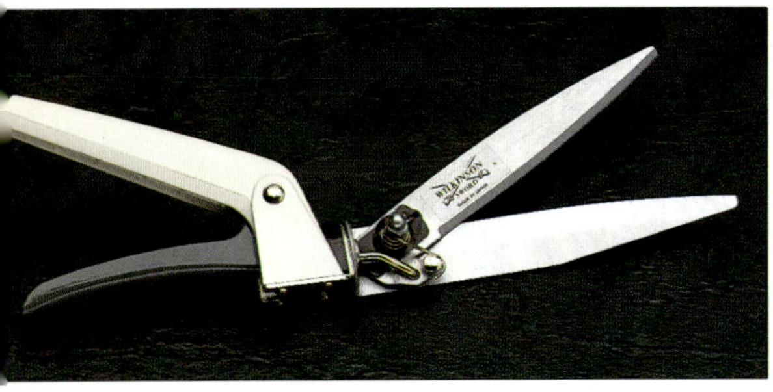

Single-handed shears (left) are used for trimming the soft growth on trees and for tidying up unwanted growth in the herbaceous border. When choosing single-handed shears, make sure that the tool feels light and comfortable in the hand.

Garden knives are used principally for general cutting jobs and for the preparation of cuttings for propagation. It is always wise to buy a good quality garden knife with a sharp, carbon steel blade that pivots, for safety, into its handle (left).

What to look for: Shears light in weight but strong, easily held and balanced, so that the blade is responsive.

Loppers

Loppers are like large secateurs, and have similar cutting actions – anvil or bypass. Depending on their size, loppers cut wood up to 36mm/1½in thick; some types have handles up to 75cm/2½ft long (the normal length is 38-45cm/15-18in) and cut wood 5cm/2in thick. Some anvil-type loppers have a compound cutting action, and can cut thick branches with ease.

What to look for: Strength, durability and firm moving parts to give an effective cutting action. Handles should be metal for strength, and easily moved. Some loppers have aluminium handles, but ordinary types are just as good for average use. As they are used in winter, handles should have rubber grips to insulate your hands from cold metal.

Pruning saws

For cutting branches that are too large for loppers you need a pruning saw. Several types are available – folding, straight-bladed and curved. Some are designed to cut on both the push and pull strokes, others just on the pull stroke. Depending on their size, they cut wood 7.5-18cm/3-7in thick. The curved-bladed Grecian type is especially effective, cutting on the pull stroke and able to get in small spaces between branches with its tapered blade.

What to look for: Saws with a comfortable handle that enables force to be applied when cutting branches, and a high-quality blade securely fixed to the handle. Some pruning saws are sold with a tubular metal handle, enabling a long handle to be fitted for cutting high branches.

Knives

At one time professional gardeners used knives for pruning, but unless the blade is exceptionally sharp and its user has years of experience, both plants and hands are easily damaged. Today, knives are reserved for propagating plants – budding, grafting and the preparation of cuttings – and for general cutting jobs.

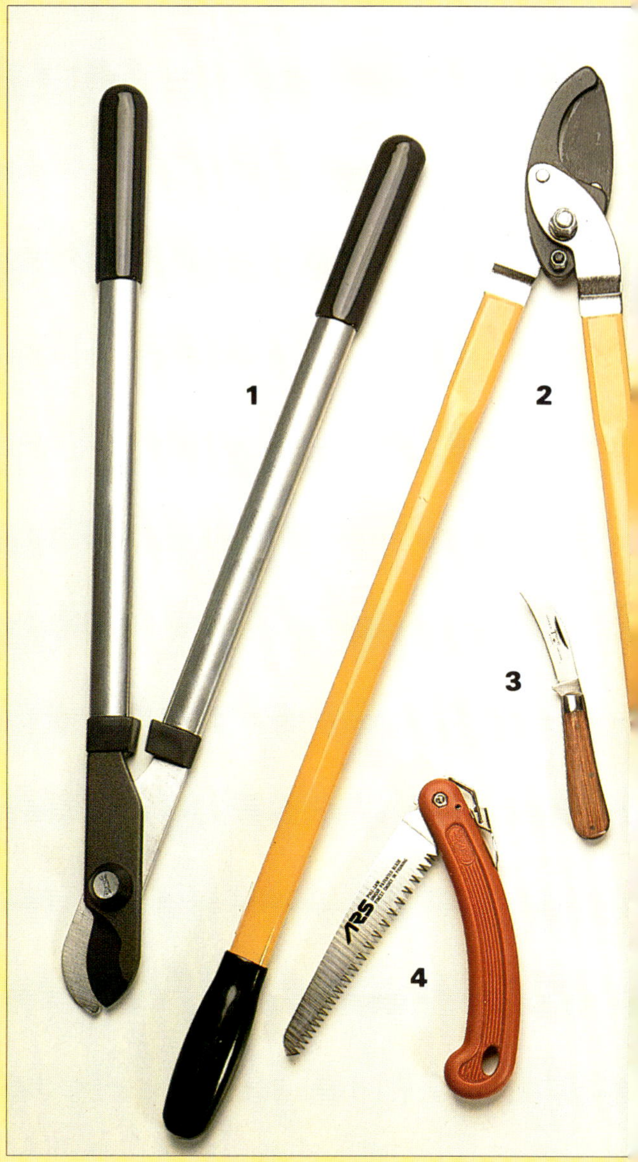

Loppers (1, 2) are great for trimming bushes or hedges above head height, or for pruning small branches. Handles vary in length. They have either a bypass action (1) or an anvil action (2). A gardening knife (3) is indispensable for many jobs. A small pruning saw (4) fits the pocket. This type cuts on the

They are available in many sizes, with blades that fold into the handle. It is false economy to buy a cheap knife, as the blade often cannot be sharpened to a keen edge: invest in a quality knife.

What to look for: A knife should have a sharp, carbon-steel blade, that pivots securely in a strong handle. Avoid knives with blades that close too easily, as this may happen

Rubber gloves are practical and cheap for potting and weeding (right) and are easily replaced when they become punctured or torn. However, make sure you buy gloves that fit properly. You may also want to discard rubber gloves in favour of fabric ones in the summer when the hands tend to sweat rather uncomfortably.

pull stroke. Hand trowels (5-7) are for planting out. This long-handled version (5) has a stainless steel blade. Handles can be in plastic. Gloves (8-10) are made of various materials. For thorny jobs heavy-duty leather and a gauntlet type (8) are best.

CHANGEABLE HEADS

Several manufacturers make tools that can quickly be attached to or detached from a handle. Additionally, there is often a range of handle lengths that enables the tool to be used while kneeling, bending or standing.

This system reduces the space needed to store the tools, as well as the cost of each tool, though having to change heads frequently can be irksome. However, it increases the range of tools you can afford.

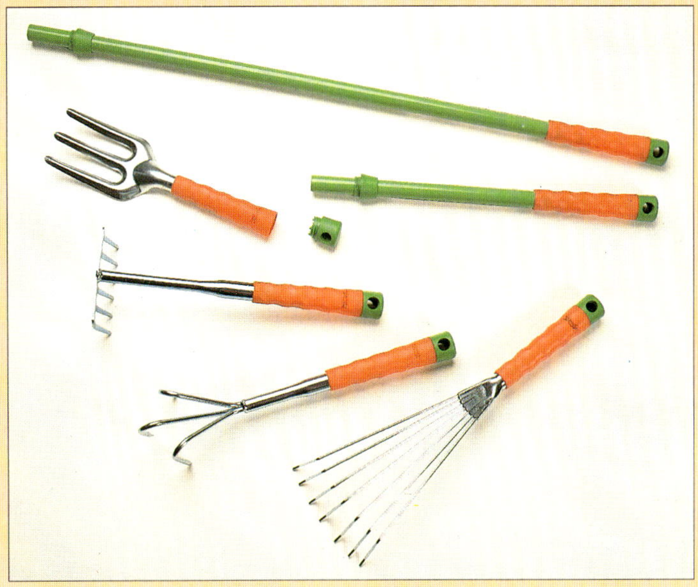

while the knife is in use – some have locking devices to prevent this happening.

Gloves

Gardening gloves protect the hands, as well as keeping them clean, and make most gardening jobs more enjoyable. The cheaper gloves are fine for potting and weeding, while tougher gloves, which are only fractionally more expensive, take the pain out of pruning prickly roses. Most gloves cover the wrists, but gauntlets give added protection when pruning roses and other prickly plants.

What to look for: Gloves should be the right size and should be suited in weight to the job. It is often better to have two pairs of cheaper gloves – one for dirty jobs – than one up-market pair.

Trowels

Hand trowels with 15cm/6in-long handles are ideal for planting out small plants. Some trowels have 30cm/12in

WHERE TO BUY?

Tools are available through garden centres, DIY outlets and other big stores, as well as through mail-order catalogues, and in local hardware or garden shops.

Many tools are impulse buys, especially in spring when the sap is rising and enthusiasm for gardening is at its height. But for value-for-money you should look at all outlets, comparing prices and quality. Before buying a tool you should always handle it; make sure it feels right and suits the size of your hands, as it should become part of you as you use it. If there are protests in the shop about you handling the tool and assessing its size, weight and general 'feel', go elsewhere.

There are bargains to be found in local hardware shops, as well as in large multiple stores and garden centres. Do shop around and seek advice from gardening friends and your local horticultural society on the best tools to buy.

handles, which provide added leverage in heavy soil, but these can be unwieldy. However, they are perfect for elderly and infirm people who garden from kneelers, as they eliminate too much bending.

What to look for: Comfortable handle, especially at the top, where pressure is exerted when forming a hole. A bulbous top is more comfortable than a narrow one. The metal part should be strong and firmly secured in the trowel's handle.

Hand forks

Like trowels, these are sold in two main handle lengths – 15cm/6in and 30cm/12in. They are ideal for weeding and for breaking up the soil's surface.

What to look for: An easily gripped handle, so that the fork can be pushed firmly into the soil. The tined part must be firmly secured in the handle of the fork.

Onion hoe

An onion hoe is like a draw hoe, but with a handle only about 40cm/16in long. It has a swan neck and an oval blade. This type of hoe is an invaluable tool for weeding between seedlings and young plants grown in rows. Professional horticulturists bend over to use these hoes, and slowly walk forward between rows of seedlings, drawing soil towards them and severing weeds with the hoe. Young home gardeners may feel lithe enough to use it in a similar way, but it can also be operated from a kneeling position.

What to look for: Lightness and strength, and a handle that fits the hand, so that the hoe's blade can be pulled easily through the soil.

Hand cultivators

Hand cultivators are used for breaking up the soil, and for weeding between rows of plants. There are long-handled versions used in the standing position. Most have three or five fixed prongs to break up the soil as the tool is used with a pulling motion, but you can buy ones with prongs that can be removed. By taking out the central one, for instance, it can be used to break up the soil or to weed either side of a row of seedlings; removing the outer pair enables the tool to be used in a more confined space.

What to look for: For general use buy one with an easily held handle of suitable length.

Daisy grubber

With the increased use of herbicides to rid lawns of daisies and other weeds, daisy grubbers have slightly lost their importance. However, for 'green' gardeners who nevertheless do not want daisies,

Plastic watering cans (1, 2) tend to be less robust than metal ones. In time the plastic collar of the rose (where it fits onto the spout) may split and the rose will fall off. Cans with long spouts (2) are ideal for situations, such as a patio crowded with pots, where you need a long reach.

Hand forks are for weeding. The long-handled version (3) can be used when standing, while small traditional ones (4) require you to bend or kneel. Shown here are a draw hoe (5), a swoe (6) and two Dutch hoes (8, 9). A sieve (7) helps you achieve a fine tilth. This one is entirely of metal and will prove durable.

Plastic watering cans are less heavy and less expensive than metal ones. A variety of roses is available for most, including the fine rose necessary for watering seedlings (far left).

A daisy grubber is useful for cutting out weeds from lawns, although a garden knife will do the same job, albeit a little less efficiently (left).

the grubber is an inexpensive and invaluable tool. The end of the tool has a narrow V-notch, with a slight bend so that daisies and other weeds can be levered out of the ground.

As with so many of the older hand-tools, made by craftsmen of an earlier generation, good second-hand examples may be available at reasonable prices from local junk shops. House clearance sales can be a source of inexpensive tools.

What to look for: A firm, easily held handle and a metal part that will not bend when used with vigour.

Sieves

Also known as riddles, sieves are used to sift soil. Finely sieved soil is ideal for covering seeds, and more coarsely sieved soil is used for filling spaces between newly-laid turves, and for any other job where friable soil is needed.

Metal-rimmed sieves are 37cm/14in wide and come in mesh sizes from 6mm/¼in to 12mm/½in, while larger, wooden-rimmed types are about 50cm/20in wide with a wider range of mesh sizes.

However, the larger sieve costs about four times the price of the small, metal-rimmed type, which is quite adequate for most jobs in a garden or potting shed. There are also plastic sieves but they are unlikely to last nearly as long and can easily be knocked out of shape. In your garden, you quickly find that a little quality goes a long way: buy the best if you can.

Watering cans

Watering cans for the garden are made of strong plastic, galvanized metal or painted galvanized metal, and have a capacity of 4.5-9l/1-2 gallons, and relatively short spouts. Cans primarily for use in the greenhouse have a capacity of 3.4-6.8l/¾-1½ gallons, and long spouts to enable plants at the back of staging or behind other plants to be reached. This makes them ideal for watering clusters of pots on patios as well. Oval and round roses are available for these cans. Painted galvanized cans are at least three times as expensive as plastic ones.

What to look for: A can that is not too heavy, and has a handle that allows the can to be tilted in a continuous flow, and that you feel you can control. Before buying one, it's a good idea to try a friend's can – check that it doesn't drip over your feet!

LOOKING AFTER AND STORING TOOLS

A tool's life depends as much on its maintenance and storage as on the way it is used and its quality. Tools that are just thrown in a damp shed after use soon deteriorate and when next needed are dirty and rusty, with cutting edges that have lost their brightness and ability to cut properly.

After use, wash away soil and dirt from all surfaces, then wipe the tool dry. Shiny surfaces and blades need a wipe with an oily rag. Wooden parts benefit from a smear of linseed oil on a soft cloth. Tools must be hung up in a dry, airy shed or garage as a damp atmosphere soon affects them.

Large Garden Tools

There is a wide range of large garden tools. Some you are sure to need, others will depend on your garden. It pays to know what to look for when you are buying.

A digging fork (above) or the slightly smaller and more lightweight border fork is an essential tool. This one has a shaft of beech and a polypropylene handle.

All gardeners need a spade. This one (above) is a top-of-the-range stainless steel model.

Several gardening tools are essential for looking after a garden, while others are useful but you can get by without them. Whatever the tool, it must feel comfortable and the right size for you. If you are large, active and strong a full-size spade is the right buy, but if you are small and not used to heavy work a smaller type – a border spade – is best.

Garden tools are available from garden centres, multiple stores and local hardware shops. Always handle the tool before buying, testing for size and balance.

Garden spades

A spade is mainly used for heavy jobs, such as digging and shovelling.

Spades come in several sizes. Digging spades have blades about 27cm deep and 19cm wide (11 × 7½in), while border spades, which are sometimes sold as 'ladies' spades', have a smaller blade.

Some spades have a tread-like ledge on the blade top. When digging heavy soil this enables increased pressure to be applied. However it makes the spade heavier and cleaning is more difficult because soil lodges under the tread.

Handle lengths vary. Choose one that feels comfortable and does not make you bend too much when you are in the upright position.

There are three types of handle: T-shaped, D-outlined and D-Y. The D-Y is most popular. It is similar to the D-type but has a Y-shape where the handle joins the shaft. Most handles are plastic but some are wooden.

Spades vary in quality, in both the metal used for the blade and the wood or metal employed to form the shaft. Stainless-steel spades are rust-proof and enable easy insertion into soil, but are more than four times as expensive as middle-of-the-range models.

Buy the best quality you can afford, as a spade is a tool you will need every year. If it is uncomfortable and too heavy it will soon put you off digging.

Garden fork

Forks are used principally for digging and are useful in winter when digging heavy soil, as the four tines (prongs) are easier to press in than a wide spade blade.

Shrub borders in spring benefit from shallow forking with a border fork to remove weeds, incorporate fertilizers and improve the soil's appearance.

Forks are made in several sizes. Digging forks (often known as garden forks) have four prongs about 27cm/11in long. Border forks have four prongs around 23cm/9in long and the overall width of the fork is less.

Potato forks have flat tines rather than oval or square ones. Unless you grow masses of potatoes, an ordinary fork suffices.

The lengths and types of handle are similar to spades.

Lever-operated tools

A Terrex spade helps to reduce backache and bending when digging. The spade's blade is pressed into the soil as you tread on a lever. The handle is then pulled back and the soil is thrown forward. It saves you lifting each spadeful of soil while your back is bent. A fork head can be fitted in place of the spade blade.

Although useful for a large area of soil, where you can dig in rows, they are difficult to use in a confined area, such as a flower bed.

Hoes

Hoes are ideal for severing weeds at soil-level and making a tilth that reduces moisture loss from the ground.

The Dutch hoe has a handle about 1.5m/5ft long and a 10-15cm/4-6in wide metal head, sharpened on its leading edge. The blade is pushed forwards through the soil, while you walk backwards.

The draw hoe has a handle about 1.5m/5ft long, attached to a curved neck that angles a sharpened blade back towards the user. The blade is drawn back through the soil as you walk forward. It is used to draw soil up around potatoes and vegetables that need blanching. It is better than a Dutch hoe for taking out a seed drill.

The push and pull hoe combines some of the virtues of Dutch and draw hoes, allowing you to sever weeds and create a tilth on both push and pull strokes. It is, however, less good for earthing up.

Garden rake

A garden rake is invaluable for levelling ground, drawing soil over seed-drills, preparing

MULTI-HEADED TOOLS

Also known as multi-change tools, these are implements – from hoes and edging irons to rakes and pruning saws – that can be clipped to the same handle.
Often, a series of handles is available, ranging in length from 30-170cm/12-66in. Additionally, there are adjustable handles that extend from 175-280cm/68-110in or from 225-380cm/88-150in, so that high branches can be pruned.

There is a cost-saving in not buying each tool with a handle permanently attached. The tool heads must be kept clean so that they can be easily and quickly attached when needed.

A Dutch hoe (left) is used mainly for weeding. It can be easily handled in a crowded border of flowers. This one has a carbon steel head and a tubular steel shaft covered with a protective epoxy coating.

Manufacturers are always coming out with new versions of tools. This is a multi-purpose lawn rake (above). The teeth on either side are of different lengths. You may find such a tool useful but this one does not look robust enough for long-term use.

You will exert quite a lot of pressure when using a lawn rake (left). Make sure it is strong. This one has a carbon steel head and an epoxy-coated aluminium shaft.

ground for laying turves and lightly covering newly-sown lawn seed.

At the end of a 1.5m/5ft handle is a metal head 25-30cm/10-12in wide. It has 10 to 14 teeth, 6-7.5cm/2½-3in long.

Most rakes have teeth at right-angles to the handle. In others the angle is not so acute, allowing you to use the rake without bending over so frequently.

The landscaping rake is a larger tool, ideal for levelling loose soil over a big area. It has a longer handle and a wider head, usually with longer tines. Some versions have a metal-reinforced back edge so that the rake can be used to level fine soil.

Lawn rakes

Lawn rakes are used to remove dead grass from a lawn and to scatter worm-casts. All have a 1.2-1.5m/4-5ft handle of wood, metal or plastic

The spring-tined lawn rake has a head of about 20 metal spring-tines that fan out to a width of around 50cm/20in. Versions with plastic tines are lighter to use and usually have a wider head.

Rubber lawn rakes usually have around 30 flexible rubber tines in a head about 45cm/18in wide. Some models have fewer tines in a 30cm/12in wide head.

Edging iron

Also known as an edging knife or half-moon edger, the edging iron is designed to cut neglected lawn edges. A shaft with a T-shaped handle is fitted to a half-moon shaped piece of metal, sharpened on its curved edge for easy entry into the soil. It is normally pressed into the soil with the foot. A spade can be used but this produces a wavy edge.

Edging shears

Edging shears are used after a lawn has been cut, to trim long, ragged edges.

The tubular metal handles

Long-handled lawn shears (right) save you from backache when tidying up around trees or fences. They generally have chromed steel blades, tubular metal handles and plastic or rubber grips.

STORING TOOLS

Like all equipment, the life-expectancy and efficiency of a tool depends on its use and the way it is stored.

After use, wash off soil and dry the tool with a clean cloth. If it is not going to be used for several weeks, wipe metal surfaces with an oily rag and wooden handles with linseed oil. Store tools in an airy shed or garage. If the storage area is damp, wrap tools such as shears in a dry cloth and place them in a plastic bag.

WHEELBARROWS

Few gardeners manage without a wheelbarrow or trolley to carry tools, move soil or transport garden waste. If you have just a few hanging baskets and window boxes it is possible to use a large plastic bucket, but for anything more a wheeled container is essential.

The traditional gardener's wheelbarrow has one wheel at the front and two legs and handles at the back. For wheeling heavy loads over rough and uneven surfaces it is very practical, but can cause backache when overloaded.

Builders' wheelbarrows are robust and strong, and are ideal when gardens are initially constructed. They have a pneumatic tyre that makes them easy to push over rough ground. Smaller barrows of galvanized metal with a tubular frame, or a polypropylene bin-like tray secured to a metal frame, are fine in small, established gardens. Some barrows have

a football-like wheel that helps to spread the load and makes pushing easier.

Traditional wheelbarrows have one wheel, but some now have two and are ideal for use on flat ground. A variation on this is a two-wheeled tipping barrow.

A hybrid between a walking-frame and a supermarket trolley is suitable for patios without steps. Mounted on four rubber-rimmed castor wheels, the tubular frame cradles two plastic trays at different heights.

For larger areas **flat-trucks,** with or without sides, help to move things around. The one-wheeled type, although manoeuvrable, has a tendency to tip over if loads are misjudged. The two-wheeled model is more stable. The four-wheeled model has a turn-table action for steering.

Always select a barrow that suits your strength, age and garden.

The besom (right) is an old country tool that is still very handy in the garden. Made from a bundle of birch twigs tightly wired to a wooden shaft, it can be used for sweeping or, as here, for brushing in a top dressing on a lawn.

Long-handled edging shears (left) are the tool for finishing off lawn edges after mowing. They trim off straggly grass and can be used while you stand up.

The edging iron or half-moon edger (right) is an invaluable tool for lawn repairs and for regular maintenance of lawn edges. It is the only tool that will cut your turf with a straight edge. Most spades have a curved blade and are not ideal for edging work. This edging knife has a wooden shaft; some have tubular steel ones.

are 81cm/32in long and are firmly secured to high-quality steel blades, with an adjustable pivot bolt to hold the blades together. It should have comfortable handle grips.

Lawn shears

Using short-handled garden shears can bring on backache. Long-handled lawn shears can be used instead for many of the same jobs. They are ideal for cutting long grass around trees and alongside fences while standing up. They are perfect for use by elderly and infirm gardeners.

Long-handled tools

The long-handled fork is designed to take the backache out of weeding. The tined head is the size of a small hand fork but is fixed to a long handle so that it can be used while you stand up.

Similar in design to a small, hand-held three-tined cultivator the long-handled version is ideal for cultivating soil without kneeling. Ensure the handle length suits your height.

A long-handled bulb planter takes the backache out of planting bulbs in grass. It cuts out a circular, pot-shaped piece of turf and soil. Place a bulb in the hole and replace the plug of grass, slightly reduced in depth, or cover the bulb with soil.

Brooms

Resembling a witch's broom, a besom is formed of brush-like, twiggy growth tied to a stout handle about 1.2m/4ft long. It is ideal for brushing worm-casts off lawns and cleaning patios and paths.

Additionally, there is a wide range of traditional brushes with bristled heads about 30cm/12in wide. Bristles come in varying degrees of stiffness. Softly-bristled American corn brooms are ideal for sweeping patios and paths.

Whatever power tools you buy most of those described here will still be useful.

Powered Tools

Powered tools have transformed gardening, removing the back-breaking toil of many routine jobs. Here we discuss the tools and what to look for.

An electric hedge trimmer makes short work of the summer chore of hedge clipping. It can also be used for trimming back shrubs and trees such as cypress. This one has a single-action blade (only one blade moves) and a good guard between the front handgrip and the blades.

Whatever the size of your garden, there are powered tools that can make gardening an easier and more pleasurable hobby. Each year they are expanded and improved, making them easier to use and more effective and reliable. They are powered by either mains electricity, rechargeable batteries or petrol.

Electrically-powered equipment is ideal in small gardens. The power can be easily turned on and off, so infirm and aged gardeners can have frequent rests without leaving a noisy motor running. Petrol-driven equipment, with either a two-stroke or a four-stroke engine, is often more convenient in large gardens. However, electrical tools can be used anywhere if you invest in a petrol-powered, 240-volt portable generator.

Hedge trimmers

Powered hedge trimmers are a real bonus when cutting a large hedge. Most are powered from the mains. Cordless models are also available, and

A nylon-line trimmer (right) is ideal for cutting grass in awkward corners or edges where the mower will not reach. It can also be used for cutting back grass or weeds which have grown too long to be tackled by a mower. This electric machine has a command feed which pays out more line at the press of a button. The spare spool of line is stored in the handle on the shaft.

Using this neat electric lawn-edging trimmer (below) is much less strenuous than working round with edging shears. It has plastic blades which are easily changed.

they run for up to 25 minutes from a recharge, allowing you to cut about 85m^2/100 square yards of privet hedge.

Petrol-driven models are robust but are heavier.

Cutting blades range in length from 33cm/13in to 75cm/30in. A few have cutting blades on one side only; others cut on both sides and can be easily used by both left- and right-handed people.

Some have dual reciprocating blades (the top and bottom blades both move), which reduces the amount of vibration and creates a smoother and cleaner cutting action. Other, less expensive models have just one movable blade.

Safety devices include a trigger that needs continual pressure while the machine is being used, and a guard between the leading handle and the cutting blades. Some also have a locking device to prevent the blades being activated accidentally.

Nylon-line trimmers

An electric or petrol-driven nylon-line trimmer is invaluable for trimming long grass around tree trunks, alongside hedges and walls and at the edges of borders. A strong nylon line rotates at high speed, cutting through grass and non-woody stems.

As the line wears it needs replacement. On some machines you have to switch off and pull out more line. Others have a 'command' feed where

SAFETY FIRST

COMMON-SENSE PRECAUTIONS

Using power tools in family gardens requires careful attention to safety. Take common-sense precautions.

Do use . . .

- power breakers when operating electrical equipment (see page 632).
- safety goggles to protect your eyes, especially when using chainsaws, compost shredders and spraying equipment.
- a harness that ensures the cable trails over one shoulder and is not likely to become entangled in equipment – especially important when using hedge trimmers.
- dust masks when cutting neglected and dusty hedges or using soil cultivators in dry conditions. Also, when dusting or spraying chemicals.
- stout shoes or boots when using lawn mowers, especially hover types. Some mowers have 'blades' that are less likely to damage your feet. Don't use hover mowers on steep banks when grass is wet.
- strong gloves when using chainsaws and compost shredders.
- ear protectors, especially when using petrol-driven equipment or if you have medical problems with your ears. However, remain alert, as you may not be aware of sounds indicating danger.

the machine is left running and a trigger mechanism feeds more line to the spinning head. Alternatively, there is an autofeed system where the spool at the base of the machine is tapped on the ground to feed out more line while the machine is still running.

The cutting action on some petrol-driven trimmers is enhanced by having two ends of nylon line.

To cut down stouter weeds and stems up to 20mm/¾in thick you will need a brushcutter. These machines have a saw-edged disc or a sharply-bladed cutting head powered by a two-stroke engine. Some can also be fitted with nylon-line trimming heads.

Some electric nylon-line trimmers have heads that can be rotated so you can trim the edges of lawns.

Lawn-edging trimmers

An electrical lawn-edging trimmer allows you to cut straight or curved lawn edges quickly. If you have a large lawn it is invaluable.

Lawn mowers

The range of lawn mowers is often bewildering for the gardener. There are two basic types for domestic lawns.

The first is the cylinder-type. The revolving blades cut when they contact a sharpened and stationary bottom plate (blade).

The higher the number of blades on the cylinder, the greater its ability to create a smooth cut. The height of the cut is easily adjusted, and a roller at the back of the machine creates a striped effect. These machines are invariably equipped with a grass box to catch mowings.

Cylinder-type mowers can be hand-propelled or powered by electricity, batteries or a petrol engine. On large machines the operator usually rides on the mower.

More recent are rotary mowers, with a blade that rotates parallel to the lawn's surface. Some are mounted on four wheels. The blade is powered from the mains or by a petrol engine, and spins at a constant speed but can be set to cut at different heights.

Some machines are moved backwards and forwards manually, while others are self-propelled. Electric mowers start at the touch of a switch, while petrol-driven ones have a 'pull-start' mechanism or a 'key' operated starter – or both. Most machines have a grass box, and some are fitted with a roller to create a striped effect. Hover mowers are rotary mowers that ride on a cushion of air. The cutting height of the blades can be adjusted. There are electric and petrol-driven models.

Because the machine hovers, cutting grassy banks and undulating lawns is easy. Hover mowers are normally hand propelled. 'Ride-on' types, suitable for large lawns, have seats mounted on powered wheels at the rear. Many

DON'T FORGET!

ELECTRICAL POWER BREAKER

Safety is essential when operating electrical tools in gardens, greenhouses and conservatories, and is achieved by using a power breaker (also known as a residual current device or earth leakage circuit breaker). It is plugged into the mains supply and the plug for the electrical tool is plugged into it. It protects you against cut or frayed cables, faulty equipment and loose or damp connections. If a fault occurs, the current is cut off in a fraction of a second. Unplug the equipment and call in a qualified electrician to diagnose the problem.

Some power breakers have a test and re-set facility to check their safe operation. Do not use electrical equipment during wet weather or in damp conditions.

A powered lawn mower really earns its keep. The traditional type is a cylinder mower (above) with rotating steel cutting blades, a grass box and roller. Blades can be set at different heights.

The rotary mower (above right) has a single blade that revolves parallel to the ground. Some can be fitted with a permanent steel blade or with the safer option of a replaceable plastic blade.

This larger model of rotary mower (far right) has a longer blade for a wider cut. The height of the cut is adjusted by levers on the wheels. For extra safety, it has an automatic blade brake which stops the rotor rapidly.

The hover mower (right) is a variation on the rotary mower. Instead of having wheels, it travels on a cushion of air. It is ideal for slopes and uneven lawns.

HIRING GARDEN TOOLS

Many garden tools can be hired from specialist shops. The economics of whether to 'hire' or 'buy' depend on the cost of buying (and it is worth shopping around) and the length of the hiring period. However, there are costs when hiring some tools that are not immediately obvious. For instance, when hiring chainsaws you may be advised to buy a spare chain and several cans of oil. The hiring company will demand a deposit on all tools, refundable if returned in good order.

Hiring at weekends is usually more expensive than on weekdays. And the cost of fetching and returning equipment – especially if distant – may influence your decision to hire or buy a tool.

Whatever the tool, ensure it is in working order, well maintained and safe to use. Ask the hiring company to confirm this. All tools should be accompanied by clear instructions about their use.

An electric lawn raker with a large capacity collection box (above) makes short work of several lawn care tasks. On a low setting, the spring-loaded metal tines on the revolving cylinder scarify the lawn. On a medium setting, they rake up grass and moss, and on a high setting they sweep up leaves. The red safety lock-off switch prevents the machine being switched on accidentally and is a sensible safety feature if there are children in the garden.

A large grass box or bag (left) saves you the chore of raking up grass cuttings.

GO ORGANIC!

FLAME GUNS

A flame gun is superb for destroying weeds. The flame is created by burning 6% paraffin with 94% air.

Before the introduction of chemical weedkillers, flame guns were widely used to clear land. As the world turns away from chemicals and towards 'green' methods of control, flame guns may once again become popular.

hover mowers have a rear roller to create a striped effect, as well as a grass box.

Lawn rakers

A powered lawn scarifier, rake and lawn sweeper greatly reduces the time needed for these tasks. Rubbish is caught in an attached box. There are electric and petrol-driven models. Some have three different height positions – low for scarifying, medium for raking and high for leaf sweeping.

Garden shredders

Also known as compost shredders, these machines are ideal for turning woody garden waste into mulching material.

Shredders are mainly used in autumn, when clearing up the garden. Unless you have a large garden that each year creates masses of woody stems, it may be wiser to hire than to buy.

Domestic types usually have a motor of either 1050 or 1300 watts; the larger machine can tackle stems up to 30mm/1¼in thick. Some shredders are on wheels and can be easily moved about the garden.

Vacuum cleaners

Vacuum cleaners for gardens are relatively new. Large models are mounted on four wheels and are ideal for clearing leaves, grass cuttings and general litter from drives, large lawns and patios. Smaller versions are hung

SHORT CUTS

CHAINSAWS

When masses of branches and trunks need cutting a power saw turns a laborious task into one easily tackled by a home gardener.

Commercial types are powered by small two-stroke petrol engines, but for home gardening electric ones are usually more convenient.

The potential for damage to yourself and others from a chainsaw is greater than with any other piece of gardening equipment. Keep children and pets indoors if possible. Safety goggles and strong gloves should be worn, and remove clothing that might trail into the chain. Avoid using one when it is raining or very damp.

Electrical types have bar lengths ranging from 25cm/10in to 40cm/16in. For added safety, most have a 'chain-break' device that stops the chain in less than a second if it jolts back after striking a knot or other resistance in the wood.

You need to oil the chain regularly by topping up the oil reservoir. Stop and unplug the chainsaw when doing this job, at the same time testing and adjusting the chain to ensure it is at the proper tension. If it is too loose it will come off the guiding bar.

over the shoulder. They are perfect for use in small, awkward areas, such as steps.

The shoulder type sometimes has a blowing mode for brushing leaves, twigs and grass clippings into piles, ready for collection. Both types are petrol-driven.

Soil cultivators

There is a wide range of soil cultivators that use rotating blades to 'dig' soil, in strips 15cm/6in to 60cm/24in wide, depending on the machine. Large machines cultivate soil deeper than small ones, but all can be used to prepare land for vegetables or for sowing a lawn or laying turf.

Large cultivators have four-stroke petrol engines, while smaller, less expensive ones have two-stroke engines.

Unless you have a large vegetable plot that needs digging each year, it is cheaper to hire one for a few days.

Power weeders

These take the hard work out of routine soil maintenance, such as hoeing and weeding in flower beds and between vegetables. They also remove moss and weeds from between paving stones.

The hardened steel blades – designed so that they do not jam or need sharpening – are at the end of a handle about 90cm/3ft long. A side handle is fitted for easy control and manoeuvrability.

A compost shredder (left) is useful for reducing garden waste to manageable proportions. It is particularly good for chopping up hedge trimmings or woody clippings from trees or shrubs. The shredded material, collected in a bag beneath the machine, can be used as a mulch or added to the compost heap. Having been shredded, the material will compost more quickly. Always wear goggles when using the machine as woody chips may shoot out from the blades. Ear protectors are optional but they can make the job of working with noisy machinery more pleasant.

A power weeder (below) takes the backache out of weeding and is small enough to manoeuvre between bedding plants.

Garden Furniture

Selecting comfortable and practical outdoor furniture is just as important as the garden's design and choice of plants. Or try making your own.

Relaxing in your garden is an important part of outdoor living, but unless it can be done in comfort much of the pleasure is lost. All too often, the selection and positioning of permanent chairs, benches and patio furniture is considered far too late in the planning of a garden.

The right view

An attractive bench positioned towards the end of a garden – either in a formal design framed by statuesque conifers in large pots, or in an informal setting, perhaps canopied by a rustic arch clothed in sprawling climbers – can become a strong visual element in the garden's design.

It also fulfils a practical function; with age, gardeners need staging posts where a moment's rest can be claimed! It is equally important that the view from benches and chairs is not obstructed.

Harmony is the key word to remember when buying furniture for the garden, patio or verandah. Here a Mediterranean-style whitewashed wall and trellis (above) set off the elegant white table and matching seats to perfection.

Range of materials

The wide range of potential materials includes wood, a combination of canvas and wood, metal, plastic-covered metals, metal and canvas, stone and reconstituted stone, and finally, plastic and moulded glass-fibre.

Furniture made from these can be grouped into three types – tables and chairs for creating an outside eating area, usually on a patio; chairs, benches and deckchairs for comfortable relaxation, either on a patio or at various positions in a garden; and furniture on which to sunbathe around a pool or on a sheltered patio.

Furniture must be in harmony with its surroundings. The key to this is to use items constructed of natural materials on surfaces that have a natural appearance. For example, wooden furniture is ideal on brick surfaces or grass, but as brightly-coloured paving slabs tend to dominate wood, then white, plastic furniture is preferable.

Wood

The natural colour and grain of wood ensures it becomes part of a garden and does not fight with all the other features for attention.

BRIGHT IDEAS

BRICK SEATS

Purpose-built permanent seats are usually only practical in warm areas. Patios are prime candidates for built-in seats, especially if they can be integrated into a retaining wall. Slatted wooden tops – moveable or permanent – make the bricks more comfortable to sit on.

The tops of walls can also be converted into seats, but take care that it is not possible to fall off them backwards.

If the wood is painted white the situation is reversed and it immediately captures the eye, often to the detriment of other attractive features. However, even this can be used to advantage when trying to create, say, a bright, Mediterranean-style patio.

Oak furniture is expensive but long-lasting; it ages to a light, brittle shade that harmonizes well with mellow-toned brick surfaces and therefore seldom looks right on brightly-coloured patios.

Benches can be placed almost anywhere in a garden. They can be set into a circular patio wall (above) to provide a welcome resting place for the weary gardener. Or use old weathered bricks and a plank to make a seat with a difference (below), around which dwarf box has been trained.

Benches are ideal for positioning around a garden, as well as on a patio. Those made of oak or teak have long lifespans, while softwood types have a shorter life but can last for a reasonable number of years if they are regularly maintained and protected from rain and snow in winter. Benches are frequently sold in sections, ready for construction at home.

Softwood picnic tables with integral seats are popular and ideal for patios and lawns. Take care, however, that the table does not tip up when several people are sitting on one side only. Such tables are often better suited to be used by children than by adults.

Collapsible wooden stools and tables (that can be stored in sheds or lofts in winter) are ideal for patio use in summer. Many are easily made by do-it-yourself enthusiasts, but do ensure they are secure and will not collapse while in use, perhaps trapping fingers.

Deckchairs are still popular and have the virtue of adapting to all human shapes, being comfortable and folding flat for easy storage. The canvas seat can be easily renewed.

Collapsible chairs resembling those used by directors on film sets are made of a wooden frame with a canvas seat and back. They are adaptable and often better than deckchairs for people who cannot bend down easily.

Metal

Metal furniture is durable and versatile. Traditional wrought-iron tables, chairs and benches have a rustic charm that harmonizes with

BRIGHT IDEAS

SUN UMBRELLAS

Large, brightly-coloured umbrellas are very welcome in summer. Most are available to go with patio tables. The supporting pole passes through the table and is anchored in a container filled with water or sand.

If you live in an area where the atmosphere is polluted, periodically wash the cover. And always collapse the shade at night and when the umbrella is not in use.

On a patio, wicker furniture has the advantage of being light and easy to move (above). But take care to protect it from the weather.

informal settings while modern furniture with formal outlines – perhaps painted white – is ideal for positioning on brightly-surfaced patios. Corrosion is the main disadvantage of furniture made of ferrous metal, but regular painting should prevent this from happening.

Metal also invariably creates a hard, unyielding surface, which is usually cold although in summer it sometimes becomes startlingly hot. Moveable cushions are the answer to this problem.

Lightweight, aluminium-framed collapsible chairs with attractive canvas seats are comfortable and usually available with adjustable back supports. Most are fitted with arm rests. Although aluminium is non-ferrous and therefore does not rust when wet, the canvas must not be allowed to become wet. Their light weight allows them to be stored away in winter. Infirm and old people find them easy to handle.

Plastic-covered metal furniture is strong and non-rusting, with the advantage that it can be wiped clean after children have spilled drinks or food.

Nothing beats a solid wooden table and chairs (below) for blending in with the garden's natural features. Oak and teak are the most durable woods, but softwood can be used for a number of years if it is properly treated with preservative.

Plastic

Plastic has revolutionized garden furniture. Moulded tables and chairs are widely available, usually in white, often in sets, and at prices that make them attractive. The chairs are usually stackable and easily stored in winter.

Designs of chairs are varied, usually providing a comfortable sitting position with good lumbar support, especially those with arms and high backs. Also, they can be left outside throughout summer, needing only a wipe with a cloth after a rain shower.

Chairs at the upper end of the price range are usually available with detachable, padded covers that make sitting easier over a long period.

Oval and round tables are most commonly seen, often with a hole in the centre so that a sun umbrella can be fitted to provide much needed shade in very hot weather.

Collapsible chairs formed of rigid, reinforced plastic frames are widely available. They can be easily stored in winter. To make them more comfortable, padded seats and back covers can be purchased.

Stone

Stone seats are a permanent feature and therefore must be carefully integrated with the rest of the garden. They should not be obtrusive, yet if the supports are attractively sculptured – perhaps in the form of lions or other animals – these should not be hidden. Additionally, such a seat needs a position offering good views of the garden.

Real stone is invariably expensive, but many companies producing statues and other garden ornaments from reconstituted stone also make attractive rectangular slabs that can be used for creating seats when they are placed on firm supports.

Use a weak mortar mix – eight parts of sand to one of cement – to fix the top securely to the supports.

Large foliaged shrubs positioned behind a stone seat, as well as sprawling ground-cover plants, will help to unify it with the surroundings.

Traditional-style wrought-iron furniture (above) looks particularly charming.

A sundial (below) or a statue can become a focal point on an uncanopied patio with built-in seating.

Make your own seats

Part of the fun of gardening is to create something not seen often in other gardens, and distinctive seats are certainly a possibility.

The simplest type of bench is a strong plank, 1.2-1.8m/4-6ft long, 25-38cm/10-15in wide and about 5cm/2in thick, secured to two supports about 45cm/18in high. The 'legs' could be two 13-18cm/5-7in thick logs, 75cm-1m/2½-3ft long that are firmly buried in the ground.

The plank is then nailed to them – but first drill holes in the plank so that it is not split by large nails.

A slightly more ambitious seat is a wooden plank integrated into a background of dwarf box (*Buxus sempervirens* 'Suffruticosa'), a small-leaved evergreen.

First construct supports from old, well-weathered bricks cemented together.

Garden Notes

GARDEN STATUES

Increasingly, statues are becoming a popular feature, either as a focal point or nestling amid plant alongside paths.

Specialist suppliers – as well as many garden centres – have a wide range of statues, from gnomes and rabbits to ornate fig-leaved gods and goddesses.

Bright Ideas

BIRD BATHS

Bird baths are ideal for encouraging garden wild life, but they can be both cruel and impractical if you or your neighbours have cats.

Placing the bath on a pedestal surrounded by 1m/3ft of gravel chippings helps to give some warning to the birds, but it is not a guarantee of success.

Place the plank on top and set it into the mortar. The dwarf box can then be trained and clipped around it.

Care of furniture

To ensure the maximum length of life, yearly maintenance and protection during winter is essential, especially for wooden furniture. Where possible, place garden furniture under cover when the weather deteriorates.

Rain, snow and freezing temperatures damage wood and by spring renovation is needed. Of course, hot summer sun can be just as damaging, drying the surface and warping thin, unseasoned wood. Use first coarse, then fine sandpaper to prepare the surface, then apply several coats of varnish, allowing each coat to dry thoroughly before applying the next. Teak furniture is maintained by cleaning and coating with teak oil.

Bird baths encourage wildlife and add character to a garden particularly when nestling amid a charming display of roses (above).

Sink into the comfort of a chair or chaise longue (below). Here, durable plastic furniture makes for affordable luxury.

If left outside in autumn, stand wooden benches and tables on bricks to prevent them resting in water. Wrap the piece of furniture in polythene sheeting, tying it firmly to the legs.

Move all wooden furniture from lawns as if it remains there in winter it encourages the legs to rot. Always put deckchairs under cover.

Check metal furniture for rust; if any is found, remove with sandpaper, then paint.

Stone and reconstituted stone seats usually need smartening up in spring. Wash with soapy water, gently rubbing with a soft brush. Then rinse thoroughly with clean water.

WHEELED FURNITURE

Occasionally, wheels are fitted to the legs at one end of a long bench and handles at the other – so that it can be moved easily. More common, however, are wheeled sunloungers, essential if the sun is to be worshipped properly and every ray absorbed.

Both wooden and plastic-covered tubular-metal types are available, and together with mattresses create soft and comfortable loungers. Some have adjustable head-rests, others are fixed.

Index

Picture Credits

John Ainsworth/The Garden Picture Library: 115 (bottom right). Gillian Beckett: 52 (centre); 151 (bottom left). G I Bernard/NHPA: 111 (centre right). 'Le Chateau' Range, Besco Baron, Rochdale: 174 (bottom). Black and Decker: 164 (centre); 165 (top); 165 (bottom); 166 (top); 167 (all pictures); 168 (all pictures); 169 (bottom). Boys Syndication: 119 (top left). Bramley Garden Furniture, Braintree: 173 (top). 'Harvest' Range, P J Bridgeman and Co Ltd, England: 172 (bottom). Brian Carter/The Garden Picture Library: 34/35 (top); 57 (centre right); 91 (top right); 118 (top left); 134/35 (top); 141 (bottom left). Pat Brindley: 7 (bottom left); 33 (top right); 36 (top inset); 41 (top right); 42 (bottom right); 75 (top right); 81 (top right); 82 (top right); 149 (top). Brian Carter/The Garden Picture Library: 34/35 (top); 57 (centre right); 91 (top right); 118 (top left); 134/35 (top); 141 (bottom left). Noel Cavanagh/The Garden Picture Library: 38 (centre right). Collections/Patrick Johns: 4 (top inset); 17 (inset); 46 (top); 49 (bottom right); 57 (bottom right); 70 (centre); 76/77 (bottom centre); 78 (centre left); 82 (centre right); 82/83 (bottom centre); 83 (top left); 89 (top right and centre right); 96 (centre right); 96/97 (bottom centre); 97 (bottom centre); 100/101 (bottom left); 105 (centre right); 108/109 (centre left); 125 (top); 131 (centre right); 145 (top right); 154 (top right); 163 (bottom). Kevin Craddock/The Garden Picture Library: 98 (bottom centre). Eric Crichton: 3; 16 (top right); 31 (top right); 39 (bottom); 43 (bottom right); 44 (centre left); 45 (top right and bottom right); 47 (top); 57 (top right); 65 (top right); 71 (bottom left); 72 (top left and bottom left); 73 (top left); 76 (centre centre); 78/79 (top centre); 80 (centre left); 87 (top right and bottom left); 106 (top centre); 113 (top right); 124 (centre); 126/7 (top); 130 (bottom left); 130/131 (centre); 140/141 (top); 153 (top and bottom). Stephen Dalton/NHPA: 112 (centre right); 113 (bottom right); 148/49 (centre and bottom). Henk Dijkman/The Garden Picture Library: 98 (bottom centre). EWA: 9 (inset); 35 (bottom right); 119 (top right and centre right). Paul Felix: 24 (top left). Fiskars, manufacturers of Wilkinson Sword garden tools: 156 (top – two pictures); 160 (left); 161 (centre left and top); 161 (bottom); 162 (top right and bottom); 163 (centre). Vaughan Fleming/The Garden Picture Library: 34 (top). John Glover/Garden Picture Library: 24/25 (bottom); 108 (bottom centre). Derek Gould: 156 (bottom left); 99 (top right); 173 (bottom). Simon Hay: 26 (top – six pictures); 27 (top left – two pictures). Neil Holmes: 31 (centre right); 32 (top centre); 37 (centre right); 62 (top); 119 (centre left); 147 (bottom). John Hooton/The Garden Picture Library: 23 (top). Roger Hyam/The Garden Picture Library: 74/75 (top centre). Insight Picture Library: 60 (centre left). Susie Johns: 26 (bottom left). Anne Kelly/The Garden Picture Library: 71 (top right). Michael Lamontagne/Garden Picture Library: 1; 134/135 (bottom). Andrew Lawson: 19 (top right); 54 (bottom left); 84/85 (top centre); 99 (top left); 105 (top right); 107 (centre centre); 130/131 (top); 142 (centre); 152 (top right). Tools courtesy of John Lewis Partnership/Marshall Cavendish: 154/155 (centre); 156/7 (top); 157 (top right); 158/159 (top). Marianne Majerns/The Garden Picture Library: 48/49 (centre). Marshall Cavendish Picture Library: 4 (centre right and bottom right); 10 (top right – four pictures); 11 (top – six pictures); 12/13 (top and centre); 12 (bottom – two pictures); 12/13 (bottom centre); 19 (top left); 20 (left – five pictures); 46 (bottom – two pictures); 47 (bottom left); 50 (bottom left – two pictures); 50 (bottom right); 53 (top right); 55 (top – three pictures); 58; 60 (top); 63 (bottom); 78 (centre right); 79 (centre left); 80/81 (centre centre); 84 (bottom left); 85 (bottom right); 89 (bottom right); 90 (top left); 91 (bottom left and centre right); 120; 121 (top right); 122 (top right – five pictures); 122 (bottom right); 122/23 (top centre); 123 (bottom left); 125 (bottom); 138 (top left, top right, centre left and bottom left); 139 (top left, top right and centre right); 144 (top left) S & O Matthews: 4 (bottom left); 42 (top); 43 (top right); 174 (top). Peter McHoy: 7 (bottom right); 19 (bottom); 21 (bottom right); 36/37 (bottom centre); 51 (bottom centre); 52/53 (bottom centre); 54 (top left); 59 (top right); 63 (top right); 64 (top left); 64/65 (top centre); 69 (top right and bottom left); 73 (bottom right); 77 (top left and bottom centre); 86/87 (top centre); 93 (top left); 93 (bottom right – two pictures); 94/95 (top centre); 100/101 (centre left); 102 (top right); 103 (top); 111 (top left); 116 (top right); 127 (bottom – four pictures); 128/129 (bottom); 129 (top); 133 (bottom right); 135 (bottom right); 137 (top right); 143 (top left); 143 (bottom); 147 (top); 163 (top). Metro Products Ltd, Oxted: 86 (centre). Tania Midgeley: 40 (top left); 97 (centre centre). Photos Horticultural: 10 (top left); 10 (centre left); 10 (bottom left); 14 (bottom left); 14 (left); 19 (centre); 20 (bottom right); 24 (bottom left); 36 (top left); 36/37 (top); 40 (bottom left); 41 (bottom right); 49 (top right); 50/51 (top); 51 (top right); 51 (centre left); 53 (bottom right); 54 (centre left); 54/55 (bottom); 59 (centre right); 62/63 (top centre); 86 (top left); 90 (bottom left); 90/91 (top centre); 95 (bottom left); 99 (bottom left); 100 (right centre); 103 (bottom left); 106/7 (bottom centre); 114 (centre right); 116 (centre left); 117 (top left); 121 (bottom right); 128/9 (top); 133 (top left and top right); 137 (bottom right); 139 (centre top); 141 (centre right); 143 (top right); 144 (top); 144 (bottom); 145 (top left); 146 (centre); 147 (centre); 148 (top); 157 (bottom left); 158 (bottom right); 162 (bottom); 169 (top). Joanne Pavia/The Garden Picture Library: 95 (top centre). Gary Rogers/The Garden Picture Library: 98 (bottom centre). David Russell/The Garden Picture Library: 27 (top right); 115 (top centre). Michael Shoebridge/Marshall Cavendish: 126 (left – four pictures); 134 (top left); 159 (bottom right). Harry Smith Collection: 4 (top); 6 (top); 8 (bottom centre); 15 (bottom right); 17 (bottom); 21 (top); 22 (top left); 25 (top); 35 (top right); 42 (centre right); 55 (centre left); 61 (top); 64 (centre left); 74 (bottom centre); 75 (bottom right); 86 (bottom centre); 88 (centre centre); 92 (centre right); 104/105 (top right and bottom right); 107 (top right); 111 (bottom centre); 117 (bottom right); 118 (bottom right); 136 (top left); 136/137 (bottom); 139 (bottom right); 150 (left); 151 (top right); 152 (bottom right); 161 (centre right); 171 (top). David Squire: 6 (bottom); 39 (top left); 40 (bottom right); 68 (top right); 109 (centre centre); 138 (centre top); 140 (left – three pictures); 171 (bottom). Sun Greenhouses, Tamworth: 66 (centre right and bottom right); 67 (top right and bottom left); 68 (bottom right). Ron Sutherland/Garden Picture Library: 8 (top); 110 (centre right); 112 (bottom centre); 170 (right); 172 (right). Brigitte Thomas/Garden Picture Library: 5 (right); 9 (background); 56 (top); 132/33 (bottom); 141 (top right). Don Wildridge: 29 (top right); 152 (bottom left). Steven Wooster/The Garden Picture Library: 28 (centre); 30/31 (centre).